The Economist

Pocket
World in
Figures
2012 Edition

THE ECONOMIST IN ASSOCIATION WITH
PROFILE BOOKS LTD

Published by Profile Books Ltd,
3A Exmouth House, Pine Street, London EC1R OJH

This edition published by Profile Books in association with
The Economist, 2011

Material researched and compiled by
Andrea Burgess, Mark Doyle, Ian Emery, Andrew Gilbert,
Conrad Heine, Carol Howard, David McKelvey, Jane Shaw,
Roxana Willis, Christopher Wilson, Simon Wright

Typeset in Officina by MacGuru Ltd
info@macguru.org.uk

Printed in Italy by
L.E.G.O Spa. Lavis

A CIP catalogue record for this book is available
from the British Library

ISBN 978 1 84668 473 9

Contents

CONTENTS

Largest amount of carbon dioxide emitted per person
Biggest increases and decreases in carbon dioxide emissions
Biggest emitters of carbon dioxide per $ of GDP
Largest forested areas   Most forested area as % of land
Fastest rates of deforestation and forestation
Highest and lowest Happy Planet Index
Biggest ecological footprint

Notes

This 2012 edition of *The Economist Pocket World in Figures*
includes new rankings on such diverse topics as Facebook
pages, migration, parliamentary seats, charitable behaviour,
top universities, a happy planet index and ecological
footprints. The world rankings consider 194 countries, all
those with a population of at least 1m or a GDP of at least
$1bn, they are listed on pages 250–54. The country profiles
cover 67 major countries. Also included are profiles of the
euro area and the world. The extent and quality of the
statistics available varies from country to country. Every care
has been taken to specify the broad definitions on which the
data are based and to indicate cases where data quality or
technical difficulties are such that interpretation of the
figures is likely to be seriously affected. Nevertheless, figures
from individual countries may differ from standard
international statistical definitions. The term "country" can
also refer to territories or economic entities.

Some country definitions
Macedonia is officially known as the Former Yugoslav Republic
of Macedonia. Data for Cyprus normally refer to Greek Cyprus
only. Data for China do not include Hong Kong or Macau.
Bosnia includes Herzegovina. Data for Sudan are for the
country before it became two countries, Sudan and South
Sudan, in 2011. For countries such as Morocco they exclude
disputed areas. Congo-Kinshasa refers to the Democratic
Republic of Congo, formerly known as Zaire. Congo-
Brazzaville refers to the other Congo. Data for the EU refer to
the 27 members as at January 1 2007, unless otherwise noted.
Euro area data normally refer to the 16 members that had
adopted the euro as at December 31 2009: Austria, Belgium,
Cyprus, France, Finland, Germany, Greece, Ireland, Italy,
Luxembourg, Malta, Netherlands, Portugal, Slovakia, Slovenia
and Spain. For more information about the EU and the euro
area see page 248.

Statistical basis
The all-important factor in a book of this kind is to be able to
make reliable comparisons between countries. Although this
is never quite possible for the reasons stated above, the best
route, which this book takes, is to compare data for the same
year or period and to use actual, not estimated, figures
wherever possible. In some cases, only OECD members are
considered. Where a country's data is excessively out of date,

it is excluded. The research for this edition of *The Economist Pocket World in Figures* was carried out in 2011 using the latest available sources that present data on an internationally comparable basis.

Data in the country profiles, unless otherwise indicated, refer to the year ending December 31 2009. Life expectancy , crude birth, death and fertility rates are based on 2005–10 averages; human development indices and energy data are for 2008; marriage and divorce, employment, health and education data refer to the latest year for which figures are available; internet hosts are as at April 2011.

Other definitions

Data shown in country profiles may not always be consistent with those shown in the world rankings because the definitions or years covered can differ.

Statistics for principal exports and principal imports are normally based on customs statistics. These are generally compiled on different definitions to the visible exports and imports figures shown in the balance of payments section.

Definitions of the statistics shown are given on the relevant page or in the glossary on pages 248–9. Figures may not add exactly to totals, or percentages to 100, because of rounding or, in the case of GDP, statistical adjustment. Sums of money have generally been converted to US dollars at the official exchange rate ruling at the time to which the figures refer.

Energy consumption data are not always reliable, particularly for the major oil producing countries; consumption per head data may therefore be higher than in reality. Energy exports can exceed production and imports can exceed consumption if transit operations distort trade data or oil is imported for refining and re-exported.

Abbreviations

bn	billion (one thousand million)	ha	hectare
EU	European Union	m	million
kg	kilogram	PPP	Purchasing power parity
km	kilometre	TOE	tonnes of oil equivalent
GDP	Gross domestic product	trn	trillion (one thousand billion)
GNI	Gross national income	...	not available

World rankings

Countries: natural facts

Countries: *the largest*[a]
'000 sq km

1	Russia	17,075		31	Tanzania	945
2	Canada	9,971		32	Nigeria	924
3	China	9,561		33	Venezuela	912
4	United States	9,373		34	Namibia	824
5	Brazil	8,512		35	Pakistan	804
6	Australia	7,682		36	Mozambique	799
7	India	3,287		37	Turkey	779
8	Argentina	2,767		38	Chile	757
9	Kazakhstan	2,717		39	Zambia	753
10	Sudan	2,506		40	Myanmar	677
11	Algeria	2,382		41	Afghanistan	652
12	Congo-Kinshasa	2,345		42	Somalia	638
13	Saudi Arabia	2,200		43	Central African Rep.	622
14	Greenland	2,176		44	Ukraine	604
15	Mexico	1,973		45	Madagascar	587
16	Indonesia	1,904		46	Kenya	583
17	Libya	1,760		47	Botswana	581
18	Iran	1,648		48	France	544
19	Mongolia	1,565		49	Yemen	528
20	Peru	1,285		50	Thailand	513
21	Chad	1,284		51	Spain	505
22	Niger	1,267		52	Turkmenistan	488
23	Angola	1,247		53	Cameroon	475
24	Mali	1,240		54	Papua New Guinea	463
25	South Africa	1,226		55	Sweden	450
26	Colombia	1,142		56	Morocco	447
27	Ethiopia	1,134			Uzbekistan	447
28	Bolivia	1,099		58	Iraq	438
29	Mauritania	1,031		59	Paraguay	407
30	Egypt	1,000		60	Zimbabwe	391

Mountains: *the highest*[b]

	Name	Location	Height (m)
1	Everest	China-Nepal	8,848
2	K2 (Godwin Austen)	China-Jammu and Kashmir	8,611
3	Kangchenjunga	India-Nepal	8,586
4	Lhotse	China-Nepal	8,516
5	Makalu	China-Nepal	8,463
6	Cho Oyu	China-Nepal	8,201
7	Dhaulagiri	Nepal	8,167
8	Manaslu	Nepal	8,163
9	Nanga Parbat	Jammu and Kashmir	8,126
10	Annapurna I	Nepal	8,091
11	Gasherbrum I	China-Jammu and Kashmir	8,068
12	Broad Peak	China-Jammu and Kashmir	8,047
13	Gasherbrum II	China-Jammu and Kashmir	8,035
14	Xixabangma Feng	China	8,012

a Includes freshwater.
b Includes separate peaks which are part of the same massif.

Rivers: *the longest*

	Name	Location	Length (km)
1	Nile	Africa	6,695
2	Amazon	South America	6,516
3	Yangtze	Asia	6,380
4	Mississippi-Missouri system	North America	5,959
5	Ob'-Irtysh	Asia	5,568
6	Yenisey-Angara-Selanga	Asia	5,550
7	Huang He (Yellow)	Asia	5,464
8	Congo	Africa	4,667
9	Río de la Plata-Paraná	South America	4,500
10	Irtysh	Asia	4,440

Deserts: *the largest*

	Name	Location	Area ('000 sq km)
1	Sahara	Northern Africa	8,600
2	Arabian	South-western Asia	2,300
3	Gobi	Mongolia/China	1,166
4	Patagonian	Argentina	673
5	Great Victoria	Western and Southern Australia	647
6	Great Basin	South-western United States	492
7	Chihuahuan	Northern Mexico	450
8	Great Sandy	Western Australia	400

Lakes: *the largest*

	Name	Location	Area ('000 sq km)
1	Caspian Sea	Central Asia	371
2	Superior	Canada/United States	82
3	Victoria	East Africa	69
4	Huron	Canada/United States	60
5	Michigan	United States	58
6	Tanganyika	East Africa	33
7	Baikal	Russia	31
	Great Bear	Canada	31

Islands: *the largest*

	Name	Location	Area ('000 sq km)
1	Greenland	North Atlantic Ocean	2,176
2	New Guinea	South-west Pacific Ocean	809
3	Borneo	Western Pacific Ocean	746
4	Madagascar	Indian Ocean	587
5	Baffin	North Atlantic Ocean	507
6	Sumatra	North-east Indian Ocean	474
7	Honshu	Sea of Japan-Pacific Ocean	227
8	Great Britain	Off coast of north-west Europe	218

Notes: Estimates of the lengths of rivers vary widely depending on eg, the path to take through a delta. The definition of a desert is normally a mean annual precipitation value equal to 250ml or less. Australia is defined as a continent rather than an island.

Population: size and growth

Largest populations
Million, 2009

1	China	1,345.8	34	Poland	38.1
2	India	1,198.0	35	Algeria	34.9
3	United States	314.7	36	Canada	33.6
4	Indonesia	230.0	37	Uganda	32.7
5	Brazil	193.7	38	Morocco	32.0
6	Pakistan	180.8	39	Iraq	30.7
7	Bangladesh	162.2	40	Nepal	29.3
8	Nigeria	154.7	41	Peru	29.2
9	Russia	140.9	42	Venezuela	28.6
10	Japan	127.2	43	Afghanistan	28.2
11	Mexico	109.6	44	Malaysia	27.5
12	Philippines	92.0		Uzbekistan	27.5
13	Vietnam	88.1	46	Saudi Arabia	25.7
14	Egypt	83.0	47	North Korea	23.9
15	Ethiopia	82.8	48	Ghana	23.8
16	Germany	82.2	49	Yemen	23.6
17	Turkey	74.8	50	Taiwan	23.0
18	Iran	74.2	51	Mozambique	22.9
19	Thailand	67.8	52	Syria	21.9
20	Congo-Kinshasa	66.0	53	Australia	21.3
21	France	62.3		Romania	21.3
22	United Kingdom	61.6	55	Côte d'Ivoire	21.1
23	Italy	59.9	56	Sri Lanka	20.2
24	South Africa	50.1	57	Madagascar	19.6
25	Myanmar	50.0	58	Cameroon	19.5
26	South Korea	48.3	59	Angola	18.5
27	Colombia	45.7	60	Chile	17.0
28	Ukraine	45.7	61	Netherlands	16.6
29	Spain	44.9	62	Burkina Faso	15.8
30	Tanzania	43.7	63	Kazakhstan	15.6
31	Sudan	42.3	64	Malawi	15.3
32	Argentina	40.3		Niger	15.3
33	Kenya	39.8	66	Cambodia	14.8

Largest populations
Million, 2050

1	India	1,614	15	Vietnam	112
2	China	1,417	16	Tanzania	109
3	United States	404	17	Japan	102
4	Pakistan	335	18	Iran	97
5	Nigeria	289		Turkey	97
6	Indonesia	288	20	Uganda	91
7	Bangladesh	222	21	Kenya	85
8	Brazil	219	22	Sudan	76
9	Ethiopia	174	23	Afghanistan	74
10	Congo-Kinshasa	148	24	Thailand	73
11	Philippines	146	25	United Kingdom	72
12	Egypt	130	26	Germany	71
13	Mexico	129	27	France	68
14	Russia	116	28	Iraq	64

Fastest growing populations
Average annual % change, 2005–10

1	Qatar	15.24	25	Chad	2.75
2	United Arab Emirates	12.26	26	Oman	2.71
3	Bahrain	11.09	27	Congo-Brazzaville	2.70
4	Liberia	4.54		French Guiana	2.70
5	Kuwait	3.79	29	Senegal	2.69
6	Niger	3.54	30	Saudi Arabia	2.65
7	Singapore	3.52		Zambia	2.65
8	Uganda	3.24	32	Sierra Leone	2.60
9	Eritrea	3.16	33	Afghanistan	2.58
10	Mali	3.08		Kenya	2.58
11	Yemen	3.05	35	West Bank & Gaza	2.55
12	Malawi	3.00	36	Mauritania	2.54
13	Burkina Faso	2.97	37	Sudan	2.51
14	Benin	2.96	38	Nigeria	2.50
15	Jordan	2.94	39	Guatemala	2.47
	Madagascar	2.94	40	Macau	2.43
17	Iraq	2.93	41	Ghana	2.39
18	Angola	2.92	42	Mozambique	2.38
19	Burundi	2.90	43	Papua New Guinea	2.36
20	Tanzania	2.88	44	Israel	2.32
21	Rwanda	2.87	45	Ethiopia	2.21
22	Equatorial Guinea	2.84	46	Cameroon	2.20
23	Gambia	2.79		Somalia	2.20
24	Congo-Kinshasa	2.78	48	Togo	2.17

Slowest growing populations
Average annual % change, 2005–10

1	Moldova	-1.06	24	Armenia	0.17
2	Bulgaria	-0.64		Slovakia	0.17
	Ukraine	-0.64	26	Faroe Islands	0.19
4	Georgia	-0.57	27	Barbados	0.21
5	Lithuania	-0.55	28	Guyana	0.22
6	Belarus	-0.47		Macedonia	0.22
	Latvia	-0.47	30	Bermuda	0.25
8	Romania	-0.26		Portugal	0.25
9	Hungary	-0.21	32	Slovenia	0.27
10	Croatia	-0.18	33	Uruguay	0.28
	Puerto Rico	-0.18	34	Greece	0.31
12	Russia	-0.12	35	Malta	0.35
13	Bosnia	-0.11	36	Netherlands	0.37
14	Estonia	-0.07	37	Albania	0.39
15	Germany	-0.06		Austria	0.39
	Virgin Islands (US)	-0.06		Trinidad & Tobago	0.39
17	Serbia	0.00	40	Martinique	0.42
	Zimbabwe	0.00	41	Jamaica	0.44
19	Cuba	0.01	42	Finland	0.45
20	Japan	0.02	43	El Salvador	0.47
21	Greenland	0.04	44	Denmark	0.48
22	Poland	0.06		South Korea	0.48
23	Montenegro	0.15	46	North Korea	0.50

Population: matters of breeding and sex

Crude birth rates
Births per 1,000 population, 2005–10

Highest				Lowest	
1	Niger	49.5	1	Hong Kong	8.2
2	Mali	47.6	2	Germany	8.4
3	Uganda	46.3	3	Japan	8.6
4	Chad	45.9	4	Bosnia	8.9
5	Afghanistan	45.1		Singapore	8.9
6	Congo-Kinshasa	44.9	6	Macau	9.0
7	Zambia	44.5	7	Austria	9.1
8	Somalia	44.2	8	Channel Islands	9.3
9	Malawi	44.0		Malta	9.3
10	Burkina Faso	43.9	10	Italy	9.4
11	Angola	43.5	11	Croatia	9.5
12	Tanzania	41.6	12	Hungary	9.8
13	Benin	40.7		Portugal	9.8
	Rwanda	40.7		Slovenia	9.8
15	Sierra Leone	40.6	15	Bulgaria	9.9
16	Liberia	40.5		Switzerland	9.9
17	Nigeria	40.4	17	South Korea	10.0
18	Guinea	39.9	18	Lithuania	10.1
19	Mozambique	39.4		Slovakia	10.1
	Timor-Leste	39.4	20	Latvia	10.2
21	Gambia	39.3		Poland	10.2
	Guinea-Bissau	39.3		Romania	10.2
23	Yemen	38.6	23	Greece	10.4
24	Senegal	38.6		Ukraine	10.4
25	Kenya	38.0	25	Cuba	10.5
26	Eritrea	37.5			

Births per 1,000 women aged 15–19, 2005-10

1	Niger	207.1	19	Afghanistan	118.7
2	Congo-Kinshasa	201.4		Congo	118.7
3	Mali	186.3	21	Nigeria	118.3
4	Angola	171.1	22	Nicaragua	112.7
5	Chad	164.5	23	Benin	111.7
6	Guinea	157.4	24	Guinea-Bissau	111.1
7	Uganda	149.9	25	Dominican Republic	108.7
8	Mozambique	149.2	26	Guatemala	107.2
9	Zambia	146.8	27	Central African Rep.	106.6
10	Sierra Leone	143.7	28	Senegal	105.9
11	Liberia	142.6	29	Nepal	103.4
12	Madagascar	134.3	30	Kenya	100.2
13	Tanzania	130.4	31	Honduras	93.1
14	Côte d'Ivoire	129.4	32	Gabon	89.9
15	Cameroon	127.8		Venezuela	89.9
16	Burkina Faso	124.8	34	India	86.3
17	Equatorial Guinea	122.9	35	Swaziland	83.9
18	Malawi	119.2	36	Ecuador	82.8

Fertility rates, 2010–15
Average number of children per woman

Highest			Lowest		
1	Niger	7.2	1	Hong Kong	1.0
2	Afghanistan	6.6		Macau	1.0
3	Mali	6.5	3	Bosnia	1.2
	Timor-Leste	6.5	4	Hungary	1.3
5	Somalia	6.4		Japan	1.3
	Uganda	6.4		Malta	1.3
7	Chad	6.2		Poland	1.3
	Zambia	6.2		Romania	1.3
9	Congo-Kinshasa	6.1		Singapore	1.3
10	Malawi	6.0		Slovakia	1.3
11	Burkina Faso	5.9		South Korea	1.3
12	Angola	5.8	12	Austria	1.4
13	Nigeria	5.6		Belarus	1.4
	Tanzania	5.6		Channel Islands	1.4
15	Benin	5.5		Croatia	1.4
	Guinea	5.5		Czech Republic	1.4
	Yemen	5.5		Germany	1.4
18	Equatorial Guinea	5.4		Italy	1.4
	Liberia	5.4		Latvia	1.4
	Rwanda	5.4		Lithuania	1.4
21	Guinea-Bissau	5.3		Portugal	1.4
22	Sierra Leone	5.2		Russia	1.4
23	Gambia	5.1		Slovenia	1.4
	Mozambique	5.1		Spain	1.4
25	Senegal	5.0		Ukraine	1.4
26	Iraq	4.9			

Sex ratio, males per 100 females, 2010

Highest			Lowest		
1	Qatar	311.1	1	Latvia	85.2
2	United Arab Emirates	228.3		Ukraine	85.2
3	Bahrain	166.2	3	Estonia	85.5
4	Kuwait	148.0	4	Russia	86.1
5	Oman	142.2	5	Netherlands Antilles	86.4
6	Saudi Arabia	124.0	6	Lithuania	86.8
7	Bhutan	112.5	7	Belarus	86.9
8	China	108.0	8	Armenia	87.1
9	Afghanistan	107.2	9	Martinique	87.7
10	India	106.8	10	Georgia	89.0
11	Jordan	105.9	11	Guadeloupe	89.3
12	Equatorial Guinea	105.2	12	Hong Kong	90.0
13	French Polynesia	105.0		Virgin Islands (US)	90.0
14	Cyprus	104.3	14	Aruba	90.2
15	Fiji	104.2	15	Moldova	90.3
16	Papua New Guinea	104.1	16	Hungary	90.4
17	Timor-Leste	104.0	17	El Salvador	90.5
18	Côte d'Ivoire	103.9	18	Kazakhstan	92.4
19	Ghana	103.6		Macau	92.4
20	Guam	103.5			

Population: age

Median age[a]

Highest, 2009			*Lowest, 2009*		
1	Japan	44.7	1	Niger	15.5
2	Germany	44.3	2	Uganda	15.7
3	Italy	43.2	3	Mali	16.3
4	Channel Islands	42.6	4	Afghanistan	16.6
5	Bermuda	42.4		Angola	16.6
6	Finland	42.0		Timor-Leste	16.6
7	Austria	41.8	7	Congo-Kinshasa	16.7
	Hong Kong	41.8		Zambia	16.7
9	Slovenia	41.7	9	Malawi	16.9
10	Bulgaria	41.6	10	Burkina Faso	17.1
11	Croatia	41.5		Chad	17.1
12	Greece	41.4	12	Yemen	17.4
	Switzerland	41.4	13	Somalia	17.5
14	Belgium	41.2		Tanzania	17.5
15	Portugal	41.0	15	Gambia	17.8
16	Netherlands	40.7		Mozambique	17.8
	Sweden	40.7		Senegal	17.8
18	Denmark	40.6	18	Benin	17.9
19	Latvia	40.2	19	West Bank & Gaza	18.1
20	Spain	40.1	20	Liberia	18.2
21	Andorra	40.0		Madagascar	18.2
22	Canada	39.9	22	Guinea	18.3
	France	39.9		Iraq	18.3
24	Hungary	39.8	24	Sierra Leone	18.4
	United Kingdom	39.8	25	Kenya	18.5
26	Estonia	39.7		Nigeria	18.5
27	Malta	39.5	27	Ethiopia	18.7
28	Bosnia	39.4		Rwanda	18.7
	Czech Republic	39.4	29	Guatemala	18.9
	Martinique	39.4	30	Eritrea	19.0
31	Lithuania	39.3		Guinea-Bissau	19.0
	Ukraine	39.3	32	Côte d'Ivoire	19.2
33	Luxembourg	38.9	33	Cameroon	19.3
34	Virgin Islands (US)	38.8		Zimbabwe	19.3
35	Cayman Islands	38.7	35	Central African Rep.	19.4
	Norway	38.7	36	Swaziland	19.5
37	Romania	38.5	37	Congo-Brazzaville	19.6
38	Cuba	38.4	38	Sudan	19.7
39	Aruba	38.3		Togo	19.7
	Belarus	38.3	40	Mauritania	19.8
41	Poland	38.0	41	Burundi	20.2
	Taiwan	38.0	42	Equatorial Guinea	20.3
43	Netherlands Antilles	37.9		Lesotho	20.3
	Russia	37.9	44	Tajikistan	20.4
	South Korea	37.9		Papua New Guinea	20.4
46	Macau	37.6	46	Ghana	20.5
	Singapore	37.6	47	Jordan	20.7
48	Serbia	37.6	48	Honduras	21.0
49	Barbados	37.5	49	Syria	21.1

a Age at which there are an equal number of people above and below.

Population: density

Highest population density
People per sq km, 2010

	Highest			Lowest	
1	Macau	20,909.8	1	Greenland	0.0
2	Singapore	7,447.2	2	Mongolia	1.8
3	Hong Kong	6,417.8	3	French Guiana	2.6
4	Bahrain	1,818.2	4	Namibia	2.8
5	Malta	1,318.1	5	Australia	2.9
6	Bermuda	1,225.3	6	Iceland	3.1
7	Maldives	1,060.0	7	Suriname	3.2
8	Bangladesh	1,032.6	8	Mauritania	3.4
9	Channel Islands	786.4	9	Canada	3.4
10	West Bank & Gaza	671.0	10	Botswana	3.5
11	Mauritius	636.8		Guyana	3.5
12	Taiwan	635.7	12	Libya	3.6
13	Barbados	635.7	13	Gabon	5.6
14	Aruba	597.2	14	Kazakhstan	5.9
15	South Korea	484.1	15	Central African Rep.	7.1
16	Puerto Rico	422.4	16	Russia	8.4
17	Lebanon	406.5	17	Chad	8.7
18	Rwanda	403.4	18	Bolivia	9.0
19	Netherlands	400.0		Oman	9.0
20	India	372.5	20	Turkmenistan	10.3
21	Martinique	368.3	21	Congo-Brazzaville	11.8
22	Haiti	360.1	22	Niger	12.2
23	Belgium	350.9	23	Mali	12.4
24	Réunion	337.1	24	Norway	12.7
25	Israel	335.0	25	Saudi Arabia	12.8
26	Japan	334.9	26	New Caledonia	13.5
27	Guam	327.7	27	Belize	13.6
28	Saint Lucia	323.3	28	Argentina	14.5
29	Sri Lanka	317.9	29	Somalia	14.6
30	Virgin Islands (US)	314.3	30	Papua New Guinea	14.8
31	Philippines	310.9	31	Algeria	14.9
32	Burundi	301.2	32	Angola	15.3
33	El Salvador	294.3	33	Bhutan	15.4
34	Guadeloupe	270.2	34	Finland	15.9
35	Vietnam	264.9		Paraguay	15.9
36	Trinidad & Tobago	261.5	36	New Zealand	16.1
37	United Kingdom	255.4	37	Sudan	17.4
38	Netherlands Antilles	250.9		Zambia	17.4
39	Jamaica	249.4	39	Uruguay	19.2
40	Germany	230.5	40	Sweden	20.8
41	Pakistan	218.1	41	Chile	22.6
42	Cayman Islands	213.0		Peru	22.6
43	Dominican Republic	204.6	43	Brazil	22.9
44	Nepal	203.6	44	Bahamas	24.7
45	North Korea	202.0	45	Equatorial Guinea	25.0
46	Italy	201.0	46	Laos	26.2
47	Antigua and Barbuda	200.7	47	Kyrgyzstan	26.7
48	Luxembourg	196.2	48	Congo-Kinshasa	28.1
49	Seychelles	190.1	49	Mozambique	29.2
50	Switzerland	185.6	50	Estonia	29.7

City living

Biggest cities[a]
Population m, 2015

1	Tokyo, Japan	37.0		Luanda, Angola	6.0
2	Delhi, India	24.2		Miami, United States	6.0
3	Mumbai, India	21.8	51	Philadelphia, US	5.8
4	São Paulo, Brazil	21.3	52	Chittagong, Bangladesh	5.7
5	Mexico City, Mexico	20.1		Shenyang, China	5.7
6	New York, US	20.0		Toronto, Canada	5.7
7	Shanghai, China	17.8	55	Foshan, China	5.5
8	Kolkata, India	16.9		Pune, India	5.5
9	Dhaka, Bangladesh	16.6	57	Chengdu, China	5.4
10	Karachi, Pakistan	14.8		Riyadh, Saudi Arabia	5.4
11	Buenos Aires, Argentina	13.4	59	Barcelona, Spain	5.3
12	Beijing, China	13.3	60	Dallas, United States	5.1
13	Los Angeles, US	13.2		Nanjing, China	5.1
14	Manila, Philippines	12.6		Singapore	5.1
15	Lagos, Nigeria	12.4	63	Xian, China	5.0
	Rio de Janeiro, Brazil	12.4	64	Atlanta, United States	4.9
17	Cairo, Egypt	11.7		Yangon, Myanmar	4.9
18	Osaka, Japan	11.4	66	Abidjan, Côte d'Ivoire	4.8
19	Istanbul, Turkey	11.2		Alexandria, Egypt	4.8
20	Paris, France	10.8		Boston, United States	4.8
21	Kinshasa, Congo-Kinshasa	10.7		Houston, United States	4.8
22	Moscow, Russia	10.6	70	Guadalajara, Mexico	4.6
23	Chongqing, China	9.8		Kabul, Afghanistan	4.6
	Seoul, South Korea	9.8		St Petersburg, Russia	4.6
	Shenzhen, China	9.8		Surat, India	4.6
26	Guangzhou, China	9.7		Sydney, Australia	4.6
	Jakarta, Indonesia	9.7		Washington, DC, US	4.6
	Lima, Peru	9.7	76	Harbin, China	4.5
29	Bogotá, Colombia	9.5	77	Detroit, United States	4.4
	Chicago, United States	9.5	78	Brasília, Brazil	4.3
31	London, UK	8.7		Nairobi, Kenya	4.3
32	Tianjin, China	8.6		Pôrto Alegre, Brazil	4.3
33	Chennai, India	8.3	81	Ankara, Turkey	4.2
	Wuhan, China	8.3		Dar es Salaam, Tanzania	4.2
35	Lahore, Pakistan	8.1		Salvador, Brazil	4.2
36	Bangalore, India	7.9	84	Hangzhou, China	4.1
37	Tehran, Iran	7.6		Monterrey, Mexico	4.1
38	Bangkok, Thailand	7.4		Recife, Brazil	4.1
	Hong Kong	7.4	87	Changchun, China	4.0
	Hyderabad, India	7.4		Fortaleza, Brazil	4.0
41	Ho Chi Minh City, Vietnam	7.1		Medellín, Colombia	4.0
42	Baghdad, Iraq	6.6		Melbourne, Australia	4.0
43	Ahmadabad, India	6.3	91	Johannesburg, S. Africa	3.9
	Belo Horizonte, Brazil	6.3		Kano, Nigeria	3.9
45	Madrid, Spain	6.2		Montréal, Canada	3.9
	Santiago, Chile	6.2	94	Curitiba, Brazil	3.8
47	Dongguan, China	6.0		Phoenix, United States	3.8
	Khartoum, Sudan	6.0			

a Urban agglomerations. Data may change from year-to-year based on reassessments of agglomeration boundaries.

Urban population

Highest, %, 2010

1	Bermuda	100.0
	Cayman Islands	100.0
	Hong Kong	100.0
	Macau	100.0
	Singapore	100.0
6	Puerto Rico	98.8
7	Guadeloupe	98.4
	Kuwait	98.4
9	Belgium	97.4
10	Qatar	95.8
11	Virgin Islands (US)	95.3
12	Malta	94.7
13	Réunion	94.0
14	Iceland	93.4
	Venezuela	93.4
16	Guam	93.2
	Netherlands Antilles	93.2
18	Uruguay	92.5
19	Argentina	92.4
20	Israel	91.9
21	Australia	89.1
22	Chile	89.0
23	Bahrain	88.6
24	Andorra	88.0
25	Lebanon	87.2
26	Denmark	86.9
27	Brazil	86.5
28	New Zealand	86.2
29	Gabon	86.0
30	France	85.3

Lowest, %, 2010

1	Burundi	11.0
2	Papua New Guinea	12.5
3	Uganda	13.3
4	Trinidad & Tobago	13.9
5	Sri Lanka	14.3
6	Ethiopia	16.7
7	Niger	17.1
8	Nepal	18.6
9	Rwanda	18.9
10	Malawi	19.8
11	Cambodia	20.1
12	Swaziland	21.4
13	Eritrea	21.6
14	Kenya	22.2
15	Afghanistan	22.6
16	Burkina Faso	25.7
17	Tajikistan	26.3
18	Tanzania	26.4
19	Lesotho	26.9
20	Chad	27.6
21	St Lucia	28.0
22	Bangladesh	28.1
	Timor-Leste	28.1
24	Guinea-Bissau	30.0
	India	30.0
26	Madagascar	30.2
27	Vietnam	30.4
28	Channel Islands	31.4
29	Yemen	31.8
30	Laos	33.2

City-liveability index[a]

100 = ideal, January 2011

Best

1	Vancouver, Canada	98.0
2	Melbourne, Australia	97.5
3	Vienna, Austria	97.4
4	Toronto, Canada	97.2
5	Calgary, Canada	96.6
6	Helsinki, Finland	96.2
7	Sydney, Australia	96.1
8	Adelaide, Australia	95.9
	Perth, Australia	95.9

10	Auckland, New Zealand	95.7
11	Zurich, Switzerland	95.6
12	Geneva, Switzerland	95.2
	Osaka, Japan	95.2
14	Hamburg, Germany	95.0
	Stockholm, Sweden	95.0
16	Montreal, Canada	94.8
	Paris, France	94.8

Worst

1	Harare, Zimbabwe	37.5
2	Dhaka, Bangladesh	38.7
3	Port Moresby, Papua NG	38.9

4	Lagos, Nigeria	39.0
5	Algiers, Algeria	39.4
6	Karachi, Pakistan	40.9

a Based on a range of factors including stability, health care, culture, education, infrastructure.

Migration

Biggest immigrant populations
Million, 2010

1	United States	42.8	11	Ukraine	5.3
2	Russia	12.3	12	Italy	4.5
3	Germany	10.8	13	Pakistan	4.2
4	Saudi Arabia	7.3	14	United Arab Emirates	3.3
5	Canada	7.2	15	Kazakhstan	3.1
6	United Kingdom	7.0	16	Jordan	3.0
7	Spain	6.9	17	Israel	2.9
8	France	6.7	18	Hong Kong	2.7
9	Australia	5.5	19	Côte d'Ivoire	2.4
10	India	5.4		Malaysia	2.4

Immigrants
As % of population, 2010

1	Qatar	86.5	11	West Bank & Gaza	43.6
2	United Arab Emirates	70.0	12	Singapore	40.7
3	Kuwait	68.8	13	Israel	40.4
4	Andorra	64.4	14	Bahrain	39.1
5	Cayman Islands	63.0	15	Hong Kong	38.8
6	Virgin Islands (US)	56.5	16	Brunei	36.4
7	Macau	54.7	17	Luxembourg	35.2
8	Channel Islands	49.8	18	Aruba	31.9
9	Jordan	45.9	19	Bermuda	30.7
10	Guam	43.9	20	Oman	28.4

Biggest emigrant populations
Number of a country's nationals who have emigrated, m, 2010

1	Mexico	11.9	11	Egypt	3.7
2	India	11.4		Kazakhstan	3.7
3	Russia	11.1	13	Germany	3.5
4	China	8.3		Italy	3.5
5	Ukraine	6.6	15	Poland	3.1
6	Bangladesh	5.4	16	West Bank & Gaza	3.0
7	Pakistan	4.7	17	Romania	2.8
	United Kingdom	4.7	18	Indonesia	2.5
9	Philippines	4.3	19	United States	2.4
10	Turkey	4.3	20	Afghanistan	2.3

Emigrants
Nationals who have emigrated as % of the current population in their original country, 2010

1	West Bank & Gaza	68.3	11	Trinidad & Tobago	26.7
2	Guyana	56.8	12	Malta	26.2
3	Antigua & Barbuda	48.3	13	Georgia	25.1
4	Albania	45.4	14	Saint Lucia	23.2
5	Barbados	41.0	15	Kazakhstan	23.1
6	Suriname	39.0	16	Macedonia	21.9
7	Bosnia	38.9	17	Moldova	21.5
8	Cape Verde	37.5	18	Fiji	21.3
9	Jamaica	36.1	19	Portugal	20.8
10	Armenia	28.2			

Refugees[a] and asylum seekers

Refugees[a], country of origin
'000, 2009

1	Afghanistan	2,887.1	11	China	180.6
2	Iraq	1,785.2	12	Central African Rep.	159.6
3	Somalia	678.3	13	Turkey	146.4
4	Congo-Kinshasa	455.9	14	Angola	141.0
5	Myanmar	406.7	15	Rwanda	129.1
6	Colombia	389.8	16	Russia	109.5
7	Sri Lanka	368.2	17	West Bank & Gaza	95.2
8	Vietnam	339.3	18	Burundi	94.2
9	Eritrea	209.2	19	Bhutan	89.1
10	Serbia	195.6	20	Croatia	76.5

Countries with largest refugee[a] populations
'000, 2009

1	Pakistan	1,740.7	11	Bangladesh	228.6
2	Iran	1,070.5	12	Venezuela	201.3
3	Syria	1,054.5	13	France	196.4
4	Germany	593.8	14	Sudan	186.3
5	Jordan	450.8	15	Congo-Kinshasa	185.8
6	Kenya	358.9	16	India	185.3
7	Chad	338.5	17	Yemen	170.9
8	China	301.0	18	Canada	169.4
9	United States	275.5	19	Uganda	127.3
10	United Kingdom	269.4	20	Ethiopia	121.9

Origin of asylum applications to industrialised countries
'000, 2009

1	Afghanistan	26.8	11	Eritrea	10.2
2	Iraq	24.3	12	Mexico	10.0
3	Somalia	22.6		Sri Lanka	10.0
4	Russia	20.4	14	Zimbabwe	8.5
5	China	20.1	15	Turkey	6.9
6	Serbia	18.6	16	Armenia	6.2
7	Nigeria	13.3		Bangladesh	6.2
8	Iran	11.5	18	Congo-Kinshasa	5.2
9	Pakistan	11.2	19	Guinea	5.0
10	Georgia	11.0		Syria	5.0

Asylum applications in industrialised countries
'000, 2009

1	United States	49.0	10	Greece	15.9
2	France	42.0	11	Austria	15.8
3	Canada	33.3	12	Netherlands	14.9
4	United Kingdom	29.8	13	Switzerland	14.5
5	Germany	27.7	14	Poland	10.6
6	Sweden	24.2	15	Turkey	7.8
7	Italy	17.6	16	Australia	6.2
8	Belgium	17.2	17	Finland	5.9
	Norway	17.2	18	Hungary	4.7

a According to UNHCR. Includes people in "refugee-like situations".

The world economy

Biggest economies
GDP, $bn, 2009

1	United States	14,119	24	Austria	381
2	Japan	5,069	25	Taiwan	377
3	China	4,985	26	Saudi Arabia	376
4	Germany	3,330	27	Iran	331
5	France[a]	2,649	28	Greece	330
6	United Kingdom	2,175	29	Venezuela	326
7	Italy	2,113	30	Denmark	310
8	Brazil	1,594	31	Argentina	307
9	Spain	1,460	32	South Africa	285
10	India	1,377	33	Thailand	264
11	Canada	1,336	34	Finland	238
12	Russia	1,232	35	Colombia	234
13	Australia	925	36	Portugal	233
14	Mexico	875	37	United Arab Emirates	230
15	South Korea	833	38	Ireland	227
16	Netherlands	792	39	Hong Kong	211
17	Turkey	615	40	Israel	195
18	Indonesia	540	40	Malaysia	193
19	Switzerland	492	42	Czech Republic	190
20	Belgium	471	43	Egypt	188
21	Poland	430	44	Singapore	182
22	Sweden	406	45	Nigeria	173
23	Norway	382	46	Chile	164

Biggest economies by purchasing power
GDP PPP, $bn, 2009

1	United States	14,119	23	Argentina	586
2	China	9,091	24	Thailand	542
3	Japan	4,135	25	South Africa	507
4	India	3,808	26	Egypt	471
5	Germany	2,975	27	Pakistan	443
6	Russia	2,686	28	Colombia	409
7	United Kingdom	2,174	29	Belgium	392
8	France	2,173	30	Malaysia	385
9	Brazil	2,008	31	Switzerland	350
10	Italy	1,953		Venezuela	350
11	Mexico	1,532	33	Sweden	348
12	Spain	1,478	34	Nigeria	341
13	South Korea	1,321	35	Greece	334
14	Canada	1,276	36	Philippines	326
15	Turkey	1,023	36	Austria	325
16	Indonesia	966	38	Romania	307
17	Australia	865	39	Hong Kong	303
18	Iran	843	40	Ukraine	291
19	Taiwan	735	41	Algeria	285
20	Poland	721	42	Norway	271
21	Netherlands	672	43	Czech Republic	268
22	Saudi Arabia	596	44	United Arab Emirates	266

Note: For a list of 194 countries with their GDPs, see pages 250–254.
a Includes overseas departments.

Regional GDP

$bn, 2010		*% annual growth 2005–10*	
World	62,910	World	3.6
Advanced economies	41,530	Advanced economies	1.1
G7	31,890	G7	0.7
Euro area (16)	12,190	Euro area (16)	0.8
Asia[a]	9,430	Asia[a]	9.2
Latin America	4,830	Latin America	4.0
Central & Eastern Europe[b]	3,710	Central & Eastern Europe[b]	3.7
Middle East & N. Africa	2,360	Middle East & N. Africa	4.5
Sub-Saharan Africa	1,060	Sub-Saharan Africa	5.4

Regional purchasing power

GDP, % of total, 2010		*$ per head, 2010*	
World	100.0	World	10,900
Advanced economies	52.3	Advanced economies	38,080
G7	39.5	G7	39,710
Euro area (16)	14.6	Euro area (16)	32,770
Asia[a]	24.0	Asia[a]	5,010
Latin America	8.6	Latin America	11,240
Central & Eastern Europe[b]	7.6	Central & Eastern Europe[b]	12,520
Middle East & N. Africa	5.0	Middle East & N. Africa	8,910
Sub-Saharan Africa	2.4	Sub-Saharan Africa	2,260

Regional population

% of total (6.9bn), 2010		*No. of countries[c], 2010*	
World	100.0	World	184
Advanced economies	15.0	Advanced economies	34
G7	10.8	G7	7
Euro area (16)	4.8	Euro area (16)	16
Asia[a]	52.3	Asia[a]	27
Latin America	8.3	Latin America	32
Central & Eastern Europe[b]	6.7	Central & Eastern Europe[b]	27
Middle East & N. Africa	6.0	Middle East & N. Africa	20
Sub-Saharan Africa	11.7	Sub-Saharan Africa	44

Regional international trade

Exports of goods & services		*Current account balances*	
% of total, 2010		*$bn, 2010*	
World	100.0	World	283
Advanced economies	63.7	Advanced economies	-96
G7	34.9	G7	-329
Euro area (16)	26.1	Euro area (16)	-77
Asia[a]	15.8	Asia[a]	308
Latin America	5.3	Latin America	-57
Central & Eastern Europe[b]	7.1	Central & Eastern Europe[b]	-1
Middle East & N. Africa	6.1	Middle East & N. Africa	153
Sub-Saharan Africa	2.0	Sub-Saharan Africa	-25

a Excludes Hong Kong, Japan, Singapore, South Korea and Taiwan.
b Includes Turkey.
c IMF definition.

Living standards

Highest GDP per head
$, 2009

1	Luxembourg	105,040	31	Martinique[b]	31,610
2	Bermuda	88,750	32	Cyprus	31,280
3	Norway	79,090	33	Hong Kong	30,070
4	Channel Islands[a]	77,130	34	New Zealand	29,350
5	Qatar	69,750	35	Greece	29,240
6	Switzerland	63,630	36	Guadeloupe[b]	28,540
7	Denmark	55,990	37	Brunei	26,850
8	Ireland	51,050	38	Israel	26,260
9	United Arab Emirates	50,070	39	Réunion[b]	26,200
10	Netherlands	47,920	40	Bahrain	26,020
11	United States	45,990	41	Puerto Rico	24,740
12	Austria	45,560	42	Aruba	24,630
13	Faroe Islands	45,190	43	Slovenia	23,730
14	Finland	44,580	44	Greenland	22,610
15	Andorra[b]	44,290	45	Portugal	21,900
16	Belgium	43,670	46	Bahamas[a]	21,680
17	Sweden	43,650	47	French Guiana[b]	20,640
18	Australia	42,280	48	Netherlands Antilles	20,300
19	France	41,050	49	Malta	19,250
20	Germany	40,670	50	Czech Republic	18,140
21	Macau	40,400	51	South Korea	17,080
22	Japan	39,740	52	French Polynesia	16,860
23	Canada	39,600	53	Taiwan	16,330
24	Iceland	38,030	54	Oman	16,210
25	New Caledonia	37,120	55	Slovakia	16,180
26	Kuwait	36,670	56	Trinidad & Tobago	15,840
27	Singapore	36,540	57	Equatorial Guinea	15,400
28	United Kingdom	35,170	58	Saudi Arabia	14,800
29	Italy	35,080	59	Virgin Islands (US)[c]	14,360
30	Spain	31,770	60	Estonia	14,240

Lowest GDP per head
$, 2009

1	Burundi	160	17	Central African Rep.	450
	Congo-Kinshasa	160		Zimbabwe	450
3	Liberia	220	19	Afghanistan	490
	Somalia	220		Timor-Leste	490
5	Malawi	310		Uganda	490
6	Ethiopia	340	22	North Korea	500
	Sierra Leone	340		Tanzania	500
8	Niger	350	24	Burkina Faso	520
9	Eritrea	370		Guinea-Bissau	520
10	Myanmar	380		Rwanda	520
11	Guinea	410	27	Bangladesh	550
12	Gambia, The	430	28	Chad	610
	Mozambique	430	29	Haiti	650
	Nepal	430	30	Mali	690
	Togo	430	31	Cambodia	710
16	Madagascar	440	32	Tajikistan	720

a 2007   b 2008   c 2004

Highest purchasing power

GDP per head in PPP (USA = 100), 2009

1	Bermuda	272.4	35	Spain	69.9
2	Qatar	198.7	36	Equatorial Guinea	69.1
3	Luxembourg	182.3		Taiwan	69.1
4	Cayman Islands	131.6	38	Cyprus	67.1
5	Macau	130.8	39	Greece	64.4
6	United Arab Emirates	125.6	40	New Zealand	63.0
7	British Virgin Is.	125.3	41	Martinique[d]	60.5
8	Norway	122.2	42	Israel	60.1
9	Channel Islands[ab]	112.9	43	Slovenia	59.0
10	Brunei[c]	111.3	44	South Korea	58.9
11	Singapore	110.1	45	Czech Republic	55.6
12	Kuwait[c]	105.7		Trinidad & Tobago	55.6
13	United States	100.0	47	Oman[d]	55.4
14	Switzerland	98.3	48	Guadeloupe[d]	54.7
15	Andorra	95.2	49	Portugal	54.2
16	Hong Kong	94.0	50	Malta	54.0
17	Ireland	88.5	51	Saudi Arabia	51.1
18	Netherlands	88.4	52	Aruba	50.3
19	Australia	86.0	53	Réunion[d]	50.0
20	Austria	84.4	54	Slovakia	49.8
21	Canada	82.2	55	Bahamas	44.2
22	Denmark	82.0		Hungary	44.2
23	Sweden	81.3		Netherlands Antilles	44.2
24	New Caledonia	80.7	58	Croatia	43.5
25	Iceland	80.0	59	Greenland	43.5
26	Belgium	79.0	60	French Polynesia	43.4
	Germany	79.0	61	Estonia	42.8
28	Finland	76.7	62	Seychelles	42.6
29	Bahrain[d]	76.5	63	Russia	41.2
30	United Kingdom	76.4	64	Poland	41.1
31	France	73.2	65	Antigua and Barbuda	40.8
32	Faroe Islands[bd]	71.3	66	French Guiana	39.5
33	Italy	70.5	67	Lithuania	37.6
	Japan	70.5	68	Libya	35.9

Lowest purchasing power

GDP per head in PPP (USA = 100), 2009

1	Somalia	0.46	13	Sierra Leone	1.76
2	Congo-Kinshasa	0.69	14	Togo	1.85
3	Zimbabwe	0.70	15	Mozambique	1.92
4	Myanmar	0.83	16	Ethiopia	2.03
5	Burundi	0.85	17	Madagascar	2.18
6	Liberia	0.86	18	Guinea	2.28
7	North Korea	1.09	19	Guinea-Bissau	2.33
8	Eritrea	1.26	20	Rwanda	2.47
9	Niger	1.50	21	Haiti	2.50
10	Central African Rep.	1.65	22	Nepal	2.51
11	Malawi	1.73	23	Burkina Faso	2.58
12	Timor-Leste	1.75		Mali	2.58

a 2005   b Estimate.   c 2007   d 2008

The quality of life

Human development index[a]
Highest, 2010

1	Norway	93.8	31	Malta	81.5
2	Australia	93.7		United Arab Emirates	81.5
3	New Zealand	90.7	33	Estonia	81.2
4	United States	90.2	34	Cyprus	81.0
5	Ireland	89.5	35	Brunei	80.5
6	Netherlands	89.0		Hungary	80.5
7	Canada	88.8	37	Qatar	80.3
8	Germany	88.5	38	Bahrain	80.1
	Sweden	88.5	39	Poland	79.5
10	Japan	88.4		Portugal	79.5
11	South Korea	87.7	41	Barbados	78.8
12	Switzerland	87.4	42	Bahamas	78.4
13	France	87.2	43	Chile	78.3
	Israel	87.2		Lithuania	78.3
15	Finland	87.1	45	Argentina	77.5
16	Iceland	86.9	46	Kuwait	77.1
17	Belgium	86.7	47	Latvia	76.9
18	Denmark	86.6		Montenegro	76.9
19	Spain	86.3	49	Croatia	76.7
20	Hong Kong	86.2		Romania	76.7
21	Greece	85.5	51	Uruguay	76.5
22	Italy	85.4	52	Libya	75.5
23	Luxembourg	85.2		Panama	75.5
24	Austria	85.1	54	Saudi Arabia	75.2
25	United Kingdom	84.9	55	Mexico	75.0
26	Singapore	84.6	56	Malaysia	74.4
27	Czech Republic	84.1	57	Bulgaria	74.3
28	Slovenia	82.8	58	Trinidad & Tobago	73.6
29	Andorra	82.4	59	Serbia	73.5
30	Slovakia	81.8	60	Belarus	73.2

Human development index[a]
Lowest, 2010

1	Zimbabwe	14.0	11	Central African Rep.	31.5
2	Congo-Kinshasa	23.9	12	Sierra Leone	31.7
3	Niger	26.1	13	Ethiopia	32.8
4	Burundi	28.2	14	Guinea	34.0
5	Mozambique	28.4	15	Afghanistan	34.9
6	Guinea-Bissau	28.9	16	Sudan	37.9
7	Chad	29.5	17	Malawi	38.5
8	Liberia	30.0		Rwanda	38.5
9	Burkina Faso	30.5	19	Gambia, The	39.0
10	Mali	30.9	20	Zambia	39.5

a GDP or GDP per head is often taken as a measure of how developed a country is, but its usefulness is limited as it refers only to economic welfare. The UN Development Programme combines statistics on average and expected years of schooling and life expectancy with income levels (now GNI per head, valued in PPP US$). The HDI is shown here scaled from 0 to 100; countries scoring over 80 are considered to have very high human development, 67–79 high, 50–79 medium and those under 50 low.

Inequality-adjusted human development index[a]
Highest, 2010

1	Norway	87.6	13	Belgium	79.4
2	Australia	86.4	14	France	79.2
3	Sweden	82.4	15	Czech Republic	79.0
4	Netherlands	81.8	16	Austria	78.7
5	Germany	81.4	17	Spain	77.9
6	Ireland	81.3	18	Luxembourg	77.5
	Switzerland	81.3	19	Slovenia	77.1
8	Canada	81.2	20	Greece	76.8
9	Iceland	81.1	21	United Kingdom	76.6
10	Denmark	81.0	22	Slovakia	76.4
11	Finland	80.6	23	Israel	76.3
12	United States	79.9	24	Italy	75.2

Gini coefficient[b]

	Highest 2000-10			*Lowest 2000-10*	
1	Namibia	74.3	1	Azerbaijan	16.8
2	Botswana	61.0	2	Denmark	24.7
3	Belize	59.6	3	Japan	24.9
4	Haiti	59.5	4	Sweden	25.0
5	Angola	58.6	5	Czech Republic	25.8
6	Colombia	58.5		Norway	25.8
7	South Africa	57.8		Slovakia	25.8
8	Bolivia	57.2	8	Finland	26.9
9	Honduras	55.3	9	Ukraine	27.6
10	Brazil	55.0	10	Serbia	28.2
11	Panama	54.9	11	Germany	28.3
12	Ecuador	54.4	12	Belarus	28.8
13	Guatemala	53.7	13	Croatia	29.0

Economic freedom index[c]
2010

1	Hong Kong	89.7	14	Estonia	75.2
2	Singapore	87.2	15	Netherlands	74.7
3	Australia	82.5	16	United Kingdom	74.5
4	New Zealand	82.3	17	Finland	74.0
5	Switzerland	81.9	18	Cyprus	73.3
6	Canada	80.8	19	Macau	73.1
7	Ireland	78.7	20	Japan	72.8
8	Denmark	78.6	21	Austria	71.9
9	United States	77.8		Sweden	71.9
10	Bahrain	77.7	23	Germany	71.8
11	Chile	77.4	24	Lithuania	71.3
12	Luxembourg	76.2	25	St Lucia	70.8
	Mauritius	76.2		Taiwan	70.8

a When there is inequality in the distribution of health, education and income, the IHDI of an average person in society is less than the ordinary HDI.

b The lower its value, the more equally household income is distributed.

c Ranks countries on the basis of indicators of how government intervention can restrict the economic relations between individuals, published by the Heritage Foundation. Scores are from 80–100 (free) to 0–49.9 (repressed) (see Glossary).

Economic growth

Highest economic growth
Average annual % increase in real GDP, 1999–2009

1	Equatorial Guinea	19.1	28	Tanzania	6.8
2	Azerbaijan	14.4	29	United Arab Emirates	6.5
3	Turkmenistan	14.2	30	Uzbekistan	6.4
4	Qatar	12.9		Trinidad & Tobago	6.4
5	Angola	11.3	32	Cape Verde	6.3
6	Myanmar	11.1	33	Jordan	6.2
7	China	10.3		Kosovo[b]	6.2
8	Sierra Leone	9.4	35	Bahrain	6.0
9	Afghanistan[a]	9.0	36	Albania	5.9
10	Nigeria	8.6	37	Bangladesh	5.8
11	Kazakhstan	8.5		Georgia	5.8
12	Armenia	8.3		Panama	5.8
13	Tajikistan	8.1	40	Ghana	5.4
	Ethiopia	8.1		Russia	5.4
	Cambodia	8.1	42	Burkina Faso	5.2
16	Bhutan	8.0		Zambia	5.2
17	Rwanda	7.7	44	Indonesia	5.1
18	Mozambique	7.5		Peru	5.1
19	Uganda	7.4		Dominican Republic	5.1
20	Vietnam	7.3		Singapore	5.1
	Sudan	7.3	48	Kuwait	5.0
22	Maldives	7.2		Sri Lanka	5.0
	Belarus	7.2		Egypt	5.0
24	Chad	7.1	51	Belize	4.9
25	Laos	7.0	52	Timor-Leste	4.8
26	India	6.9		Iran	4.8
	Mongolia	6.9			

Lowest economic growth
Average annual % change in real GDP, 1999–2009

1	Zimbabwe[b]	-6.1	20	Belgium	1.5
2	Eritrea	-0.7	21	Malta[b]	1.6
3	Côte d'Ivoire	0.4		Netherlands	1.6
4	Italy	0.5		Togo	1.6
	Liberia[b]	0.5	24	Austria	1.7
6	Japan	0.6		Mexico	1.7
7	Haiti	0.7		Switzerland	1.7
8	Denmark	0.8		United Kingdom	1.7
	Fiji	0.8	28	Guyana	1.8
	Germany	0.8		United States	1.8
11	Central African Rep.	0.9	30	Norway	1.9
	Portugal	0.9		Sweden	1.9
13	Jamaica	1.0	32	Finland	2.0
14	Bahamas	1.1	33	Canada	2.1
	St. Lucia	1.1		El Salvador	2.1
16	Barbados	1.3	35	Hungary	2.2
17	Brunei	1.4		Paraguay	2.2
	France	1.4	37	Swaziland	2.3
	Gabon	1.4		Uruguay	2.3

a 2002–09   b 2000–09

Highest economic growth
Average annual % increase in real GDP, 1989–99

1	Equatorial Guinea	29.2	10	Chile	6.4
2	China	9.9		Mozambique	6.4
3	Eritrea[a]	7.7	12	Taiwan	6.3
4	Vietnam	7.4		Uganda	6.3
5	Singapore	7.3	14	Cambodia	6.2
6	Malaysia	7.1	15	Cape Verde	6.1
7	Ireland	6.7		Laos	6.1
8	South Korea	6.6		Panama	6.1
9	Maldives	6.5			

Lowest economic growth
Average annual % change in real GDP, 1989–99

1	Ukraine[a]	-9.5	11	Kyrgyzstan[a]	-2.8
2	Sierra Leone	-7.8	12	Romania	-2.5
3	Moldova[a]	-7.5	13	Djibouti[b]	-1.6
4	Tajikistan[a]	-5.9	14	Burundi	-1.3
5	Congo-Kinshasa	-5.6	15	Belarus[a]	-1.1
6	Bulgaria	-5.4	16	Macedonia[b]	-0.9
7	Azerbaijan[a]	-4.8	17	Zambia	-0.6
	Turkmenistan[a]	-4.8	18	Albania	-0.5
9	Kazakhstan[a]	-4.0	19	Mongolia	-0.4
	Russia[a]	-4.0	20	Rwanda	-0.3

Highest services growth
Average annual % increase in real terms, 2001–09

1	Afghanistan[c]	15.7	10	Azerbaijan	10.1
2	Equatorial Guinea	15.1	11	Moldova	10.0
3	Turkmenistan	15.0	12	India	9.6
4	Nigeria[d]	13.4	13	Bhutan	9.5
5	Angola	11.8	14	Sudan	9.4
6	China	11.4	15	Mongolia	9.0
7	Congo-Kinshasa	11.1	16	Uzbekistan	8.9
8	Ethiopia	10.7	17	Uganda	8.7
9	Armenia	10.5	18	Cambodia	8.4

Lowest services growth
Average annual % change in real terms, 2001–09

1	Zimbabwe	-4.3		Finland	1.1
2	United Arab Emirates[e]	-2.3	9	Bahamas[f]	1.2
3	Guinea	-1.3		Côte d'Ivoire	1.2
4	Slovakia	0.2	11	Germany	1.3
5	Eritrea	0.5		Japan[g]	1.3
6	Italy	0.6	13	Haiti	1.4
7	Denmark	1.1		Portugal	1.4

a 1992–99   b 1991–99   c 2002–09   d 2002–07   e 2001–06   f 2001–07
g 2001–08
Note: Rankings of highest and lowest industrial growth 2001–09 can be found on page 46 and highest and lowest agricultural growth 2001–09 on page 49.

Trading places

Biggest exporters

% of total world exports (goods, services and income), 2009

1	Euro area (16)	16.46	22	Austria		1.23
2	United States	11.77		Luxembourg		1.23
3	Germany	8.77	24	Australia		1.22
4	China	7.86	25	Saudi Arabia		1.21
5	United Kingdom	4.72	26	United Arab Emirates		1.14
6	Japan	4.63	27	Hong Kong		1.12
7	France	4.46	28	Malaysia		1.08
8	Netherlands	4.23	29	Brazil		1.03
9	Italy	3.12	30	Norway		1.02
10	South Korea	2.44		Thailand		1.02
11	Canada	2.37	32	Poland		0.97
12	Belgium	2.21	33	Denmark		0.95
13	Spain	2.20	34	Turkey		0.81
14	Russia	2.07	35	Czech Republic		0.75
15	Switzerland	2.05	36	Indonesia		0.74
16	Singapore	1.54	37	Hungary		0.63
17	Ireland	1.50	38	Finland		0.58
18	India	1.49	39	Iran		0.48
19	Taiwan	1.39	40	South Africa		0.45
20	Mexico	1.36	41	Portugal		0.43
21	Sweden	1.31	42	Israel		0.40

Most trade dependent

Trade[a] as % of GDP, 2009

1	Guyana[a]	91.3
2	Malaysia	89.7
3	Vietnam	89.2
4	United Arab Emirates	86.1
5	Singapore	78.1
6	Iraq[a]	77.8
7	Zimbabwe	75.6
8	Aruba	74.5
	Lesotho	74.5
10	Slovakia	72.9
11	Equatorial Guinea	72.1
12	Bahrain	68.4
13	Trinidad & Tobago[a]	67.8
14	Netherlands	66.0
15	Panama	62.6
16	Czech Republic	61.6
17	Oman	61.2
18	Netherlands Antilles	61.0
19	Cambodia	60.9
20	Kyrgyzstan	60.3
21	Qatar	60.2
	Suriname	60.2

Least trade dependent

Trade[a] as % of GDP, 2009

1	North Korea	4.5
2	Bermuda	9.3
3	United States	9.6
4	Brazil	10.7
5	Japan	11.9
6	Central African Rep.	12.3
7	Greece	13.7
8	Cuba	14.2
9	Euro area (16)	14.5
10	United Kingdom	15.2
11	Colombia	15.8
12	Pakistan	16.4
13	Rwanda	17.3
14	India	17.6
15	Argentina	17.7
	Sudan	17.7
17	Spain	17.8
18	New Zealand	18.2
19	Turkey	18.6
20	Iceland	18.8
21	Australia	19.1

Notes: The figures are drawn wherever possible from balance of payment statistics so have differing definitions from trade statistics taken from customs or similar sources. For Hong Kong and Singapore, domestic exports and retained imports only are used. Euro area data exclude intra-euro area trade.
a 2008

Biggest traders of goods[a]
% of world, 2010

Exports		Imports	
1 China	10.4	1 United States	12.8
2 United States	8.4	2 China	9.1
3 Germany	8.3	3 Germany	6.9
4 Japan	5.1	4 Japan	4.5
5 Netherlands	3.8	5 France	3.9
6 France	3.4	6 United Kingdom	3.6
7 South Korea	3.1	7 Netherlands	3.4
8 Italy	2.9	8 Italy	3.1
9 Belgium	2.7	9 South Korea	2.8
United Kingdom	2.7	10 Canada	2.6
11 Russia	2.6	11 Belgium	2.5
12 Canada	2.5	12 India	2.1
13 Mexico	2.0	13 Mexico	2.0
14 Taiwan	1.8	Spain	2.0
15 Saudi Arabia	1.7	15 Russia	1.6
16 Spain	1.6	Taiwan	1.6
17 United Arab Emirates[b]	1.5	17 Australia	1.3
18 Australia	1.4	18 Brazil	1.2
India	1.4	Thailand	1.2
20 Brazil	1.3	Turkey	1.2
Malaysia	1.3		
Switzerland	1.3		
Thailand	1.3		

Biggest earners from services and income
% of world exports of services and income, 2009

1 Euro area (16)	19.30	22 Russia	1.20
2 United States	17.21	23 South Korea	1.18
3 United Kingdom	8.06	24 Australia	1.10
4 Germany	7.34	25 Norway	1.04
5 France	5.41	26 Taiwan	0.81
6 Japan	4.81	27 Greece	0.69
7 Netherlands	3.79	28 Finland	0.68
8 China	3.77	29 Malaysia	0.63
9 Luxembourg	3.32	30 Turkey	0.61
10 Hong Kong	2.99	31 Brazil	0.58
11 Spain	2.85	32 Poland	0.57
12 Switzerland	2.70	Thailand	0.57
13 Ireland	2.67	34 Hungary	0.55
14 Italy	2.61	35 Portugal	0.54
15 Belgium	2.42	36 Saudi Arabia	0.47
16 Singapore	2.28	37 Israel	0.44
17 Canada	1.74	38 Czech Republic	0.40
18 Sweden	1.67	39 Egypt	0.36
19 India	1.65	40 Kuwait	0.34
20 Austria	1.42	41 Mexico	0.32
21 Denmark	1.29	42 Macau	0.31

a Individual countries only.
b Estimate.

Balance of payments: current account

Largest surpluses
$m, 2009

1	China	297,142	26	Argentina	8,632
2	Germany	165,470	27	Venezuela	8,561
3	Japan	142,190	28	Philippines	8,552
4	Norway	50,122	29	Trinidad & Tobago[a]	8,519
5	Russia	49,365	30	United Arab Emirates	7,845
6	South Korea	42,668	31	Macau	7,828
7	Taiwan	42,056	32	Israel	7,592
8	Switzerland	38,972	33	Finland	6,814
9	Netherlands	36,581	34	Chile	4,217
10	Singapore	32,628	35	Brunei	3,977
11	Malaysia	31,801	36	Belgium	3,522
12	Sweden	31,460	37	Luxembourg	3,495
13	Kuwait	28,605	38	Bangladesh	3,345
14	Iraq[a]	26,973	39	Latvia	2,284
15	Saudi Arabia	22,765	40	Côte d'Ivoire	1,670
16	Thailand	21,861	41	Lithuania	1,646
17	Nigeria	21,659	42	Gabon[b]	1,485
18	Hong Kong	18,278	43	Timor-Leste	1,363
19	Denmark	11,222	44	Estonia	893
20	Austria	10,995	45	Bolivia	814
21	Indonesia	10,743	46	Uzbekistan	735
22	Iran	10,282	47	Bermuda	579
23	Azerbaijan	10,178	48	Bahrain	560
24	Qatar	10,015	49	West Bank & Gaza[a]	535
25	Libya	9,381	50	Cuba[c]	528

Largest deficits
$m, 2009

1	United States	-378,430	22	Mexico	-6,242
2	Spain	-80,375	23	Morocco	-5,362
3	Italy	-66,199	24	Colombia	-5,001
4	Euro area (16)	-64,500	25	Bulgaria	-4,751
5	France	-51,860	26	Kazakhstan	-4,249
6	Australia	-43,836	27	Sudan	-3,908
7	Canada	-38,380	28	New Zealand	-3,624
8	United Kingdom	-37,050	29	Pakistan	-3,583
9	Greece	-35,913	30	Egypt	-3,349
10	India	-26,626	31	Croatia	-3,315
11	Brazil	-24,302	32	Turkmenistan	-2,981
12	Portugal	-23,952	33	Slovakia	-2,810
13	Turkey	-14,410	34	Yemen	-2,565
14	South Africa	-11,327	35	Serbia	-2,412
15	Poland	-9,598	36	Ethiopia	-2,191
16	Angola	-7,572	37	Dominican Republic	-2,159
17	Lebanon	-7,555	38	Czech Republic	-2,147
18	Romania	-7,298	39	Equatorial Guinea	-2,093
19	Ireland	-6,488	40	Burkina Faso[a]	-1,994
20	Belarus	-6,389	41	Cyprus	-1,915
21	Vietnam	-6,274	42	Senegal	-1,884

Note: Euro area data exclude intra-euro area trade.   a 2008   b 2006   c 2007

Largest surpluses as % of GDP
%, 2009

1	Timor-Leste	244.3	26	Saudi Arabia	6.1
2	Iraq[a]	41.0	27	Aruba	6.0
3	Trinidad & Tobago[a]	40.2		China	6.0
4	Brunei	37.1	29	Philippines	5.3
5	Macau	36.0	30	South Korea	5.1
6	Kuwait	26.1	31	Germany	5.0
7	Azerbaijan	23.7	32	Bolivia	4.7
8	Singapore	17.9		Estonia	4.7
9	Malaysia	16.5	34	Netherlands	4.6
10	Libya	15.0	35	French Polynesia	4.5
11	Gabon[b]	13.4	36	Lithuania	4.4
12	Norway	13.1	37	Gambia, The	4.0
13	Nigeria	12.5		Russia	4.0
14	Taiwan	11.1	39	Israel	3.9
15	Qatar	10.2	40	Bangladesh	3.7
16	Bermuda	10.1	41	Denmark	3.6
17	Hong Kong	8.7	42	United Arab Emirates	3.4
	Latvia	8.7	43	Iran	3.1
19	Thailand	8.3	44	Austria	2.9
20	West Bank & Gaza[a]	8.1		Finland	2.9
21	Switzerland	7.9	46	Argentina	2.8
22	Sweden	7.7		Japan	2.8
23	Côte d'Ivoire	7.2	48	Bahrain	2.7
24	Luxembourg	6.7	49	Chile	2.6
25	Suriname	6.5		Venezuela	2.6

Largest deficits as % of GDP
%, 2009

1	Liberia	-61.7	22	Burundi	-12.4
2	Montenegro	-30.1	23	Georgia	-12.3
3	Maldives	-27.4		Mauritania	-12.3
4	Zimbabwe	-25.4	25	Niger	-12.1
5	Burkina Faso[a]	-24.5	26	Mozambique	-12.0
6	Antigua & Barbuda	-23.1	27	Mali	-11.8
7	Chad	-22.5	28	Bahamas	-11.7
8	Lebanon	-21.9	29	Guinea-Bissau[a]	-11.1
9	Madagascar	-20.7	30	Congo-Kinshasa	-11.0
10	Netherlands Antilles	-20.6	31	Greece	-10.9
11	Equatorial Guinea	-20.1	32	Iceland	-10.8
12	St Lucia	-19.8	33	Guinea	-10.4
13	Kosovo	-17.6	34	Portugal	-10.3
14	Armenia	-15.7	35	Angola	-10.0
15	Albania	-15.6	36	Cape Verde	-9.9
16	Turkmenistan	-14.9		Moldova	-9.9
17	Sierra Leone	-14.9	38	Bulgaria	-9.8
18	Senegal	-14.7		New Caledonia	-9.8
19	Swaziland	-13.8	40	Haiti	-9.7
20	Nicaragua	-13.7		Yemen	-9.7
21	Belarus	-13.0			

a 2008   b 2006

Official reserves[a]

$m, end-2010

1	China	2,913,725	16	Algeria	170,457
2	Japan	1,096,065	17	France	165,851
3	Euro area (16)	788,033	18	Italy	158,480
4	United States	488,928	19	Mexico	120,583
5	Russia	479,222	20	Malaysia	106,501
6	Saudi Arabia	470,374	21	Libya	106,136
7	Taiwan	381,997	22	Indonesia	96,211
8	India	300,480	23	Poland	93,473
9	South Korea	292,143	24	Turkey	85,960
10	Brazil	288,574	25	Denmark	76,511
11	Switzerland	270,337	26	Israel	70,914
12	Hong Kong	268,731	27	Philippines	62,324
13	Singapore	225,725	28	Canada	57,153
14	Germany	215,972	29	Norway	52,860
15	Thailand	172,028	30	Argentina	52,208

Official gold reserves

Market prices, $m, end-2010

1	Euro area (16)	487,652	14	Saudi Arabia	14,592
2	United States	367,538	15	United Kingdom	14,027
3	Germany	153,677	16	Lebanon	12,959
4	Italy	110,796	17	Spain	12,720
5	France	110,051	18	Austria	12,650
6	China	47,646	19	Belgium	10,274
7	Switzerland	47,000	20	Algeria	7,843
8	Russia	35,636	21	Philippines	6,963
9	Japan	34,575	22	Libya	6,493
10	Netherlands	27,674	23	Sweden	5,681
11	India	25,203	24	South Africa	5,650
12	Portugal	17,288	25	Turkey	5,247
13	Venezuela	16,529	26	Greece	5,046

Workers' remittances

Inflows, $m, 2009

1	India	49,468	16	Indonesia	6,793
2	China	48,729	17	Vietnam	6,626
3	Mexico	21,914	18	Morocco	6,270
4	Philippines	19,766	19	Serbia	5,406
5	France	15,551	20	Russia	5,359
6	Germany	10,879	21	Ukraine	5,073
7	Bangladesh	10,523	22	Romania	4,929
8	Belgium	10,437	23	Brazil	4,234
9	Spain	9,904	24	Colombia	4,180
10	Nigeria	9,585	25	Australia	4,089
11	Poland	8,816	26	Guatemala	4,026
12	Pakistan	8,717	27	Netherlands	3,691
13	Lebanon	7,558	28	Jordan	3,597
14	Egypt	7,150	29	Portugal	3,585
15	United Kingdom	6,847	30	El Salvador	3,482

a Foreign exchange, SDRs, IMF position and gold at market prices.

Exchange rates

The Economist's Big Mac index

		Big Mac prices in local currency	in $	Implied PPP[a] of the $	Actual $ exchange rate	Under (-)/ over (+) valuation against $, %
Countries with the most under-valued currencies, March 2011						
1	Ukraine	15.00	1.89	3.82	7.93	-52
	Hong Kong	14.80	1.90	3.77	7.79	-52
3	Sri Lanka	210.00	1.91	53.42	110.01	-51
	Estonia	22.00	1.94	5.60	11.34	-51
5	China	13.20	2.01	3.36	6.57	-49
6	Egypt	13.00	2.20	3.31	5.91	-44
7	Thailand	70.00	2.31	17.81	30.34	-41
	Malaysia	7.04	2.32	1.79	3.04	-41
9	Philippines	102.00	2.35	25.95	43.49	-40
10	Pakistan	210.00	2.46	53.42	85.40	-37
11	Russia	72.00	2.52	18.32	28.57	-36
12	Taiwan	75.00	2.54	19.08	29.49	-35
13	Indonesia	22,780.00	2.59	5,795.21	8,782.00	-34
14	Saudi Arabia	10.00	2.67	2.54	3.75	-32
	Mexico	32.00	2.67	8.14	11.97	-32
16	South Africa	18.95	2.74	4.82	6.90	-30
17	Poland	8.45	2.90	2.15	2.91	-26
	Lithuania	7.30	2.92	1.86	2.50	-26
19	United Arab Em.	11.00	2.99	2.80	3.67	-24
20	South Korea	3,400.00	3.03	864.96	1,121.75	-23
21	Latvia	1.60	3.13	0.41	0.51	-21
22	Singapore	4.50	3.53	1.14	1.27	-10
23	Czech Republic	63.62	3.60	16.18	17.66	-8
	Peru	10.00	3.61	2.54	2.77	-8
25	New Zealand	5.07	3.72	1.29	1.36	-5
	Chile	1,800.00	3.73	457.92	482.45	-5
27	Hungary	760.00	3.83	193.34	198.47	-3
28	United Kingdom	2.39	3.83	1.64[b]	1.60[b]	-2
	Japan	320.00	3.85	81.41	83.05	-2
Countries with the most over-valued currencies, March 2011						
1	Norway	45.00	7.96	11.45	5.65	103
2	Sweden	48.40	7.57	12.31	6.40	93
3	Switzerland	6.50	6.96	1.65	0.93	77
4	Brazil	8.82	5.31	2.24	1.66	35
5	Denmark	28.50	5.27	7.25	5.40	34
6	Euro area[c]	3.51	4.85	1.12[d]	1.38[d]	23
7	Australia	4.56	4.56	1.16	1.00	16
8	Israel	15.90	4.46	4.04	3.57	13
	Canada	4.22	4.33	1.07	0.98	10
10	Argentina	16.00	3.97	4.07	4.03	1
11	Turkey	6.25	3.95	1.59	1.58	0.5

a Purchasing-power parity: local price in the 40 countries listed divided by United States price ($3.93, average of four cities).
b Dollars per pound.   c Weighted average of prices in euro area.   d Dollars per euro.

Public finance

Government debt
As % of GDP, 2010

1	Japan	199.7		16	Israel	76.1
2	Greece	147.3		17	Netherlands	71.4
3	Italy	126.8		18	Spain	66.1
4	Iceland	120.2		19	Poland	62.4
5	Portugal	103.1		20	Finland	57.4
6	Ireland	102.4		21	Denmark	55.5
7	Belgium	100.7		22	Norway	49.5
8	France	94.1		23	Sweden	49.1
9	United States	93.6		24	Slovenia	47.5
10	Euro area (15)	92.7		25	Czech Republic	46.6
11	Germany	87.0		26	Slovakia	44.5
12	Hungary	85.6		27	Switzerland	40.2
13	Canada	84.2		28	New Zealand	38.7
14	United Kingdom	82.4		29	South Korea	33.9
15	Austria	78.6		30	Australia	25.3

Government spending
As % of GDP, 2010

1	Ireland	67.0		16	Hungary	48.6
2	Denmark	58.2		17	Germany	46.7
3	France	56.2		18	Norway	46.0
4	Finland	55.1		19	Poland	45.8
5	Belgium	53.1		20	Israel	45.5
	Sweden	53.1		21	Czech Republic	45.2
7	Austria	53.0		22	Spain	45.0
8	Netherlands	51.2		23	Canada	43.8
9	United Kingdom	51.0		24	New Zealand	43.0
10	Portugal	50.7		25	United States	42.3
11	Italy	50.6		26	Luxembourg	41.2
12	Euro area (15)	50.5		27	Slovakia	41.0
13	Iceland	50.0		28	Japan	40.7
14	Greece	49.5		29	Estonia	40.0
15	Slovenia	49.0		30	Turkey	37.1

Tax revenue
As % of GDP, 2009

1	Denmark	48.2		14	Portugal[a]	35.2
2	Sweden	46.4		15	Czech Republic	34.8
3	Italy	43.5		16	Poland[a]	34.3
4	Belgium	43.2			United Kingdom	34.3
5	Finland	43.1		18	Iceland	34.1
6	Austria	42.8		19	Israel	31.4
7	France	41.9		20	Canada	31.1
8	Norway	41.0		21	New Zealand	31.0
9	Hungary	39.1		22	Spain	30.7
	Netherlands[a]	39.1		23	Switzerland	30.3
11	Slovenia	37.9		24	Greece	29.4
12	Luxembourg	37.5		25	Slovakia	29.3
13	Germany	37.0		26	Japan[a]	28.1

Note: Includes only OECD countries.   a 2008

Democracy

Democracy index
Most democratic = 100, 2010

Most			Least		
1	Norway	9.80	1	North Korea	1.08
2	Iceland	9.65	2	Chad	1.52
3	Denmark	9.52	3	Turkmenistan	1.72
4	Sweden	9.50	4	Uzbekistan	1.74
5	New Zealand	9.26	5	Myanmar	1.77
6	Australia	9.22	6	Central African Rep.	1.82
7	Finland	9.19	7	Saudi Arabia	1.84
8	Switzerland	9.09	8	Equatorial Guinea	1.84
9	Canada	9.08	9	Iran	1.94
10	Netherlands	8.99	10	Libya	1.94
11	Luxembourg	8.88	11	Guinea-Bissau	1.99
12	Ireland	8.79	12	Laos	2.10
13	Austria	8.49	13	Congo-Kinshasa	2.15
14	Germany	8.38	14	Djibouti	2.20
15	Malta	8.28	15	Syria	2.31

Parliamentary seats
Lower chambers, seats per 100,000 population, 2011

Most			Least		
1	Antigua & Barbuda	22.09	1	India	0.05
2	Bahamas	13.67	2	United States	0.14
3	St. Lucia	11.25	3	Pakistan	0.19
4	Belize	10.67	4	Nigeria	0.23
5	Barbados	10.00	5	Brazil	0.26
6	Gabon	7.73	6	Philippines	0.30
7	Bhutan	6.71	7	Russia	0.32
8	Lesotho	5.71	8	Colombia	0.36
9	Swaziland	5.50	9	Japan	0.38
10	Bahrain	5.00	10	Mexico	0.46
11	Slovenia	4.50	11	Uzbekistan	0.55
12	Congo-Brazzaville	3.70	12	Egypt	0.62
13	Ireland	3.69	13	Argentina	0.64

Women in parliament
Lower chambers, women as % of total seats, April 2011

1	Rwanda	56.3	15	Denmark	38.0
2	Andorra	53.6	16	Uganda	37.2
3	Sweden	45.0	17	Spain	36.6
4	South Africa	44.5	18	Tanzania	36.0
5	Cuba	43.2	19	New Zealand	33.6
6	Iceland	42.9	20	Nepal	33.2
7	Finland	42.5	21	Germany	32.8
8	Norway	39.6	22	Macedonia	32.5
9	Belgium	39.3	23	Ecuador	32.3
	Netherlands	39.3	24	Burundi	32.1
11	Mozambique	39.2	25	Belarus	31.8
12	Angola	38.6	26	Guyana	30.0
	Costa Rica	38.6	27	Timor-Leste	29.2
14	Argentina	38.5	28	Switzerland	29.0

Inflation

Consumer price inflation

Highest, 2010, %

1	Venezuela	29.1
2	Congo-Kinshasa[a]	17.3
3	Sierra Leone	16.6
4	Guinea	15.5
5	Angola	14.5
6	Pakistan	13.9
7	Nigeria	13.7
8	Zambia[b]	13.4
9	Mozambique	12.7
10	Jamaica	12.6
11	India	12
12	Nepal[b]	11.6
13	Egypt	11.3
14	Sudan[b]	11.2
15	Yemen	11.2
	Argentina	10.8
17	Ghana	10.7
18	Trinidad & Tobago	10.5
19	Iran	10.1
20	Mongolia	10.1
	Chad[b]	10
22	Ukraine	9.4
23	Madagascar	9.2

Lowest, 2010, %

1	Qatar	-4.9
2	Latvia	-1.1
3	Ireland	-0.9
4	Burkina Faso	-0.8
5	Japan	-0.7
6	Haiti[b]	0.0
	Laos[b]	0.0
8	Switzerland	0.7
9	Niger	0.8
10	Belize	0.9
	United Arab Emirates	0.9
12	Côte d'Ivoire[b]	1.0
	Croatia	1.0
	Morocco	1.0
	St. Lucia[b]	1.0
	Slovakia	1.0
	Taiwan	1.0
18	Germany	1.1
	Mali	1.1
20	El Salvador	1.2
	Finland	1.2
	Sweden	1.2

Highest average annual consumer price inflation, 2005–10, %

1	Zimbabwe[c]	28,118.0
2	Venezuela	24.1
3	Myanmar[d]	20.2
4	Guinea	18.8
5	Ethiopia	17.4
6	Congo-Kinshasa[e]	15.8
7	Iran	15.5
8	Ukraine	14.3
9	Ghana	13.6
10	Angola	13.2
11	Pakistan	12.6
12	Kenya	12.5
13	Jamaica	12.3
14	Egypt	11.6
15	Zambia[d]	11.4
16	Sri Lanka	11.3
17	Tajikistan	11.2
18	Mongolia	10.9
19	Kyrgyzstan	10.8
	Liberia[d]	10.8
	Vietnam	10.8
	Yemen	10.8

Lowest average annual consumer price inflation, 2005–10, %

1	Japan	-0.1
2	Switzerland	0.9
3	Lebanon	1.0
4	Taiwan	1.2
5	Ireland	1.4
6	France	1.5
	Netherlands	1.5
	Sweden	1.5
9	Germany	1.6
10	Canada	1.7
	Portugal	1.7
12	Austria	1.8
13	Finland	1.9
	Italy	1.9
15	Belgium	2.0
16	Denmark	2.1
17	Antigua & Barbuda	2.2
	Hong Kong	2.2
	Luxembourg	2.2
	Morocco	2.2
	United States	2.2
22	Norway	2.3

---

a 2008 b 2009 c Estimates. Reports in early 2011 quote CPI at around 3%.
d 2005–09 e 2005–08

Commodity prices

2010, % change on a year earlier			2005–10, % change	
1	Coconut oil	129.3	1 Rubber	300.8
2	Cotton	127.0	2 Cotton	280.8
3	Rubber	84.1	3 Tin	250.0
4	Wool (NZ)	66.2	4 Sugar	248.2
5	Timber	62.8	5 Gold	225.1
6	Palm oil	58.3	6 Palm oil	212.7
7	Coffee	57.3	7 Corn	210.1
8	Tin	54.4	8 Copper	199.7
9	Corn	48.8	9 Coconut oil	197.2
10	Wheat	44.3	10 Soya oil	186.1
11	Soya oil	39.6	11 Wheat	169.7
12	Lamb	36.9	12 Soyabeans	159.7
13	Soyabeans	30.7	13 Coffee	149.5
14	Nickel	28.2	14 Soya meal	148.9
15	Copper	26.3	15 Lead	144.0
16	Beef (Aus)	24.5	16 Oil[a]	116.3
17	Gold	23.5	17 Tea	103.2
18	Soya meal	21.0	18 Cocoa	98.8
19	Sugar	18.6	19 Rice	89.2
20	Beef (US)	18.5	20 Zinc	87.3
21	Wool (Aus)	17.3	21 Nickel	69.1
22	Hides	11.9	22 Lamb	66.7
23	Oil[a]	11.4	23 Wool (Aus)	38.8
24	Aluminium	6.9	24 Wool (NZ)	32.3
25	Lead	0.0	25 Beef (Aus)	31.7
26	Tea	-5.5	26 Aluminium	30.9

The Economist's house-price indicators

Q4 2010[b], % change on a year earlier			1997–2011[b], % change	
1	Hong Kong	20.1	1 South Africa	421
2	Singapore	17.6	2 Australia	215
3	France	8.6	3 United Kingdom	178
4	China	6.4	4 Sweden	175
5	Belgium	6.0	5 Belgium	164
6	Australia	5.8	6 Spain	157
7	Sweden	5.2	7 France	152
8	Switzerland	4.2	8 Ireland	118
9	South Africa	2.9	9 New Zealand	111
10	Denmark	2.7	10 Denmark	98
11	Germany	2.6	11 Italy	93
12	Canada	2.4	12 Netherlands	90
13	Netherlands	1.7	13 Canada	69
14	New Zealand	0.9	14 United States	56
15	United Kingdom	-1.1	15 Switzerland	37
16	Italy	-1.6	16 Singapore	21
17	Spain	-3.5	17 Hong Kong	-1
18	Japan	-4.1	18 Japan	-38
	United States	-4.1		
20	Ireland	-10.8		

a West Texas Intermediate. b Or latest.

Debt

Highest foreign debt[a]
$bn, 2009

1	China	428.4	24	Pakistan	53.7
2	Russia	381.3	25	Colombia	52.2
3	Brazil	276.9	26	Saudi Arabia	51.0
4	South Korea	259.0	27	Qatar	49.0
5	Turkey	251.4	28	Croatia	44.0
6	India	237.7	29	South Africa	42.1
7	Mexico	192.0	30	Bulgaria	40.6
8	Poland	169.0	31	Serbia	33.4
9	Indonesia	157.5	32	Egypt	33.3
10	Argentina	120.2	33	Lithuania	31.7
11	Romania	117.5	34	Peru	29.6
12	Hungary	112.0	35	Latvia	29.0
13	Kazakhstan	109.9	36	Vietnam	28.7
14	Ukraine	93.2	37	Hong Kong	28.0
15	United Arab Emirates	85.0	38	Lebanon	24.9
16	Chile	71.6	39	Bangladesh	23.8
17	Malaysia	66.4		Morocco	23.8
18	Philippines	62.9	41	Slovakia	22.0
19	Israel	61.0	42	Tunisia	21.7
20	Thailand	58.5	43	Sudan	20.1
21	Czech Republic	57.0	44	Belarus	17.2
22	Taiwan	55.0		Sri Lanka	17.2
23	Venezuela	54.5	46	Estonia	17.0

Highest foreign debt burden[a]
Foreign debt as % of GDP, 2009

1	Liberia	316		Tunisia	54
2	Guinea-Bissau	203	23	Romania	53
3	Latvia	161	24	Togo	50
4	Estonia	128	25	El Salvador	49
5	Hungary	124		United Arab Emirates	49
6	Croatia	100	27	Côte d'Ivoire	46
7	Kazakhstan	96	28	Bosnia	45
8	Bulgaria	85		South Korea	45
9	Mauritania	83	30	Guinea	44
10	Jamaica	82		Israel	44
11	Lebanon	80	32	Chile	43
12	Laos	78		Czech Republic	43
13	Qatar	73	34	Argentina	41
	Sudan	73	35	Tajikistan	39
15	Lithuania	72	36	Cambodia	38
16	Serbia	71	37	Uruguay	37
17	Ukraine	62	38	Armenia	36
18	Macedonia	59		Kyrgyzstan	36
19	Poland	56		Nicaragua	36
20	Moldova	55		Slovakia	36
21	Panama	54			

a Foreign debt is debt owed to non-residents and repayable in foreign currency; the figures shown include liabilities of government, public and private sectors. Developed countries have been excluded.

Highest foreign debt[a]
As % of exports of goods and services, 2009

1	Eritrea	811	22	Armenia	148
2	Guinea-Bissau	647		Qatar	148
3	Sudan	352	24	Turkey	144
4	Liberia	347	25	Burundi	143
5	Zimbabwe	335	26	Hungary	137
6	Latvia	320	27	Sri Lanka	136
7	Croatia	252		Togo	136
8	Laos	233	29	Poland	134
9	Serbia	223	30	Bulgaria	132
10	Jamaica	178	31	Guatemala	126
11	Estonia	171	32	Brazil	125
12	Cuba	166	33	Ukraine	123
	Romania	166	34	Uruguay	121
14	El Salvador	162	35	Lithuania	120
15	Kazakhstan	157	36	Israel	114
	Pakistan	157		Tajikistan	114
17	Argentina	156	38	Haiti	113
18	Burkina Faso	154	39	Colombia	111
	Nepal	154	40	Moldova	109
20	Mauritania	153	41	Bosnia	106
21	Guinea	152	42	Lebanon	105

Highest debt service ratio[b]
Average, %, 2009

1	Kazakhstan	80.2	24	Philippines	18.5
2	Latvia	57.7	25	Guatemala	18.4
3	Croatia	41.9		Indonesia	18.4
4	Turkey	41.6	27	Lebanon	18.0
5	Ecuador	40.8	28	Russia	17.7
6	Hungary	39.4	29	Argentina	17.3
7	Tajikistan	38.4	30	Nicaragua	17.2
8	Serbia	37.1	31	Cuba	17.1
9	Zimbabwe	36.7	32	Mexico	16.0
10	Ukraine	36.2	33	Sri Lanka	15.6
11	Jamaica	33.9	34	Pakistan	15.0
12	Romania	31.4	35	Moldova	14.9
13	Lithuania	31.0	36	Macedonia	14.8
14	Poland	28.8	37	Bolivia	14.4
15	El Salvador	25.2	38	Kyrgyzstan	14.0
16	Brazil	23.4	39	Czech Republic	13.5
17	Estonia	23.0	40	Slovakia	12.7
18	Chile	22.6	41	Morocco	12.5
19	Colombia	22.4	42	Dominican Republic	12.1
20	Bulgaria	21.3		Qatar	12.1
21	Uruguay	21.0	44	Israel	11.9
22	Armenia	20.9	45	Peru	11.8
23	Kosovo	20.8	46	Papua New Guinea	11.7

b Debt service is the sum of interest and principal repayments (amortisation) due on outstanding foreign debt. The debt service ratio is debt service expressed as a percentage of the country's exports of goods and services.

Aid

Largest recipients of bilateral and multilateral aid[a]
$m, 2009

1	Afghanistan	6,070	24	Colombia	1,060
2	Ethiopia	3,820	25	Indonesia	1,049
3	Vietnam	3,744	26	Senegal	1,018
4	West Bank & Gaza	3,026	27	Mali	985
5	Tanzania	2,934	28	Rwanda	934
6	Iraq	2,791	29	Egypt	925
7	Pakistan	2,781	30	Morocco	912
8	India	2,393	31	Georgia	908
9	Côte d'Ivoire	2,366	32	Nepal	855
10	Congo-Kinshasa	2,354	33	Kosovo	788
11	Sudan	2,289	34	Nicaragua	774
12	Mozambique	2,013	35	Malawi	772
13	Uganda	1,786	36	Jordan	761
14	Kenya	1,778	37	Zimbabwe	737
15	Nigeria	1,659	38	Bolivia	726
16	Ghana	1,583	39	Cambodia	722
17	Turkey	1,362	40	Sri Lanka	704
18	Zambia	1,269	41	Benin	683
19	Bangladesh	1,227	42	Ukraine	668
20	China	1,132	43	Somalia	662
21	Haiti	1,120	44	Cameroon	649
22	Burkina Faso	1,084	45	Lebanon	641
23	South Africa	1,075	46	Serbia	608

Largest recipients of bilateral and multilateral aid[a]
$ per head, 2009

1	West Bank & Gaza	749.0	23	Côte d'Ivoire	112.3
2	Kosovo	435.3	24	Haiti	111.6
3	Cape Verde	384.2	25	Bosnia & Herzegovina	110.1
4	Suriname	302.1	26	Maldives	107.3
5	St. Lucia	241.6	27	Zambia	98.0
6	Guyana	228.3	28	Macedonia	94.8
7	Georgia	213.1	29	Rwanda	93.4
8	Afghanistan	203.7	30	Guinea-Bissau	90.4
8	Timor-Leste	191.8	31	Iraq	88.6
10	Djibouti	188.6	32	Mozambique	88.0
11	Bhutan	179.2	33	Mauritania	87.1
12	Armenia	171.3	34	Belize	84.4
13	Lebanon	151.9	35	Fiji	83.7
14	Namibia	150.3	36	Serbia	83.1
15	Botswana	143.4	37	Senegal	81.2
16	Mongolia	139.4	38	Congo-Brazzaville	76.9
17	Nicaragua	134.8	39	Sierra Leone	76.7
18	Liberia	127.9	40	Benin	76.5
19	Jordan	127.8	41	Mali	75.7
20	Montenegro	121.6	42	Togo	75.4
21	Mauritius	121.5	43	Gambia	75.0
21	Albania	113.3	44	Oman	74.4

a Israel also receives aid, but does not disclose amounts.

Largest bilateral and multilateral donors[a]
$m, 2009

1	United States	28,831	15	Belgium	2,610
2	France	12,600	16	Switzerland	2,310
3	Germany	12,079	17	Finland	1,290
4	United Kingdom	11,491	18	Austria	1,142
5	Japan	9,469	19	Ireland	1,006
6	Spain	6,584	20	United Arab Emirates	834
7	Netherlands	6,426	21	South Korea	816
8	Sweden	4,548	22	Turkey	707
9	Norway	4,086	23	Greece	607
10	Canada	4,000	24	Portugal	513
11	Italy	3,297	25	Luxembourg	415
12	Saudi Arabia	3,134	26	Taiwan	411
13	Denmark	2,810	27	Poland	375
14	Australia	2,762	28	New Zealand	309

Largest bilateral and multilateral donors[a]
% of GDP, 2009

1	Sweden	1.12	15	United Arab Emirates	0.33
2	Norway	1.06	16	Iceland	0.32
3	Luxembourg	1.04	17	Austria	0.30
4	Denmark	0.88		Canada	0.30
5	Saudi Arabia	0.83	19	Australia	0.29
6	Netherlands	0.82	20	New Zealand	0.28
7	Belgium	0.55	21	Portugal	0.23
8	Finland	0.54	22	United States	0.21
	Ireland	0.54	23	Kuwait	0.20
10	United Kingdom	0.52	24	Greece	0.19
11	France	0.47	25	Japan	0.18
12	Spain	0.46	26	Italy	0.16
13	Switzerland	0.45	27	Slovenia	0.15
14	Germany	0.35	28	Taiwan	0.13

Resource flow donors[b]
% of GNI, 2009

1	United Kingdom	3.10	12	Austria	0.87
2	Ireland	2.27	13	United States	0.82
3	Sweden	1.77	14	Netherlands	0.77
	Switzerland	1.77		South Korea	0.77
5	France	1.43	16	Germany	0.76
6	Finland	1.34	17	Belgium	0.68
7	Denmark	1.18	18	Canada	0.56
8	Luxembourg	1.08	19	Portugal	0.55
9	Norway	1.06	20	New Zealand	0.35
10	Japan	0.95	21	Australia	0.34
11	Spain	0.89	22	Italy	0.27

a China also provides aid, but does not disclose amounts.
b Including other official flows eg, export credits, private grants and flows.

Industry and services

Largest industrial output
$bn, 2009

1	United States[a]	2,848		23	Thailand	114
2	China	2,308		24	Austria	100
3	Japan[a]	1,360		25	Belgium	92
4	Germany	787		26	Argentina	90
5	Italy	476		27	Sweden	89
6	France	451		28	Malaysia	85
7	United Kingdom	412		29	South Africa	81
8	Spain	355		30	Colombia	74
9	Russia	354		31	Libya[a]	68
10	India	349		32	Egypt	67
11	Taiwan	347		33	Algeria	66
12	Brazil	344		34	Chile	65
13	Saudi Arabia[a]	329		35	Czech Republic	64
14	Mexico	292			Ireland	64
15	South Korea	274		37	Denmark	60
16	Australia[a]	266		38	Finland	58
17	Indonesia	257		39	Greece	52
18	Netherlands	169		40	Philippines	49
19	Turkey	140		41	Portugal	47
20	Norway	137		42	Angola	45
21	Switzerland	125			Singapore	45
22	Poland	116		44	Kazakhstan	44

Highest growth in industrial output
Average annual % increase in real terms, 2001–09

1	Turkmenistan	32.7		11	Sudan	10.1
2	Azerbaijan	21.1		12	Cape Verde	10.0
3	Afghanistan[b]	14.3		13	Zambia	9.6
4	Equatorial Guinea	13.5		14	Ethiopia	9.4
5	Bhutan	12.7			Tanzania	9.4
6	Angola	12.5		16	Uganda	9.3
7	Belarus	11.8		17	Burkina Faso[c]	9.2
8	China	11.7			Trinidad & Tobago	9.2
9	Cambodia	10.6		19	Vietnam	9.1
10	Slovakia	10.3				

Lowest growth in industrial output
Average annual % change in real terms, 2001–09

1	Zimbabwe	-5.6		11	Cameroon[d]	-0.6
2	Moldova	-3.9			Norway	-0.6
3	Malta	-1.8		13	France	-0.5
4	Italy	-1.7		14	Fiji	-0.3
5	Portugal	-1.6		15	Greece	-0.2
6	Denmark	-1.4			St. Lucia	-0.2
	United Kingdom	-1.4		17	Belgium	0.0
8	Germany	-1.2			Central African Rep.[c]	0.0
9	Jamaica	-1.0		19	Côte d'Ivoire	0.1
10	Canada	-0.7			Spain	0.1

a 2008   b 2002–09   c 2001–06   d 2001–07

Largest manufacturing output
$bn, 2009

1	United States[a]	1,752	21	Austria		64
2	China	1,691	22	Poland		62
3	Japan[a]	970	23	Argentina		60
4	Germany	568	24	Belgium		59
5	Italy	306	25	Sweden		57
6	France	254	26	Ireland		49
7	United Kingdom	218		Malaysia		49
8	South Korea	208	28	Czech Republic		40
9	Brazil	200	29	Saudi Arabia[a]		39
10	India	196		South Africa		39
11	Spain	172	31	Finland		38
12	Russia	162	32	Denmark		35
13	Mexico	144	33	Norway		33
14	Indonesia	143		Philippines		33
15	Australia[a]	96		Singapore		33
16	Turkey	93	36	Romania		32
17	Taiwan	90	37	Colombia		31
	Thailand	90	38	Greece		30
19	Netherlands	89	39	Egypt		29
20	Switzerland	88		Hungary[a]		29

Largest services output
$bn, 2009

1	United States[a]	10,362	27	Argentina	172
2	Japan[a]	3,433	28	South Africa	170
3	Germany	2,163	29	Portugal	154
4	China	2,162	30	Finland	143
5	France	1,900	31	Ireland	140
6	United Kingdom	1,534	32	Singapore[a]	136
7	Italy	1,389	33	Saudi Arabia[a]	135
8	Spain	966	34	Colombia	125
9	Brazil	927	35	Thailand	119
10	India	674	36	Czech Republic	103
11	Russia	673	37	Romania	99
12	Australia[a]	625	38	Malaysia	89
13	Netherlands	524		Philippines	89
14	Mexico	511	40	Egypt	88
15	South Korea	457	41	Hungary[a]	87
16	Turkey	353	42	Chile	84
17	Switzerland	334	43	Pakistan	83
18	Belgium	327	44	Peru	70
19	Taiwan[a]	287	45	Ukraine	62
20	Sweden	259	46	Kazakhstan	59
21	Poland	251	47	Slovakia	50
22	Austria	239	48	Bangladesh	45
23	Greece	234		Morocco	45
24	Denmark	204	50	Algeria	41
25	Norway	200		Luxembourg	41
26	Indonesia	184	52	Cuba[a]	39

a 2008

Agriculture

Largest agricultural output
$bn, 2009

1	China	516	16	Germany	24
2	India	211		Philippines	24
3	United States[a]	165	18	Australia[a]	23
4	Indonesia	83	19	Argentina	21
5	Brazil	82	20	South Korea	20
6	Japan[a]	71	21	Malaysia	18
7	Russia	51	22	Bangladesh	16
	Turkey	51		Colombia	16
9	France	42	24	Sudan	15
10	Mexico	36	25	Algeria	14
	Spain	36		Ethiopia	14
12	Italy	35		Poland	14
13	Pakistan	33		United Kingdom	14
14	Thailand	31	29	Morocco	13
15	Egypt	25	30	Netherlands	12

Most economically dependent on agriculture
% of GDP from agriculture, 2009

1	Liberia[a]	61.3	14	Ghana	31.7
2	Central African Rep.	55.5	15	Mozambique	31.5
3	Sierra Leone	51.4	16	Malawi	30.5
4	Ethiopia	50.7	17	Sudan	29.7
5	Congo-Kinshasa	42.9	18	Kyrgyzstan[a]	29.2
6	Mali[b]	36.5	19	Madagascar	29.1
7	Papua New Guinea	35.9	20	Tanzania	28.8
8	Cambodia	35.3	21	Gambia, The	27.5
9	Laos[a]	34.7	22	Uganda	24.7
10	Rwanda	34.2	23	Côte d'Ivoire	24.4
11	Nepal	33.8	24	Mongolia	23.5
12	Nigeria[b]	32.7	25	Kenya	22.6
13	Afghanistan	32.5	26	Tajikistan	22.4

Least economically dependent on agriculture
% of GDP from agriculture, 2009

1	Macau[a]	0.0		United States[a]	1.2
2	Hong Kong	0.1	15	Austria	1.5
3	Luxembourg	0.3		Japan[a]	1.5
4	Trinidad & Tobago	0.4	17	France	1.7
5	Belgium	0.7		Netherlands	1.7
	Brunei[b]	0.7		Sweden	1.7
	United Kingdom	0.7		Taiwan	1.7
8	Bermuda	0.8	21	Italy	1.8
	Germany	0.8		Malta	1.8
10	Denmark	0.9		United Arab Emirates[b]	1.8
11	Ireland	1.0	24	Libya[a]	1.9
12	Norway	1.2	25	Seychelles	2.0
	Switzerland	1.2	26	Cyprus[a]	2.1

a 2008   b 2007

Highest growth in agriculture
Average annual % increase in real terms, 2001–09

1	Angola	14.4	10	Uzbekistan	6.4
2	Turkmenistan	12.7	11	Ethiopia	6.2
3	Jordan	9.7	12	Mongolia	6.1
4	Mozambique	8.5	13	Hungary	5.7
5	Afghanistan[a]	7.9		Romania	5.7
	Tajikistan	7.9	15	Cambodia	5.5
7	Morocco	7.2	16	Armenia	5.4
8	Nigeria[b]	7.0	17	Azerbaijan	5.2
9	Iran[c]	6.8		Belarus	5.2

Lowest growth in agriculture
Average annual % change in real terms, 2001–09

1	Zimbabwe	-11.7	9	Ireland	-3.1
2	Trinidad & Tobago	-6.2	10	St. Lucia	-2.8
3	Hong Kong	-5.0	11	Paraguay	-2.5
4	Bahamas[c]	-4.6	12	Estonia	-1.9
5	Lesotho	-3.6	13	Eritrea	-1.8
6	Malta	-3.5	14	Samoa	-1.7
7	Cyprus	-3.4	15	Bulgaria	-1.6
8	Luxembourg	-3.2	16	Maldives	-1.4

Biggest producers
'000 tonnes, 2009

Cereals

1	China	483,680	6	Brazil	71,288
2	United States	419,810	7	France	70,040
3	India	246,774	8	Germany	49,748
4	Russia	95,079	9	Canada	49,059
5	Indonesia	82,029	10	Bangladesh	46,812

Meat

1	China	78,214	6	Mexico	5,641
2	United States	41,616	7	France	5,537
3	Brazil	22,465	8	Spain	5,311
4	Germany	7,903	9	Canada	4,477
5	Russia	6,570	10	Argentina	4,439

Fruit

1	China	114,139	6	Indonesia	17,058
2	India	68,358	7	Mexico	16,122
3	Brazil	37,687	8	Philippines	15,911
4	United States	27,116	9	Spain	14,373
5	Italy	18,123	10	Turkey	14,081

Vegetables

1	China	459,558	5	Egypt	20,275
2	India	90,757	6	Iran	16,351
3	United States	37,813	7	Russia	14,827
4	Turkey	26,733	8	Italy	13,645

a 2002–09   b 2002–07   c 2001–07

Commodities

Wheat

Top 10 producers, 2009–10 '000 tonnes		Top 10 consumers, 2009–10 '000 tonnes	
1 EU27	138,700	1 EU27	126,400
2 China	115,100	2 China	106,500
3 India	80,700	3 India	76,500
4 Russia	61,700	4 Russia	41,600
5 United States	60,400	5 United States	30,900
6 Canada	26,800	6 Pakistan	23,300
7 Pakistan	24,000	7 Turkey	17,700
8 Australia	21,900	8 Egypt	17,100
9 Ukraine	20,900	9 Iran	15,400
10 Turkey	18,500	10 Ukraine	11,800

Rice[a]

Top 10 producers, 2009–10 '000 tonnes		Top 10 consumers, 2009–10 '000 tonnes	
1 China	136,570	1 China	134,320
2 India	89,130	2 India	85,730
3 Indonesia	36,370	3 Indonesia	38,000
4 Bangladesh	31,000	4 Bangladesh	31,600
5 Vietnam	24,979	5 Vietnam	19,150
6 Thailand	20,260	6 Philippines	13,300
7 Myanmar	10,597	7 Thailand	10,200
8 Philippines	9,772	8 Myanmar	9,855
9 Japan	7,711	9 Brazil	8,400
10 Brazil	7,657	10 Japan	8,200

Sugar[b]

Top 10 producers, 2009 '000 tonnes		Top 10 consumers, 2009 '000 tonnes	
1 Brazil	33,454	1 India	24,131
2 EU27	16,631	2 EU27	17,862
3 India	15,655	3 China	15,000
4 China	13,629	4 Brazil	12,199
5 Thailand	7,945	5 United States	9,705
6 United States	6,855	6 Russia	5,652
7 Mexico	5,181	7 Mexico	5,153
8 Australia	4,523	8 Indonesia	5,125
9 Russia	3,602	9 Pakistan	4,625
10 Pakistan	3,500	10 Egypt	2,750

Coarse grains[c]

Top 5 producers, 2009–10 '000 tonnes		Top 5 consumers, 2009–10 '000 tonnes	
1 United States	349,000	1 United States	295,300
2 China	164,900	2 China	170,800
3 EU27	153,400	3 EU27	146,500
4 Brazil	58,600	4 Brazil	50,200
5 India	33,900	5 Mexico	40,900

Tea

Top 10 producers, 2009		*Top 10 consumers, 2009*	
'000 tonnes		*'000 tonnes*	
1 China	1,203	1 China	801
2 India	979	2 India	719
3 Kenya	314	3 Russia	182
4 Sri Lanka	289	4 Turkey	176
5 Turkey	199	5 Japan	153
6 Indonesia	136	6 United Kingdom	130
7 Vietnam	130	7 Pakistan	123
8 Japan	86	8 United States	103
9 Argentina	69	9 Iran	100
10 Thailand	62	10 Egypt	84

Coffee

Top 10 producers, 2009–10		*Top 10 consumers, 2009–10*	
'000 tonnes		*'000 tonnes*	
1 Brazil	2,368	1 United States	1,299
2 Vietnam	1,092	2 Brazil	1,103
3 Indonesia	683	3 Germany	504
4 Colombia	486	4 Japan	440
5 Ethiopia	416	5 Italy	345
6 India	289	6 France	320
7 Mexico	252	7 Spain	203
8 Guatemala	230	8 Indonesia	200
9 Honduras	215	9 Canada	198
10 Peru	197	10 United Kingdom	196

Cocoa

Top 10 producers, 2008–09		*Top 10 consumers, 2008–09*	
'000 tonnes		*'000 tonnes*	
1 Côte d'Ivoire	1,222	1 United States	710
2 Ghana	662	2 Germany	310
3 Indonesia	490	3 France	230
4 Nigeria	250	4 United Kingdom	227
5 Cameroon	227	5 Russia	188
6 Brazil	157	6 Brazil	161
7 Ecuador	134	7 Japan	157
8 Togo	105	8 Spain	100
9 Papua New Guinea	59	9 Italy	90
10 Dominican Republic	55	10 Canada	84

a Milled.
b Raw.
c Includes: maize (corn), barley, sorghum, oats, rye, millet, triticale and other.

Copper

Top 10 producers[a], 2009		*Top 10 consumers[b], 2009*	
'000 tonnes		*'000 tonnes*	
1 Chile	5,390	1 China	7,419
2 Peru	1,275	2 United States	1,785
3 United States	1,204	3 Germany	1,317
4 Indonesia	997	4 Japan	1,060
5 China	961	5 South Korea	850
6 Australia	854	6 Italy	619
7 Russia	742	7 Taiwan	532
8 Zambia	601	8 India	477
9 Canada	495	9 Brazil	468
10 Poland	439	10 Russia	421

Lead

Top 10 producers[a], 2009		*Top 10 consumers[b], 2009*	
'000 tonnes		*'000 tonnes*	
1 China	1,908	1 China	3,860
2 Australia	566	2 United States	1,290
3 United States	409	3 South Korea	309
4 Peru	302	4 Germany	306
5 Mexico	140	5 Spain	237
6 Bolivia	85	6 Italy	205
7 India	83	7 Japan	190
8 Russia	78	8 United Kingdom	189
9 Canada	69	9 India	180
Sweden	69	10 Brazil	174

Zinc

Top 10 producers[a], 2009		*Top 10 consumers[c], 2009*	
'000 tonnes		*'000 tonnes*	
1 China	3,092	1 China	4,888
2 Peru	1,509	2 United States	920
3 Australia	1,290	3 India	532
4 Canada	699	4 Japan	433
5 United States	690	5 South Korea	392
6 India	681	6 Germany	379
7 Mexico	458	7 Belgium	335
8 Bolivia	431	8 France	225
9 Kazakhstan	419	9 Italy	217
10 Ireland	387	10 Spain	210

Tin

Top 5 producers[a], 2009		*Top 5 consumers[b], 2009*	
'000 tonnes		*'000 tonnes*	
1 China	128.0	1 China	143.0
2 Indonesia	84.0	2 United States	26.9
3 Peru	37.5	3 Japan	23.0
4 Bolivia	19.6	4 South Korea	15.2
5 Brazil	10.0	5 Germany	14.5

Nickel

Top 10 producers[a], 2009
'000 tonnes

1	Russia	274.8
2	Indonesia	190.6
3	Australia	166.0
4	Philippines	143.5
5	Canada	136.6
6	New Caledonia	92.8
7	China	81.1
8	Cuba	65.0
9	Colombia	51.8
10	Brazil	36.2

Top 10 consumers[b], 2009
'000 tonnes

1	China	541.3
2	Japan	147.6
3	South Korea	93.0
4	United States	90.9
5	Taiwan	64.2
6	Germany	62.2
7	Italy	44.2
8	South Africa	42.5
9	United Kingdom	32.4
10	India	24.5

Aluminium

Top 10 producers[d], 2009
'000 tonnes

1	China	12,846
2	Russia	3,815
3	Canada	3,030
4	Australia	1,943
5	United States	1,727
6	Brazil	1,536
7	India	1,479
8	Norway	1,098
9	United Arab Emirates	1,010
10	Bahrain	858

Top 10 consumers[e], 2009
'000 tonnes

1	China	14,276
2	United States	3,854
3	Japan	1,523
4	India	1,458
5	Germany	1,277
6	South Korea	1,038
7	Brazil	799
8	Russia	750
9	Italy	661
10	Canada	571

Precious metals

Gold [a]
Top 10 producers, 2009
tonnes

1	China	314.0
2	United States	223.0
3	Australia	222.0
4	South Africa	206.2
5	Russia	184.8
6	Peru	182.4
7	Indonesia	115.4
8	Canada	97.4
9	Ghana	91.1
10	Uzbekistan	73.2

Silver [a]
Top 10 producers, 2009
tonnes

1	Mexico	3,999
2	Peru	3,637
3	China	2,800
4	Australia	1,864
5	Chile	1,276
6	Bolivia	1,259
7	United States	1,254
8	Poland	1,232
9	Canada	596
10	Kazakhstan	548

Platinum
Top 3 producers, 2009
tonnes

1	South Africa	131.4
2	Russia	22.3
3	United States/Canada	7.4

Palladium
Top 3 producers, 2009
tonnes

1	Russia	75.8
2	South Africa	67.2
3	United States/Canada	21.4

a Mine production. b Refined consumption. c Slab consumption.
d Primary refined production. e Primary refined consumption.

Rubber (natural and synthetic)

Top 10 producers, 2009			Top 10 consumers, 2009		
'000 tonnes			'000 tonnes		
1	China	3,500	1	China	7,614
2	Thailand	3,354	2	United States	2,135
3	Indonesia	2,480	3	Japan	1,468
4	United States	1,962	4	India	1,226
5	Japan	1,303	5	Brazil	725
6	South Korea	1,149	6	Thailand	620
7	Russia	971	7	South Korea	608
8	India	924	8	Malaysia	599
9	Malaysia	906	9	Germany	592
10	Germany	743	10	Indonesia	499

Raw wool

Top 10 producers[a], 2009–10			Top 10 consumers[a], 2009–10		
'000 tonnes			'000 tonnes		
1	Australia	244	1	China	405
2	China	167	2	India	82
3	New Zealand	145	3	Italy	68
4	India	36	4	Turkey	45
5	Iran	33	5	Iran	35
6	South Africa	30	6	New Zealand	17
7	Argentina	29		Russia	17
	United Kingdom	29	8	South Korea	16
9	Uruguay	28	9	Morocco	15
10	Russia	25	10	Belgium	14

Cotton

Top 10 producers, 2009–10			Top 10 consumers, 2009–10		
'000 tonnes			'000 tonnes		
1	China	6,925	1	China	10,099
2	India	5,050	2	India	4,232
3	United States	2,654	3	Pakistan	2,307
4	Pakistan	2,019	4	Turkey	1,300
5	Brazil	1,194	5	Brazil	1,002
6	Uzbekistan	850	6	Bangladesh	794
7	Australia	387	7	United States	754
8	Turkey	380	8	Indonesia	461
9	Turkmenistan	250	9	Mexico	420
10	Argentina	225	10	Thailand	390

Major oil seeds[b]

Top 5 producers, 2009–10			Top 5 consumers, 2009–10		
'000 tonnes			'000 tonnes		
1	United States	100,410	1	China	103,784
2	Brazil	71,250	2	United States	61,759
3	Argentina	58,550	3	EU25	46,198
4	China	72,540	4	Brazil	39,135
5	EU27	51,915	5	Argentina	38,999

Oil[c]

Top 10 producers, 2010
'000 barrels per day

1	Russia	10,270
2	Saudi Arabia[d]	10,007
3	United States	7,513
4	Iran[d]	4,245
5	China	4,071
6	Canada	3,336
7	Mexico	2,958
8	United Arab Emirates[d]	2,849
9	Kuwait[d]	2,508
10	Venezuela[d]	2,471

Top 10 consumers, 2010
'000 barrels per day

1	United States	19,148
2	China	9,057
3	Japan	4,451
4	India	3,319
5	Russia	3,199
6	Saudi Arabia[d]	2,812
7	Brazil	2,604
8	Germany	2,441
9	South Korea	2,384
10	Canada	2,276

Natural gas

Top 10 producers, 2010
Billion cubic metres

1	United States	611.0
2	Russia	588.9
3	Canada	159.8
4	Iran[d]	138.5
5	Qatar[d]	116.7
6	Norway	106.4
7	China	96.8
8	Saudi Arabia[d]	83.9
9	Indonesia[d]	82.0
10	Algeria[d]	80.4

Top 10 consumers, 2010
Billion cubic metres

1	United States	683.4
2	Russia	414.1
3	Iran[d]	136.9
4	China	109.0
5	Japan	94.5
6	Canada	93.8
	United Kingdom	93.8
8	Saudi Arabia[d]	83.9
9	Germany	81.3
10	Italy	76.1

Coal

Top 10 producers, 2010
Million tonnes oil equivalent

1	China	1,800.4
2	United States	552.2
3	Australia	235.4
4	India	216.1
5	Indonesia[d]	188.1
6	Russia	148.8
7	South Africa	143.0
8	Kazakhstan	56.2
9	Poland	55.5
10	Colombia	48.3

Top 10 consumers, 2010
Million tonnes oil equivalent

1	China	1,713.5
2	United States	524.6
3	India	277.6
4	Japan	123.7
5	Russia	93.8
6	South Africa	88.7
7	Germany	76.5
8	South Korea	76.0
9	Poland	54.0
10	Australia	43.4

Oil reserves[c]

Top proved reserves, end 2010
% of world total

1	Saudi Arabia[d]	19.1		5	Kuwait[d]	7.3
2	Venezuela[d]	15.3		6	United Arab Emirates[d]	7.1
3	Iran[d]	9.9		7	Russia	5.6
4	Iraq[d]	8.3		8	Libya[d]	3.4

a Clean basis.   b Soybeans, sunflower seed, cottonseed, groundnuts and rapeseed.
c Includes crude oil, shale oil, oil sands and natural gas liquids.   d Opec members.

Energy

Largest producers
Million tonnes oil equivalent, 2008

1	China	1,993	15	United Arab Emirates	181
2	United States	1,706	17	United Kingdom	167
3	Russia	1,254	18	South Africa	163
4	Saudi Arabia	579	19	Algeria	162
5	India	468	20	Kuwait	153
6	Euro area	463	21	Kazakhstan	148
7	Canada	407	22	France	137
8	Indonesia	347	23	Germany	134
9	Iran	327	24	Qatar	125
10	Australia	302	25	Iraq	118
11	Mexico	234	26	Angola	106
12	Brazil	228	27	Libya	104
13	Nigeria	227	28	Colombia	94
14	Norway	220	29	Malaysia	93
15	Venezuela	181	30	Japan	89

Largest consumers
Million tonnes oil equivalent, 2008

1	United States	2,284	16	Italy	176
2	China	2,116	17	Saudi Arabia	162
3	Euro area	1,226	18	Spain	139
4	Russia	687	19	Ukraine	136
5	India	621	20	South Africa	134
6	Japan	496	21	Australia	130
7	Germany	335	22	Nigeria	111
8	Canada	267	23	Thailand	107
9	France	266	24	Turkey	99
10	Brazil	249	25	Poland	98
11	South Korea	227	26	Pakistan	83
12	United Kingdom	208	27	Netherlands	80
13	Iran	202	28	Argentina	76
14	Indonesia	199	28	Malaysia	73
15	Mexico	181	30	Kazakhstan	71

Energy efficiency[a]

Most efficient			Least efficient		
GDP per unit of energy use, 2008			*GDP per unit of energy use, 2008*		
1	Hong Kong	20.0	1	Congo-Kinshasa	0.8
2	Peru	15.4	2	Uzbekistan	1.3
3	Panama	13.8	3	Trinidad & Tobago	1.7
4	Singapore	12.5		Turkmenistan	1.7
5	Colombia	12.0	5	Mozambique	1.9
6	Botswana	11.6		Togo	1.9
	Ireland	11.6	7	Ethiopia	2.0
8	Malta	11.4	8	Zambia	2.1
9	Albania	11.0	9	Iceland	2.2
10	Switzerland	10.9	10	Kazakhstan	2.3
11	United Kingdom	10.0		Ukraine	2.3

a 2005 PPP $ per kg of oil equivalent.

Net energy importers
% of commercial energy use, 2008

Highest			Lowest		
1	Hong Kong	100	1	Congo-Brazzaville	-868
	Malta	100	2	Angola	-865
	Netherlands Antilles	100	3	Norway	-640
	Singapore	100	4	Gabon	-552
5	Luxembourg	98	5	Brunei	-482
6	Cyprus	97	6	Kuwait	-481
	Moldova	97	7	Libya	-469
8	Jordan	96	8	Qatar	-418
	Lebanon	96	9	Azerbaijan	-338
	Morocco	96	10	Algeria	-337
11	Ireland	90	11	Oman	-286
12	Jamaica	88	12	Turkmenistan	-265

Largest consumption per head
Kg of oil equivalent, 2008

1	Qatar	18,830	12	Finland	6,635
2	Iceland	16,556	13	Saudi Arabia	6,514
3	Trinidad & Tobago	14,557	14	Norway	6,222
4	United Arab Emirates	13,030	15	Australia	6,071
5	Bahrain	11,896	16	Oman	5,903
6	Netherlands Antilles	11,078	17	Belgium	5,471
7	Kuwait	9,637	18	Sweden	5,379
8	Brunei	9,251	19	Netherlands	4,845
9	Luxembourg	8,429	20	Russia	4,838
10	Canada	8,008	21	South Korea	4,669
11	United States	7,503	22	Kazakhstan	4,525

Sources of electricity
% of total, 2008

Oil			Gas		
1	Malta	100.0	1	Bahrain	100.0
	Netherlands Antilles	100.0		Qatar	100.0
	Yemen	100.0		Turkmenistan	100.0
4	Cyprus	99.7	4	Trinidad & Tobago	99.6
5	Eritrea	99.3	5	Brunei	99.0

Hydropower			Nuclear power		
1	Albania	100.0	1	France	77.1
	Paraguay	100.0	2	Lithuania	74.2
3	Mozambique	99.9	3	Slovakia	58.1
4	Zambia	99.7	4	Belgium	54.5
5	Nepal	99.6	5	Ukraine	46.7

Coal		
1	Botswana	100.0
2	Mongolia	96.1
3	South Africa	94.2
4	Poland	92.2
5	Estonia	91.0

Workers of the world

Highest % of population in labour force
2009 or latest

1	Qatar	70.8		Vietnam	53.9
2	Guam	70.2	22	New Zealand	53.8
3	Cayman Islands	68.4		Sweden	53.8
4	United Arab Emirates	62.7	24	Portugal	53.3
5	Iceland	62.3	25	Russia	53.1
6	Macau	60.4		United States	53.1
7	Serbia	60.0	27	Hong Kong	53.0
8	China	59.5		Kazakhstan	53.0
9	Bermuda	59.4	29	Cambodia	52.9
10	Barbados	59.3		Denmark	52.9
11	Thailand	57.1		Georgia	52.9
12	Canada	56.3		Latvia	52.9
13	Kuwait	56.0	33	Armenia	52.8
14	Switzerland	55.5	34	Aruba	52.5
15	Burundi	55.1	35	Guadeloupe	52.5
16	Bahamas	54.6		Trinidad & Tobago	52.5
17	Netherlands	54.5	37	Brazil	52.4
18	Norway	54.1	38	Estonia	51.9
19	Myanmar	54.0		Germany	51.9
20	Mongolia	53.9	40	Bosnia	51.8

Most male workforce
Highest % men in workforce, 2009 or latest

1	Qatar	88.1
2	United Arab Emirates	84.4
3	Iraq	83.3
4	Saudi Arabia	83.2
5	West Bank & Gaza	81.8
6	Oman	81.2
7	Pakistan	80.6
8	Bahrain	79.5
9	Syria	79.1
10	Yemen	78.9
11	Libya	77.5
12	Egypt	77.0
	Jordan	77.0
14	Kuwait	75.0
15	Lebanon	74.9
16	Turkey	74.3
16	Morocco	74.2
18	Afghanistan	73.4
19	Tunisia	73.3
20	India	72.4
21	Sudan	70.6
22	Iran	70.2
23	Algeria	68.4
	Niger	68.4
25	Malta	67.7

Most female workforce
Highest % women in workforce, 2009 or latest

1	Papua New Guinea	55.6
2	Rwanda	52.9
3	Burundi	52.6
4	Lesotho	52.5
5	Martinique	52.4
6	Mozambique	52.0
7	Sierra Leone	51.4
8	Laos	50.4
9	Netherlands Antilles	50.0
	Russia	50.0
11	Kazakhstan	49.8
	Moldova	49.8
13	Malawi	49.7
14	Armenia	49.6
	Azerbaijan	49.6
	Guadeloupe	49.6
17	Belarus	49.5
18	Tanzania	49.4
19	Ghana	49.2
	Madagascar	49.2
21	Estonia	49.1
22	Ukraine	49.0
23	Lithuania	48.7
24	Vietnam	48.6
25	Bermuda	48.5

Lowest % of population in labour force
2009 or latest

1	Iraq	23.8		21	Saudi Arabia	37.3
2	West Bank & Gaza	23.9		22	Honduras	37.5
3	Yemen	26.3			Morocco	37.5
4	Mali	29.0		24	Sierra Leone	37.6
5	Afghanistan	30.5		25	Congo	37.7
6	Niger	31.4		26	Belize	38.2
7	Sudan	31.9			Chad	38.2
8	Nigeria	32.3			Oman	38.2
9	Egypt	33.0		29	Papua New Guinea	38.5
10	Syria	34.0		30	Swaziland	38.6
11	Turkey	34.2		31	Somalia	38.8
12	Jordan	34.3			South Africa	38.8
13	Lebanon	34.4		33	Guatemala	38.9
14	Namibia	36.0		34	Timor-Leste	39.1
15	Tunisia	36.3		35	Cameroon	39.6
16	Pakistan	36.5		36	Côte d'Ivoire	39.7
17	Libya	36.9			Israel	39.7
	Puerto Rico	36.9		38	Zimbabwe	40.1
19	Suriname	37.1		39	Fiji	40.3
20	Zambia	37.2		40	Nicaragua	40.5

Highest rate of unemployment
% of labour force[a], 2009 or latest

1	Namibia	33.8		26	Jordan	12.9
2	Macedonia	32.2		27	Nicaragua	12.2
3	Bosnia	29.0		28	Slovakia	12.1
4	Martinique	28.1		29	Colombia	12.0
5	Guinea-Bissau	26.3		30	Ireland	11.7
6	West Bank & Gaza	25.7		31	Jamaica	11.4
7	Réunion	24.5		32	Algeria	11.3
8	South Africa	23.8		33	Syria	10.9
9	Botswana	23.4		34	Iran	10.4
10	Guadeloupe	22.7		35	Netherlands Antilles	10.3
11	Spain	18.0		36	Hungary	10.0
12	Ethiopia	16.7			Morocco	10.0
13	Serbia	16.6		38	Chile	9.7
13	Georgia	16.5		39	Greece	9.5
15	Iraq	15.3			Portugal	9.5
16	Yemen	15.0		41	Egypt	9.4
17	Bahamas	14.2		42	Greenland	9.3
	Dominican Republic	14.2		43	Croatia	9.1
	Tunisia	14.2		43	France	9.1
20	Burundi	14.0		45	Mali	8.8
	Turkey	14.0			Ukraine	8.8
22	Albania	13.8		47	Bolivia	8.7
23	Estonia	13.7		48	Argentina	8.6
	Lithuania	13.7		49	Afghanistan	8.5
25	Puerto Rico	13.4				

a ILO definition.

The business world

Global competitiveness

2011

	Overall	Government	Infrastructure
1	Hong Kong	Hong Kong	United States
2	United States	Singapore	Sweden
3	Singapore	Switzerland	Denmark
4	Sweden	United Arab Emirates	Switzerland
5	Switzerland	Sweden	Canada
6	Taiwan	Qatar	Finland
7	Canada	Australia	Germany
8	Qatar	New Zealand	Norway
9	Australia	Canada	Iceland
10	Germany	Taiwan	Singapore
11	Luxembourg	Norway	Japan
12	Denmark	Chile	Netherlands
13	Norway	Denmark	Austria
14	Netherland	Finland	Australia
15	Finland	Luxembourg	Israel
16	Malaysia	Israel	Taiwan
17	Israel	Malaysia	United Kingdom
18	Austria	Netherlands	France
19	China	United States	Belgium
20	United Kingdom	Estonia	South Korea
21	New Zealand	Kazakhstan	Hong Kong
22	South Korea	South Korea	Luxembourg
23	Belgium	Thailand	New Zealand
24	Ireland	Germany	Ireland
25	Chile	Indonesia	Portugal
26	Japan	United Kingdom	Spain
27	Thailand	Austria	Malaysia
28	United Arab Emirates	Czech Republic	China
29	France	India	Czech Republic
30	Czech Republic	Ireland	Italy
31	Iceland	Jordan	Slovenia
32	India	South Africa	Greece
33	Estonia	China	Estonia
34	Poland	Turkey	Poland
35	Spain	Poland	Hungary
36	Kazakhstan	Peru	Lithuania
37	Indonesia	Philippines	Qatar
38	Mexico	Spain	Russia
39	Turkey	Belgium	United Arab Emirates
40	Portugal	Iceland	Chile
41	Philippines	Bulgaria	Slovakia
42	Italy	Slovakia	Romania
43	Peru	Mexico	Croatia
44	Brazil	France	Turkey

Notes: Overall competitiveness of 59 economies is calculated by combining four factors: economic performance, government efficiency, business efficiency and infrastructure. Column 1 is based on 331 criteria, using hard data and survey data. Column 2 measures government efficiency, looking at public finance, fiscal policy, institutional and societal frameworks and business legislation. Column 3 includes basic, technological and scientific infrastructure, health and environment, and education.

The business environment

		2011–15 score	2006–2010 score	2006–2010 ranking
1	Singapore	8.74	8.79	1
2	Switzerland	8.53	8.44	2
3	Finland	8.51	8.30	5
4	Hong Kong	8.50	8.40	3
5	Sweden	8.44	8.20	8
6	Australia	8.40	8.21	6
	Canada	8.40	8.37	4
	Denmark	8.40	8.20	7
9	New Zealand	8.35	7.95	12
10	Germany	8.21	8.08	10
	Netherlands	8.21	8.13	9
12	Norway	8.19	7.91	13
13	United States	8.09	8.07	11
14	Taiwan	8.06	7.67	18
15	Chile	7.93	7.81	15
16	France	7.85	7.63	19
17	Austria	7.79	7.73	17
	Ireland	7.79	7.85	14
19	United Kingdom	7.68	7.58	20
20	Belgium	7.67	7.79	16
21	Qatar	7.63	7.31	21
22	Spain	7.58	7.19	23
23	Israel	7.55	7.30	22
24	Malaysia	7.45	7.16	24
25	Japan	7.35	7.06	26
26	Czech Republic	7.32	7.15	25
	South Korea	7.32	6.93	32
	United Arab Emirates	7.32	7.04	27
29	Poland	7.31	7.01	29
30	Slovakia	7.29	6.98	31
31	Estonia	7.27	6.98	30
32	Slovenia	7.10	6.79	34
33	Bahrain	7.05	7.03	28
34	Mexico	6.92	6.68	36
35	Kuwait	6.83	6.46	39
36	Cyprus	6.82	6.82	33
37	Hungary	6.77	6.58	37
38	Thailand	6.74	6.42	41
39	Brazil	6.71	6.50	38
40	Costa Rica	6.66	6.38	42
41	Portugal	6.62	6.78	35
42	Latvia	6.55	6.04	47
43	Peru	6.52	6.19	44
44	China	6.51	5.99	49
	Saudi Arabia	6.51	6.06	46
46	Lithuania	6.50	6.30	43

Note: Scores reflect the opportunities for, and hindrances to, the conduct of business, measured by countries' rankings in ten categories including market potential, tax and labour-market policies, infrastructure, skills and the political environment. Scores reflect average and forecast average over given date range.

Business creativity and research

Innovation index[a]
2010

1	United States	5.65		13	Netherlands	4.77
2	Switzerland	5.60		14	United Kingdom	4.65
3	Finland	5.56		15	Belgium	4.59
4	Japan	5.52		16	Iceland	4.53
5	Sweden	5.45			Luxembourg	4.53
6	Israel	5.30		18	Norway	4.49
7	Taiwan	5.23		19	Austria	4.48
8	Germany	5.19			France	4.48
9	Singapore	5.04		21	Australia	4.41
10	Denmark	4.89		22	Ireland	4.25
11	Canada	4.87		23	Qatar	4.11
12	South Korea	4.81		24	Malaysia	4.10

Technological readiness index[b]
2010

1	Sweden	6.12		13	Belgium	5.22
2	Luxembourg	6.11		14	United Arab Emirates	5.19
3	Iceland	5.99		15	Finland	5.17
	Netherlands	5.99		16	Canada	5.14
5	Hong Kong	5.96		17	United States	5.10
6	Denmark	5.62		18	Austria	5.09
7	Switzerland	5.60		19	South Korea	5.05
8	United Kingdom	5.58		20	Taiwan	5.04
9	Norway	5.56		21	Ireland	4.99
10	Germany	5.36		22	Barbados	4.98
11	Singapore	5.35		23	Australia	4.97
12	France	5.28		24	Estonia	4.94

Brain drain[c]

Highest, 2010			Lowest, 2010		
1	Bosnia	2.0	1	Switzerland	6.3
	Kyrgyzstan	2.0	2	Qatar	6.0
	Lesotho	2.0	3	United States	5.9
	Libya	2.0	4	Singapore	5.8
	Mauritania	2.0	5	United Arab Emirates	5.5
	Serbia	2.0	6	Sweden	5.4
	Swaziland	2.0	7	Norway	5.3
8	Burundi	2.1	8	Canada	5.2
	Guyana	2.1		Hong Kong	5.2
	Moldova	2.1		Netherlands	5.2
	Nepal	2.1		United Kingdom	5.2
	Venezuela	2.1			

a The innovation index is a measure of the adoption of new technology, and the interaction between the business and science sectors. It includes measures of the investment into research institutions and protection of intellectual property rights.

b The technological readiness index measures the ability of the economy to adopt new technologies. It includes measures of information and communication technology (ICT) usage, the regulatory framework with regard to ICT, and the availability of new technology to business.

c Scores: 1=talented people leave for other countries, 7=they always remain in home country.

Total expenditure on R&D

% of GDP, 2008			*$bn, 2008*	
1	Israel	4.86	1	United States	398.1
2	Sweden	3.75	2	Japan	150.8
3	Finland	3.50	3	Germany	84.2
4	Japan	3.44	4	China	66.5
5	South Korea	3.21	5	France	57.6
6	Switzerland	2.90	6	United Kingdom	49.8
7	Taiwan	2.77	7	South Korea	33.7
8	United States	2.76	8	Canada	27.6
9	Denmark	2.72	9	Italy	27.2
10	Singapore	2.68	10	Spain	21.5
11	Austria	2.67	11	Sweden	18.0
12	Iceland	2.65	12	Brazil	17.9
13	Germany	2.53	13	Russia	17.3
14	Australia	2.07	14	Australia	16.2
15	France	2.02	15	Netherlands	13.3
16	Belgium	1.92	16	Taiwan	11.1
17	United Kingdom	1.88	17	Austria	11.0
18	Canada	1.84	18	Switzerland	10.5
19	Netherlands	1.71	19	Israel	9.8
20	Slovenia	1.66	20	Belgium	9.7
21	Luxembourg	1.62	21	Finland	9.4
	Norway	1.62	22	Denmark	9.3
23	China	1.54	23	India	9.1
24	Portugal	1.51	24	Norway	7.3
25	Czech Republic	1.47	25	Singapore	5.0

Patents

No. of patents granted to residents *Total, average 2006–08*			*No. of patents in force* *Per 100,000 people, 2008*	
1	Japan	141,203	1	Luxembourg	5,605
2	United States	82,284	2	Hong Kong	2,856
3	South Korea	80,688	3	Ireland	1,782
4	China	34,537	4	Taiwan	1,415
5	Taiwan	33,402	5	South Korea	1,285
6	Russia	19,943	6	Sweden	1,150
7	Germany	13,691	7	Japan	995
8	France	9,894	8	Singapore	970
9	Italy	5,257	9	Finland	838
10	Ukraine	2,452	10	New Zealand	798
11	United Kingdom	2,369	11	France	707
12	Spain	2,086	12	United Kingdom	636
13	Netherlands	1,781	13	Germany	622
14	Canada	1,761	14	United States	615
15	Kazakhstan	1,459	15	Australia	496
16	India	1,385	16	Canada	389
17	Poland	1,383	17	Norway	380
18	Sweden	1,252	18	Portugal	373
19	Australia	978	19	Iceland	327
20	Austria	961	20	Estonia	290
21	Finland	700	21	Greece	285

Business costs and FDI

Office occupancy costs
Rent, taxes and operating expenses, $ per sq. metre, November 2010

1	London (West End), UK	2,085	12	Dubai, UAE	1,026
2	Hong Kong (Central, CBD)	1,983	13	Hong Kong (Citywide)	996
3	Tokyo (Inner Central), Japan	1,702	13	Geneva, Switzerland	927
4	Mumbai, India	1,404	15	Zurich, Switzerland	906
5	Moscow, Russia	1,381	16	Luxembourg City, Lux.	889
6	Tokyo (Outer Central), Japan	1,370	17	Istanbul, Turkey	848
7	London (City), UK	1,341	18	Milan, Italy	846
8	Paris (Ile-de-France), France	1,246	19	Stockholm, Sweden	789
			20	Abu Dhabi, UAE	776
9	São Paulo, Brazil	1,174	21	Seoul (CBD), South Korea	764
10	Rio de Janeiro, Brazil	1,124	22	Frankfurt am Main, Germany	756
11	New Delhi, India	1,089	23	Edinburgh, UK	753
			24	Manchester, UK	736
			25	Singapore	727

Minimum wage
Minimum wage as a ratio of the median wage of full-time workers, 2009

1	Turkey	0.71	11	Netherlands	0.47
2	France	0.60	12	United Kingdom	0.46
3	New Zealand	0.59	13	Poland	0.45
4	Australia	0.54		Romania	0.45
	Portugal	0.54		Slovakia	0.45
6	Belgium	0.51	16	Lithuania	0.44
	Ireland	0.51		Spain	0.44
8	Slovenia	0.49	18	Canada	0.43
9	Greece	0.48		Luxembourg	0.43
	Hungary	0.48			

Foreign direct investment[a]

Inflows, $m, 2009

1	United States	129,883
2	China	95,000
3	France	59,628
4	Hong Kong	48,449
5	United Kingdom	45,676
6	Russia	38,722
7	Germany	35,606
8	Saudi Arabia	35,514
9	India	34,613
10	Belgium	33,782
11	Italy	30,538
12	Luxembourg	27,273
13	Netherlands	26,949
14	Brazil	25,949
15	British Virgin Islands	25,310
16	Ireland	24,971
17	Australia	22,572

Outflows, $m, 2009

1	United States	248,074
2	France	147,161
3	Japan	74,699
4	Germany	62,705
5	Hong Kong	52,269
6	China	48,000
7	Russia	46,057
8	Italy	43,918
9	Canada	38,832
10	Norway	34,203
11	Sweden	30,287
12	British Virgin Islands	26,535
13	Ireland	20,750
14	United Kingdom	18,463
15	Australia	18,426
16	Netherlands	17,780
17	Spain	16,335

Note: CBD is Central Business District.
a Investment in companies in a foreign country.

Business red tape, corruption and piracy

Number of days taken to register a new company

Lowest, 2011		Highest, 2011	
1 New Zealand	1	1 Suriname	694
2 Australia	2	2 Guinea-Bissau	216
3 Georgia	3	3 Congo-Brazzaville	160
Macedonia	3	4 Venezuela	141
Rwanda	3	5 Equatorial Guinea	136
Singapore	3	6 Brazil	120
7 Belgium	4	7 Brunei	105
Hungary	4	Haiti	105
9 Albania	5	9 Laos	100
Belarus	5	10 Zimbabwe	90
Canada	5	11 Cambodia	85
Iceland	5	12 Congo-Kinshasa	84
Saudi Arabia	5	Eritrea	84
		14 Timor-Leste	83

Corruption perceptions index[a]

2010, 10 = least corrupt

Lowest		Highest	
1 Denmark	9.3	1 Somalia	1.1
New Zealand	9.3	2 Afghanistan	1.4
Singapore	9.3	Myanmar	1.4
4 Finland	9.2	4 Iraq	1.5
Sweden	9.2	5 Sudan	1.6
6 Canada	8.9	Turkmenistan	1.6
7 Netherlands	8.8	Uzbekistan	1.6
8 Australia	8.7	8 Chad	1.7
Switzerland	8.7	9 Burundi	1.8
10 Norway	8.6	10 Angola	1.9
11 Iceland	8.5	Equatorial Guinea	1.9
Luxembourg	8.5	12 Congo-Kinshasa	2.0
13 Hong Kong	8.4	Guinea	2.0
14 Ireland	8.0	Kyrgyzstan	2.0
15 Austria	7.9	Venezuela	2.0
Germany	7.9		

Business software piracy

% of software that is pirated, 2009

1 Georgia	95	10 Belarus	87
2 Zimbabwe	92	Venezuela	87
3 Bangladesh	91	12 Indonesia	86
Moldova	91	13 Iraq	85
5 Armenia	90	Ukraine	85
Yemen	90	Vietnam	85
7 Sri Lanka	89	16 Algeria	84
8 Azerbaijan	88	Pakistan	84
Libya	88		

a This index ranks countries based on how much corruption is perceived by business people, academics and risk analysts to exist among politicians and public officials.

Businesses and banks

Largest non-bank businesses
By market capitalisation, $bn
End December 2009

1	PetroChina	China	353.2
2	Exxon Mobil	United States	323.7
3	Microsoft	United States	270.6
4	Wal-Mart Stores	United States	203.7
5	BHP Billiton	Australia/United Kingdom	201.1
6	Petrobras	Brazil	199.2
7	Google	United States	196.7
8	Apple	United States	189.6
9	China Mobile	China	188.5
10	Royal Dutch Shell	United Kingdom/Netherlands	186.6
11	BP	United Kingdom	181.8
12	Johnson & Johnson	United States	177.7
13	Nestlé	Switzerland	177.1
	Procter & Gamble	United States	177.1
15	IBM	United States	172.0
16	AT&T	United States	165.4
17	General Electric	United States	161.1
18	China Petroleum & Chemical Corp	China	159.3
19	Chevron	United States	154.5
20	Berkshire Hathaway	United States	153.6
21	Total	France	151.4
22	Roche	Switzerland	147.4
23	Pfizer	United States	146.8
24	Gazprom	Russia	144.4

End March 2011

1	Exxon Mobil	United States	417.2
2	PetroChina	China	326.3
3	Apple	United States	321.1
4	BHP Billiton	Australia/United Kingdom	248.6
5	Petrobras	Brazil	247.3
6	Royal Dutch Shell	United Kingdom/Netherlands	228.6
7	Chevron	United States	215.8
8	Microsoft	United States	213.3
9	General Electric	United States	212.9
10	Berkshire Hathaway	United States	206.7
11	Nestlé	Switzerland	199.2
12	IBM	United States	198.9
13	Gazprom	Russia	190.8
14	Google	United States	189.1
15	China Mobile	China	184.9
16	Wal-Mart Stores	United States	181.7
17	AT&T	United States	180.9
18	Procter & Gamble	United States	172.5
19	Oracle	United States	169.2
20	Vale	Brazil	168.2
21	Pfizer	United States	162.4
22	Johnson & Johnson	United States	162.1
23	Coca-Cola	United States	152.2
24	Vodafone	United Kingdom	146.2

Largest banks
By market capitalisation, $bn
End December 2009

1	Industrial and Commercial Bank of China	China	269.0
2	China Construction Bank	China	201.5
3	HSBC Holdings	United Kingdom	199.2
4	JPMorgan Chase	United States	171.1
5	Bank of China	China	154.0
6	Bank of America	United States	149.6
7	Wells Fargo	United States	138.0
8	Banco Santander	Spain	136.2
9	BNP Paribas	France	94.9
10	Citigroup	United States	93.5
11	Itaú Unibanco	Brazil	90.1
12	Royal Bank of Canada	Canada	75.7
13	Commonwealth Bank of Australia	Australia	75.6
14	Mitsubishi UFJ Financial Group	Japan	68.7
15	BBVA	Spain	68.4

End March 2011

1	Industrial and Commercial Bank of China	China	251.1
2	China Construction Bank	China	232.7
3	JPMorgan Chase	United States	183.6
4	HSBC Holdings	United Kingdom	182.3
5	Wells Fargo	United States	167.1
6	Bank of China	China	146.0
7	Bank of America	United States	134.9
8	Citigroup	United States	128.4
9	Itaú Unibanco	Brazil	99.7
10	Banco Santander	Spain	98.1
11	Royal Bank of Canada	Canada	88.2
12	BNP Paribas	France	87.8
13	Commonwealth Bank of Australia	Australia	84.1
14	Sberbank	Russia	81.1
15	Toronto-Dominion Bank	Canada	78.1

Central bank staff
Per 100,000 population, 2010

Highest			Lowest		
1	Cayman Islands	310.7	1	China	0.2
2	Bermuda	219.7	2	Ethiopia	0.5
3	Barbados	86.8		Somalia	0.5
4	Panama	80.1	4	Pakistan	0.8
5	Bahamas	76.0	5	India	1.8
6	Aruba	71.7	6	Myanmar	2.1
7	Suriname	63.7	7	Indonesia	2.3
8	Belize	52.8	8	Brazil	2.4
9	Qatar	51.9		North Korea	2.4
10	Russia	49.9	10	Bangladesh	2.5
11	Bahrain	48.0		Eritrea	2.5
12	Montenegro	46.7		Mexico	2.5

Stockmarkets

Largest market capitalisation
$bn, end 2010

1	United States	17,139		23	Indonesia	360
2	China	4,763		24	Saudi Arabia	353
3	Japan	4,100		25	Chile	342
4	United Kingdom	3,107		26	Italy	318
5	Canada	2,160		27	Turkey	307
6	France	1,926		28	Thailand	278
7	India	1,616		29	Belgium	269
8	Brazil	1,546		30	Norway	251
9	Australia	1,455		31	Denmark	232
10	Germany	1,430		32	Israel	218
11	Switzerland	1,229		33	Colombia	209
12	Spain	1,172		34	Poland	190
13	South Korea	1,089		35	Philippines	157
14	Hong Kong	1,080		36	Qatar	124
15	South Africa	1,013		37	Kuwait	120
16	Russia	1,005		38	Finland	118
17	Taiwan	804		39	United Arab Emirates	105
18	Netherlands	661		40	Luxembourg	101
19	Sweden	581		41	Peru	100
20	Mexico	454		42	Iran	87
21	Malaysia	411		43	Egypt	82
22	Singapore	370			Portugal	82

Largest gains in global stockmarkets
$ terms, % increase December 31 2009 to January 5th 2011

1	Thailand (SET)	58.0		24	Norway (OSEAX)	13.0
2	Indonesia (JSX)	56.1		25	United States (DJIA)	12.4
3	Argentina (MERV)	48.8		26	Japan (Topix)	12.3
4	Chile (IGPA)	44.7		27	Australia (All Ord)	10.0
5	Colombia (IGBC)	41.5			Japan (Nikkei 225)	10.0
6	Malaysia (KLSE)	37.3		29	Egypt (Case 30)	9.9
7	Mexico (IPC)	28.8		30	Saudi Arabia (Tadawul)	9.4
8	South Korea (KOSPI)	28.0		31	Hong Kong (Hang Seng)	8.4
9	Sweden (OMXS30)	27.5		32	Czech Republic (PX)	8.3
10	Pakistan (KSE)	27.2		32	Brazil (BVSP)	8.1
11	South Africa (JSE AS)	26.6		34	United Kingdom (FTSE 100)	6.9
12	Denmark (OMXCB)	26.3		35	Germany (DAX)[a]	6.7
13	Turkey (ISE)	26.0		36	Switzerland (SMI)	6.6
14	Israel (TA-100)	24.1		37	Austria (ATX)	5.7
15	Russia (RTS, $ terms)	22.5		37	Netherlands (AEX)	-2.4
16	Singapore (STI)	21.9		39	Belgium (Bel 20)	-4.0
17	China (SSEB, $ terms)	21.7		40	Hungary (BUX)	-6.6
18	Canada (S&P TSX)	20.1		41	France (CAC 40)	-9.1
19	India (BSE)	19.3		42	Euro area (FTSE Euro 100)	-9.2
19	United States (NAScomp)	19.1		43	China (SSEA)	-10.8
21	Taiwan (TWI)	18.4		44	Euro area (DJ STOXX 50)	-12.4
22	United States (S&P 500)	14.5		45	Italy (FTSE/MIB)	-19.0
23	Poland (WIG)	14.3		46	Spain (Madrid SE)	-26.3

a Total return index.

Highest growth in value traded
$ terms, $bn, 2010

1	United States	30,455		23	Thailand	218
2	China	8,030		24	Norway	217
3	Japan	4,280		25	Saudi Arabia	203
4	United Kingdom	3,007		26	Denmark	145
5	South Korea	1,627		27	Israel	133
6	Hong Kong	1,598		28	Indonesia	130
7	Germany	1,405		29	Belgium	111
8	Canada	1,366		30	Mexico	109
9	Australia	1,222		31	Finland	102
10	India	1,057		32	Malaysia	90
11	Spain	938		33	Poland	77
12	Brazil	901		34	Chile	54
13	Taiwan	893		35	Austria	48
14	Switzerland	869		36	Greece	43
15	France	828		37	Kuwait	42
16	Russia	800		38	Egypt	37
17	Netherlands	592		39	Portugal	31
18	Italy	539		40	Vietnam	29
19	Sweden	440		41	Philippines	27
20	Turkey	422			United Arab Emirates	27
21	South Africa	340		43	Hungary	26
22	Singapore	282		44	Qatar	18

Number of listed companies
2010

1	India	4,987		25	Russia	345
2	United States	4,279		26	Iran	341
3	Canada	3,805		27	Turkey	337
4	Japan	3,553		28	Mongolia	336
5	Spain	3,310		29	Sweden	331
6	China	2,063		30	Bangladesh	302
7	United Kingdom	2,056		31	Italy	291
8	Australia	1,913		32	Greece	287
9	South Korea	1,781		33	Jordan	277
10	Hong Kong	1,396		34	Philippines	251
11	Romania	1,383		35	Switzerland	246
12	Malaysia	957		35	Sri Lanka	241
13	France	901		37	Chile	227
14	Taiwan	752		38	Croatia	221
15	Pakistan	644		39	Kuwait	215
16	Israel	596			Nigeria	215
17	Germany	571		41	Egypt	211
18	Poland	569		42	Peru	199
19	Thailand	541		43	Denmark	196
20	Singapore	461		44	Norway	195
21	Indonesia	420		45	Nepal	190
22	Bulgaria	390		46	Ukraine	183
23	Brazil	373		47	Vietnam	164
24	South Africa	360				

Transport: roads and cars

Longest road networks
Km, 2009 or latest

1	United States	6,486,176	21	Saudi Arabia	239,519
2	China	3,799,417	22	Bangladesh	239,226
3	India	3,428,048	23	Argentina	230,418
4	Brazil	1,841,534	24	Philippines	201,433
5	Canada	1,419,300	25	Romania	199,298
6	Japan	1,201,340	26	Nigeria	195,431
7	France	1,030,227	27	Iran	175,867
8	Russia	952,957	28	Vietnam	169,976
9	Australia	815,455	29	Ukraine	169,533
10	Sweden	697,794	30	Colombia	164,385
11	Spain	680,347	31	Hungary	162,028
12	Germany	664,833	32	Belgium	153,947
13	Italy	489,982	33	Congo-Kinshasa	153,497
14	Turkey	427,235	34	Netherlands	140,111
15	Indonesia	404,343	35	Czech Republic	129,143
16	United Kingdom	398,156	36	Greece	118,936
17	Poland	383,305	37	Malaysia	115,261
18	South Africa	365,081	38	Egypt	111,175
19	Mexico	361,866	39	Algeria	109,733
20	Pakistan	263,590	40	Austria	107,400

Densest road networks
Km of road per km² land area, 2009 or latest

1	Macau	21.3		Sweden	1.6
2	Malta	7.1		Trinidad & Tobago	1.6
3	Singapore	5.2		United Kingdom	1.6
4	Bahrain	5.1	25	Sri Lanka	1.5
5	Belgium	5.0	26	Ireland	1.4
6	Barbados	3.7	27	Austria	1.3
7	Netherlands	3.4		Cyprus	1.3
8	Japan	3.2		Estonia	1.3
9	Puerto Rico	2.8		Spain	1.3
10	Jamaica	2.0	31	Lithuania	1.2
	Luxembourg	2.0		Poland	1.2
12	France	1.9	33	Latvia	1.1
	Germany	1.9		Netherlands Antilles	1.1
	Hong Kong	1.9		South Korea	1.1
	Slovenia	1.9		Taiwan	1.1
16	Bangladesh	1.7	37	India	1.0
	Denmark	1.7		Mauritius	1.0
	Hungary	1.7	39	Greece	0.9
	Switzerland	1.7		Israel	0.9
20	Czech Republic	1.6		Portugal	0.9
	Italy	1.6		Slovakia	0.9

Most crowded road networks

Number of vehicles per km of road network, 2009 or latest

1	Kuwait	270.9	26	Luxembourg	68.6
2	Hong Kong	241.0	27	Malaysia	68.0
3	Macau	237.6	28	Iran	67.5
4	United Arab Emirates	219.6		Mexico	67.5
5	Singapore	218.2	30	Germany	66.8
6	Taiwan	169.7	31	Netherlands	62.2
7	South Korea	157.3	32	Switzerland	61.2
8	Netherlands Antilles	153.8	33	Croatia	59.6
9	Israel	127.9	34	Honduras	59.0
10	Malta	122.8	35	Trinidad & Tobago	58.4
11	Thailand	121.4	36	Bulgaria	53.3
12	Bahrain	114.2	37	Greece	52.4
13	Jordan	112.5	38	Saudi Arabia	50.3
14	Puerto Rico	110.0	39	Armenia	49.3
15	Dominican Republic	104.6	40	Indonesia	49.1
16	Qatar	98.1		Serbia	49.1
17	Mauritius	93.8	42	Japan	48.5
18	Guatemala	91.0	43	Poland	46.0
19	United Kingdom	87.6	44	Austria	43.8
20	Italy	83.6		Tunisia	43.8
21	Haiti	81.7	46	Bahamas	43.7
22	El Salvador	81.5	47	Ukraine	43.2
23	Barbados	78.3	48	Cyprus	42.5
24	Brunei	73.1	49	Spain	40.9
25	Portugal	69.9	50	Fiji	39.6

Most car journeys

Km travelled by car per person per year, 2009

1	Peru	38,553	21	South Africa	15,934
2	United States	34,560	22	Romania	15,462
3	Tunisia	25,225	23	China	15,435
4	Pakistan	25,199	24	Norway	15,310
5	Ecuador	23,570	25	Australia	14,951
6	Chile	22,671	26	Austria	14,742
7	South Korea	21,763	27	Latvia	14,537
8	Singapore	21,563	28	Germany	14,402
9	Morocco	18,455	29	Netherlands	14,317
10	Croatia	17,723	30	United Kingdom	14,068
11	Finland	17,639	31	Portugal	13,337
12	Canada	17,498	32	Switzerland	13,290
13	Denmark	16,903	33	New Zealand	13,062
14	Thailand	16,823	34	Luxembourg	12,876
15	Israel	16,721	35	France	12,700
16	Greece	16,470	36	Estonia	12,635
17	Hong Kong	16,261	37	Japan	12,403
18	Belgium	16,212	38	Italy	11,917
19	Sweden	16,077	39	India	10,516
20	Ireland	15,951	40	Iceland	10,453

Highest car ownership
Number of cars per 1,000 population, 2009 or latest

#	Country		#	Country	
1	Luxembourg	663	26	Greece	438
2	Iceland	659	27	United States	435
3	New Zealand	655	28	Ireland	433
4	Brunei	610	29	Kuwait	426
5	Italy	601	30	Latvia	421
6	Malta	558	31	Czech Republic	417
7	Canada	555	32	Portugal	414
8	Australia	535	33	Poland	395
9	Guam	531	34	Estonia	387
10	Switzerland	528	35	United Arab Emirates	384
11	Austria	510	36	Denmark	379
12	Slovenia	509	37	Netherlands Antilles	360
13	Germany	502	38	Lebanon	357
14	France	496	39	Croatia	344
15	United Kingdom	495	40	Barbados	343
16	Spain	490	41	Qatar	335
17	Lithuania	489	42	Hungary	305
18	Finland	487	43	Bahamas	290
19	Belgium	469		Bahrain	290
20	Saudi Arabia	468	45	Bulgaria	285
21	Sweden	467	46	Slovakia	271
22	Netherlands	466	47	Israel	259
23	Cyprus	460	48	Taiwan	254
	Norway	460	49	South Korea	248
25	Japan	446	50	New Caledonia	244

Lowest car ownership
Number of cars per 1,000 population, 2009 or latest

#	Country		#	Country	
1	Bangladesh	1		Myanmar	4
	Chad	1		Niger	4
	Ethiopia	1	23	Gambia, The	5
	Malawi	1		Guinea	5
	Rwanda	1		Liberia	5
	Somalia	1		Papua New Guinea	5
	Tanzania	1	27	Benin	6
8	Burundi	2		Togo	6
	Central African Rep	2	29	Burkina Faso	7
	Congo-Brazzaville	2		Equatorial Guinea	7
	Eritrea	2	31	Congo-Kinshasa	8
	Sudan	2		India	8
	Uganda	2		Zambia	8
14	Guinea-Bissau	3	34	Cameroon	9
	Lesotho	3		Kenya	9
	Madagascar	3		Philippines	9
	Mali	3	37	Pakistan	10
	Nepal	3		Senegal	10
19	Ghana	4	39	Bhutan	12
	Mozambique	4	40	Sierra Leone	13

Car production

Number of cars produced, '000, 2009

1	Japan	8,630	21	Ukraine	361
2	China	7,436	22	Tunisia	311
3	Germany	4,587	22	Malaysia	306
4	South Korea	3,752	24	Indonesia	305
5	United States	3,377	25	Argentina	298
6	Brazil	2,585	26	Australia	264
7	India	1,799	27	Romania	252
8	Spain	1,601	28	South Africa	233
9	France	1,559	29	Slovenia	187
10	Canada	1,286	30	Pakistan	186
11	Mexico	1,153	31	Hungary	180
12	Russia	1,151	32	Taiwan	160
13	Iran	1,149	33	Venezuela	133
14	Czech Republic	895	34	Sweden	103
15	United Kingdom	851	35	Portugal	96
16	Poland	761	36	Colombia	86
17	Turkey	599	37	Egypt	66
18	Italy	591	38	Netherlands	57
19	Slovakia	497	39	Austria	47
20	Belgium	390	40	Morocco	32

Cars sold

New car registrations, '000, 2009

1	China	8,094	21	Netherlands	385
2	United States	6,867	22	Saudi Arabia	362
3	Japan	4,739	23	Malaysia	356
4	Germany	3,875	24	Argentina	334
5	Russia	2,735	25	Poland	322
6	France	2,206	26	Austria	317
7	Italy	2,130	27	Turkey	311
8	United Kingdom	1,943	28	Switzerland	263
9	Brazil	1,701	29	Pakistan	228
10	India	1,697	30	Greece	217
11	Iran	1,107	31	Sweden	208
12	Spain	919	32	Egypt	203
13	South Korea	871	33	Costa Rica	197
14	Canada	800	34	Taiwan	184
15	Australia	774	35	Thailand	180
16	Mexico	698	36	Indonesia	165
17	Nigeria	470	37	Portugal	159
18	Belgium	469	38	Czech Republic	158
19	Venezuela	457	39	Chile	146
20	South Africa	410	40	Romania	112

Transport: planes and trains

Most air travel
Million passenger-km[a] per year, 2010

1	United States	1,230,882	16	India	71,894
2	China	292,362	17	Ireland	69,974
3	United Kingdom	226,169	18	Brazil	62,738
4	Germany	168,303	19	Thailand	51,404
5	France	139,285	20	Italy	50,809
6	Japan	121,887	21	Qatar	37,032
7	Canada	105,526	22	Turkey	34,566
8	United Arab Emirates	97,141	23	Malaysia	31,247
9	Australia	95,080	24	Saudi Arabia	29,869
10	Netherlands	90,130	25	Mexico	29,040
11	Hong Kong	83,862	26	New Zealand	27,338
12	Singapore	78,850	27	Switzerland	25,391
13	South Korea	77,222	28	South Africa	24,979
14	Russia	76,927	29	Indonesia	24,005
15	Spain	74,373	30	Portugal	23,392

Busiest airports

Total passengers, m, 2010		*Total cargo, m tonnes, 2010*	
1 Atlanta, Hartsfield	88.0	1 Memphis, Intl.	3.70
2 London, Heathrow	66.0	2 Hong Kong, Intl.	3.39
3 Beijing, Capital	65.4	3 Shanghai, Pudong Intl.	2.54
4 Chicago, O'Hare	64.2	4 Seoul, Incheon	2.31
5 Tokyo, Haneda	61.9	5 Paris, Charles de Gaulle	2.05
6 Paris, Charles de Gaulle	57.9	6 Anchorage, Intl.	1.99
7 Los Angeles, Intl.	56.5	7 Louisville, Standiford Field	1.95
8 Dallas, Ft. Worth	56.0	8 Dubai, Intl.	1.93
9 Frankfurt, Main	50.9	9 Frankfurt, Main	1.89
10 Denver, Intl.	50.2	10 Tokyo, Narita	1.85
11 Madrid, Barajas	48.3	11 Singapore, Changi	1.66
12 New York, JFK	45.9	12 Miami, Intl.	1.56
13 Hong Kong, Intl.	45.6	13 Los Angeles, Intl.	1.51
14 Amsterdam, Schiphol	43.6	14 Beijing, Capital	1.48
15 Dubai Intl.	40.9	15 Taiwan, Taoyuan Intl.	1.36

Average daily aircraft movements, take-offs and landings, 2010

1 Atlanta, Hartsfield	2,658	11	Philadelphia, Intl.	1,295
2 Chicago, O'Hare	2,268	12	London, Heathrow	1,278
3 Dallas, Ft. Worth	1,750	13	Frankfurt, Main	1,269
4 Los Angeles, Intl.	1,738	14	Phoenix, Skyharbor	
5 Denver, Intl.	1,663		Intl.	1,253
6 Houston, George Bush		15	Madrid, Barajas	1,192
Intercont.	1,474	16	Detroit, Metro	1,185
7 Paris, Charles de Gaulle	1,439	17	Minneapolis, St Paul	1,185
8 Las Vegas, McCarran		18	New York, JFK	1,142
Intl.	1,400	18	Newark	1,128
9 Charlotte/Douglas, Intl.	1,396	20	Toronto, Pearson Intl.	1,116
10 Beijing, Capital	1,338			

---

a Air passenger–km data refer to the distance travelled by aircraft of national origin.

Longest railway networks
'000 km, 2010

1	United States	228.5	21	Turkey	9.6
2	Russia	85.3	22	Czech Republic	9.5
3	China	65.5	23	Australia	8.6
4	India	63.3	24	Hungary	8.0
5	Canada	58.3	25	Pakistan	7.8
6	Germany	33.7	26	Iran	7.6
7	France	33.6	27	Finland	5.9
8	United Kingdom	31.5	28	Belarus	5.5
9	Brazil	29.8	29	Chile	5.4
10	Mexico	26.7	30	Egypt	5.2
11	Argentina	25.0	31	Austria	5.1
12	South Africa	22.1	32	Sudan	4.5
13	Ukraine	21.7	33	Thailand	4.4
14	Japan	20.0	34	Uzbekistan	4.2
15	Poland	19.7	35	Bulgaria	4.1
16	Italy	18.0		Norway	4.1
17	Spain	15.3	37	Serbia	3.8
18	Kazakhstan	14.2	38	Algeria	3.6
19	Romania	10.8		Belgium	3.6
20	Sweden	10.0		Slovakia	3.6

Most rail passengers
Km per person per year, 2010

1	Switzerland	2,258	13	Kazakhstan	879
2	Japan	1,910	14	Belarus	779
3	Slovakia	1,420	15	Italy	735
4	Denmark	1,322	16	Finland	733
5	France	1,320	17	Sweden	721
6	Austria	1,227	18	Luxembourg	690
7	Ukraine	1,097	19	Taiwan	671
8	Russia	1,075	20	South Korea	661
9	Belgium	972	21	India	636
10	Germany	961	22	Czech Republic	624
11	Netherlands	922	23	China	588
12	United Kingdom	887	24	Norway	546

Most rail freight
Million tonnes-km per year, 2010

1	China	2,523,917	13	Poland	34,266
2	United States	2,468,738	14	Austria	23,104
3	Russia	1,865,305	15	France	22,840
4	India	521,371	16	Uzbekistan	22,227
5	Canada	322,741	17	Iran	20,540
6	Brazil	267,700	18	Japan	20,432
7	Ukraine	218,091	19	Latvia	17,164
8	Kazakhstan	197,302	20	Czech Republic	13,592
9	South Africa	113,342	21	Lithuania	13,431
10	Germany	105,794	22	Italy	12,037
11	Australia	64,172	23	Argentina	12,025
12	Belarus	42,742	24	Turkmenistan	11,547

Transport: shipping

Merchant fleets
Number of vessels, by country of domicile, 2010

1	Japan	3,751	11	Denmark	940
2	China	3,633	12	Indonesia	868
3	Germany	3,627	13	Italy	844
4	Greece	3,150	14	Netherlands	800
5	Russia	1,987	15	United Kingdom	794
6	Norway	1,968	16	Hong Kong	680
7	United States	1,865	17	Taiwan	637
8	Turkey	1,222	18	Vietnam	544
9	South Korea	1,200	19	India	509
10	Singapore	985	20	Malaysia	480

By country of domicile, deadweight tonnage, m, January 2010

1	Greece	186.1	11	Taiwan	29.5
2	Japan	183.3	12	United Kingdom	26.2
3	China	104.5	13	Italy	22.5
4	Germany	103.9	14	Russia	19.4
5	South Korea	44.9	15	Canada	18.3
6	United States	41.3	16	Bermuda	17.2
7	Norway	40.5		India	17.2
8	Hong Kong	34.4	18	Turkey	16.8
9	Denmark	33.2	19	Iran	13.7
10	Singapore	32.6	20	Saudi Arabia	13.2

Maritime trading
% of value of world trade generated, January 2009

1	United States	10.7		Singapore	2.1
2	China	8.8	15	Spain	2.0
3	Germany	8.2	16	Mexico	1.9
4	Japan	4.8	17	India	1.6
5	France	4.1	18	Taiwan	1.5
6	Netherlands	3.8	19	Australia	1.3
7	Italy	3.3		Saudi Arabia	1.3
	United Kingdom	3.3		Switzerland	1.3
9	Belgium	2.9	22	Brazil	1.2
10	Hong Kong	2.7		Thailand	1.2
	South Korea	2.7	24	Malaysia	1.1
12	Canada	2.6		Poland	1.1
13	Russia	2.1			

% of world fleet deadweight tonnage, by country of ownership, January 2010

1	Japan	15.7	10	Italy	1.9
2	China	9.0	11	Russia	1.7
3	Germany	8.9	12	Canada	1.6
4	South Korea	3.9	12	India	1.5
5	United States	3.5	14	Belgium	1.1
6	Hong Kong	3.0		Malaysia	1.1
7	Singapore	2.8		Saudi Arabia	1.1
8	United Kingdom	2.7	17	Netherlands	0.8
9	Taiwan	2.5	18	Brazil	0.7

Note: Deadweight tonnage is the weight the ships can safely carry.

Tourism

Most tourist arrivals
Number of arrivals, '000, 2009

1	France	74,200	21	Macau	10,402
2	United States	54,884	22	Netherlands	9,921
3	Spain	52,231	23	Croatia	9,335
4	China	50,875	24	Hungary	9,058
5	Italy	43,239	25	United Arab Emirates	8,618
6	United Kingdom	28,199	26	Morocco	8,341
7	Turkey	25,506	27	Switzerland	8,294
8	Germany	24,224	28	South Korea	7,818
9	Malaysia	23,646	29	Singapore	7,488
10	Mexico	21,454	30	South Africa	7,012
11	Austria	21,355	31	Tunisia	6,901
12	Ukraine	20,741	32	Belgium	6,814
13	Russia	19,420	33	Japan	6,790
14	Hong Kong	16,926	34	Romania	6,384
15	Canada	15,771	35	Indonesia	6,324
16	Greece	14,915	36	Syria	6,092
17	Thailand	14,145	37	Czech Republic	6,032
18	Egypt	11,914	38	Bulgaria	5,739
19	Poland	11,890	39	Australia	5,584
20	Saudi Arabia	10,896	40	Bahrain	5,575

Biggest tourist spenders
$m, 2009

1	Germany	94,933	11	Spain	21,406
2	United States	88,242	12	Australia	20,806
3	United Kingdom	70,721	13	Belgium	20,437
4	France	47,346	14	South Korea	17,462
5	China	39,585	15	Norway	17,145
6	Italy	32,855	16	Hong Kong	16,503
7	Canada	28,854	17	Saudi Arabia	16,472
8	Russia	26,694	18	Sweden	16,403
9	Japan	26,290	19	Singapore	15,245
10	Netherlands	23,404	20	United Arab Emirates	13,851

Largest tourist receipts
$m, 2009

1	United States	93,917	13	Thailand	15,901
2	Spain	53,177	14	Malaysia	15,772
3	France	49,398	15	Greece	14,506
4	Italy	40,249	16	Switzerland	13,945
5	China	39,675	17	Canada	13,707
6	Germany	34,709	18	Russia	13,501
7	United Kingdom	30,038	19	Poland	12,993
8	Australia	25,594	20	Netherlands	12,365
9	Turkey	21,250	21	Belgium	12,314
10	Austria	19,404	22	Sweden	12,100
11	Macau	18,901	23	Croatia	12,079
12	Hong Kong	16,463	24	Portugal	11,714

Education

Primary enrolment
Number enrolled as % of relevant age group

Highest			Lowest		
1	Madagascar	160	1	Somalia	33
2	Sierra Leone	158	2	Eritrea	48
3	Rwanda	151	3	Djibouti	54
4	Burundi	147	4	Papua New Guinea	55
5	Angola	128	5	Niger	67
6	Brazil	127	6	Côte d'Ivoire	74
7	Belize	122		Sudan	74
	Benin	122	8	Burkina Faso	79
	Syria	122	9	Equatorial Guinea	82
	Uganda	122	10	Oman	84
11	Indonesia	121		Senegal	84
12	Colombia	120	12	Gambia, The	85
	Congo-Brazzaville	120		Pakistan	85
	Guinea-Bissau	120			

Highest secondary enrolment
Number enrolled as % of relevant age group

1	Australia	149	11	Belgium	108
2	Netherlands	121		Georgia	108
3	Spain	120	13	Portugal	104
4	Denmark	119		Uzbekistan	104
	New Zealand	119	15	Guyana	103
6	Ireland	118		Kazakhstan	103
7	France	113		Sweden	103
8	Norway	112	18	Germany	102
9	Finland	110		Greece	102
	Iceland	110			

Highest tertiary enrolment[a]
Number enrolled as % of relevant age group

1	Cuba	118	12	Australia	77
2	South Korea	98		Belarus	77
3	Finland	94		Lithuania	77
4	Greece	91		Russia	77
5	Slovenia	87	16	Iceland	75
6	United States	83	17	Norway	73
7	Ukraine	79	18	Spain	71
	Venezuela	79		Sweden	71
9	Denmark	78	20	Latvia	69
	New Zealand	78		Poland	69
	Puerto Rico	78			

Notes: Latest available year 2005–10. The gross enrolment ratios shown are the actual number enrolled as a percentage of the number of children in the official primary age group. They may exceed 100 when children outside the primary age group are receiving primary education.

a Tertiary education includes all levels of post-secondary education including courses leading to awards not equivalent to a university degree, courses leading to a first university degree and postgraduate courses.

Least literate
% adult population

1	Mali	26.2			Guinea-Bissau	55.2
2	Burkina Faso	28.7		16	Côte d'Ivoire	55.3
	Niger	28.7		17	Pakistan	55.5
4	Chad	33.6		18	Bangladesh	55.9
5	Guinea	39.5		19	Morocco	56.1
6	Sierra Leone	40.9		20	Togo	56.9
7	Benin	41.7		21	Mauritania	57.5
8	Gambia, The	46.5		22	Liberia	59.1
9	Haiti	48.7			Nepal	59.1
10	Senegal	49.7		24	Papua New Guinea	60.1
11	Timor-Leste	50.6		25	Nigeria	60.8
12	Bhutan	52.8		26	Yemen	62.4
13	Mozambique	55.1		27	India	62.8
14	Central African Rep.	55.2		28	Madagascar	64.5

Top universities[b]
2010

1	Harvard, US		14	California, San Diego, US
2	California, Berkeley, US		15	Pennsylvania, US
3	Stanford University, US		16	Washington, US
4	Mass. Inst. of Tech., US		17	Wisconsin - Madison, US
5	Cambridge, UK		18	The Johns Hopkins, US
6	California Institute of Technology, US		19	California, San Francisco, US
7	Princeton University, US		20	Tokyo, Japan
8	Columbia University, US		21	University College London, UK
9	Chicago, US		22	Michigan - Ann Arbor, US
10	Oxford, UK		23	Swiss Federal Institute of Technology Zurich
11	Yale University, US		24	Kyoto, Japan
12	Cornell, US		25	Illinois at Urbana-Champaign, US
13	California, Los Angeles, US			

Education spending
% of GDP

Highest				Lowest		
1	Timor-Leste	16.8		1	Congo-Kinshasa	2.0
2	Cuba	13.6			Myanmar	2.0
3	Lesotho	12.4		3	Eritrea	2.2
4	Maldives	11.2		4	Turkmenistan	2.3
5	Moldova	9.6		5	Indonesia	2.4
6	Djibouti	8.4		6	Mauritania	2.5
7	Burundi	8.3			Qatar	2.5
8	Denmark	7.8		8	Pakistan	2.6
	Swaziland	7.8		9	United Arab Emirates	2.8
10	Iceland	7.4		10	Syria	2.9
11	Tunisia	7.1		11	Brunei	3.0
12	Kenya	7.0			Congo-Brazzaville	3.0
					Oman	3.0

b Based on academic peer review, employer review, faculty/student ratio, research strength and international factors.

Life expectancy

Highest life expectancy
Years, 2010–15

1	Japan	83.7	25	Luxembourg	80.3
2	Hong Kong	82.8		Malta	80.3
3	Switzerland	82.5	27	Cyprus	80.2
4	Andorra[a]	82.4		Martinique	80.2
5	Iceland	82.3	29	Greece	80.1
6	Australia	82.2		United Kingdom	80.1
7	France	81.9	31	South Korea	80.0
8	Italy	81.6	32	United States	79.9
	Spain	81.6	33	Channel Islands	79.8
	Sweden	81.6		Guadeloupe	79.8
11	Israel	81.5	35	Faroe Islands[a]	79.7
12	Canada	81.4		Virgin Islands (US)	79.7
	Macau	81.4	37	Costa Rica	79.4
14	Norway	81.3		Portugal	79.4
15	New Zealand	81.0		Puerto Rico	79.4
	Singapore	81.0	40	Chile	79.1
17	Austria	80.8		Cuba	79.1
	Belgium	80.8		Slovenia	79.1
19	Bermuda[a]	80.7	43	Denmark	79.0
	Cayman Islands[a]	80.7	44	Taiwan[a]	78.3
21	Netherlands	80.6	45	Barbados	78.2
22	Finland	80.5		Kuwait	78.2
	Germany	80.5	47	United Arab Emirates	78.1
	Ireland	80.5	48	Brunei	77.7

Highest male life expectancy
Years, 2010–15

1	Iceland	80.8	10	Canada	79.2
2	Andorra[a]	80.4		Norway	79.2
3	Switzerland	80.2	12	New Zealand	79.1
4	Japan	80.1	13	France	78.6
5	Australia	80.0		Italy	78.6
6	Hong Kong	79.9		Spain	78.6
7	Sweden	79.6	16	Netherlands	78.5
8	Israel	79.4		Netherlands Antilles	78.5
	Macau	79.4		Singapore	78.5

Highest female life expectancy
Years, 2010–15

1	Japan	87.2	10	Belgium	83.9
2	Hong Kong	85.7		Iceland	83.9
3	France	85.1	12	Canada	83.6
4	Spain	84.7		Finland	83.6
	Switzerland	84.7		Sweden	83.6
6	Andorra[a]	84.6	15	Cayman Islands[a]	83.4
	Italy	84.6		Israel	83.4
8	Australia	84.4		Norway	83.4
9	Bermuda[a]	84.0		Singapore	83.4

a 2011 estimate.

Lowest life expectancy
Years, 2010–15

1	Afghanistan	45.5	26	Malawi	56.3
2	Lesotho	46.9	27	Kenya	56.9
3	Central African Rep.	48.6	28	Djibouti	57.1
4	Swaziland	48.7		Senegal	57.1
5	Congo	48.8	30	Ethiopia	57.2
6	Sierra Leone	48.9	31	Gambia, The	57.5
7	Nigeria	49.1	32	Ghana	58.0
8	Mozambique	49.2	33	Mauritania	58.2
9	Angola	49.3	34	Tanzania	58.3
10	Zambia	49.4	35	Côte d'Ivoire	59.6
11	Guinea-Bissau	49.6	36	Sudan	59.8
12	Chad	50.0	37	Guinea	60.1
13	Mali	50.2		Liberia	60.1
14	Zimbabwe	50.4	39	Eritrea	61.4
15	Somalia	51.5	40	Haiti	62.1
16	Rwanda	52.0	41	Namibia	62.2
17	Equatorial Guinea	52.1	42	Madagascar	62.3
18	Burundi	52.4		Papua New Guinea	62.3
19	Cameroon	52.7	44	Gabon	62.5
20	South Africa	52.9	45	Timor-Leste	63.2
21	Niger	53.8	46	Benin	63.3
22	Burkina Faso	54.5		Cambodia	63.3
	Congo-Brazzaville	54.5	48	Togo	64.0
24	Botswana	55.5	49	Myanmar	64.5
25	Uganda	55.6	50	Yemen	64.9

Lowest male life expectancy
Years, 2010–15

1	Afghanistan	45.5	11	Mozambique	48.8
2	Lesotho	46.9	12	Mali	49.5
3	Angola	47.2	13	Swaziland	49.7
	Central African Rep.	47.2	14	Rwanda	50.0
	Congo-Kinshasa	47.2		Somalia	50.0
6	Sierra Leone	47.6	16	Zimbabwe	50.5
7	Guinea-Bissau	48.1	17	Burundi	50.7
8	Nigeria	48.6	18	Equatorial Guinea	50.9
9	Chad	48.7	19	South Africa	51.8
	Zambia	48.7	20	Cameroon	52.0

Lowest female life expectancy
Years, 2010–15

1	Afghanistan	45.5	10	Congo-Kinshasa	50.4
2	Lesotho	46.6	11	Mali	50.9
3	Swaziland	47.6	12	Guinea-Bissau	51.2
4	Mozambique	49.4	13	Chad	51.3
5	Nigeria	49.7	14	Angola	51.4
6	Zimbabwe	49.8	15	Somalia	53.0
7	Central African Rep.	50.0	16	Equatorial Guinea	53.3
	Zambia	50.0	17	Cameroon	53.4
9	Sierra Leone	50.3	18	South Africa	53.8

Death rates and infant mortality

Highest death rates
Number of deaths per 1,000 population, 2010–15

#	Country	Rate	#	Country	Rate
1	Afghanistan	18.2	49	Denmark	10.4
2	Lesotho	16.3		Djibouti	10.4
3	Ukraine	16.1		Greece	10.4
4	Congo	15.8	52	Gambia, The	10.3
	Guinea-Bissau	15.8		Kenya	10.3
6	Central African Rep.	15.7		North Korea	10.3
7	Chad	15.5	55	Montenegro	10.2
8	Nigeria	15.3		Slovenia	10.2
9	Angola	15.2	57	Slovakia	10.1
10	Russia	15.1	58	Tanzania	10.0
	South Africa	15.1	59	Côte d'Ivoire	9.8
12	Mozambique	14.7		Japan	9.8
13	Belarus	14.6		Senegal	9.8
	Bulgaria	14.6		Sweden	9.8
15	Sierra Leone	14.5		United Kingdom	9.8
	Somalia	14.5	64	Belgium	9.7
	Zambia	14.5		Finland	9.7
18	Mali	14.2		Guinea	9.7
	Swaziland	14.2		Macedonia	9.7
20	Latvia	13.9	68	Channel Islands	9.6
21	Equatorial Guinea	13.8	69	Austria	9.5
	Lithuania	13.8		Liberia	9.5
23	Rwanda	13.5		Mauritania	9.5
24	Hungary	13.4		Sudan	9.5
25	Moldova	13.3	73	Uruguay	9.2
26	Cameroon	13.2	74	Thailand	9.1
27	Niger	13.1	75	Armenia	9.0
28	Estonia	13.0		France	9.0
29	Burundi	12.9	77	Gabon	8.9
	Zimbabwe	12.9		Haiti	8.9
31	Romania	12.6		Spain	8.9
32	Georgia	12.5	80	Myanmar	8.8
33	Congo-Brazzaville	12.3		Netherlands	8.8
34	Botswana	12.1	82	Faroe Islands[a]	8.7
35	Croatia	12.0	83	Norway	8.5
	Serbia	12.0		Switzerland	8.5
37	Burkina Faso	11.8	85	Malta	8.4
38	Uganda	11.1		Namibia	8.4
39	Germany	11.0	87	Trinidad & Tobago	8.3
40	Czech Republic	10.9	88	Benin	8.2
41	Kazakhstan	10.8		Madagascar	8.2
42	Ethiopia	10.7		Martinique	8.2
43	Malawi	10.6		Puerto Rico	8.2
44	Bosnia	10.5	92	Greenland[a]	8.1
	Ghana	10.5		Guadeloupe	8.1
	Italy	10.5		India	8.1
	Poland	10.5		Luxembourg	8.1
	Portugal	10.5	96	Mauritius	8.0

Note: Both death and, in particular, infant mortality rates can be underestimated in certain countries where not all deaths are officially recorded.   a 2011 estimate.

Highest infant mortality
Number of deaths per 1,000 live births, 2010–15

1	Afghanistan	146.9	23	Malawi	74.0
2	Angola	105.3	24	Gambia, The	72.2
3	Guinea-Bissau	104.5	25	Ethiopia	70.9
4	Nigeria	103.2	26	Mauritania	68.8
5	Somalia	101.2	27	Ghana	67.0
6	Mali	99.6	28	Uganda	66.9
7	Sierra Leone	99.0	29	Togo	65.7
8	Central African Rep.	97.3	30	Myanmar	63.4
9	Rwanda	92.4	31	Sudan	61.9
10	Burundi	91.0	32	Haiti	60.9
11	Equatorial Guinea	90.9	33	Lesotho	60.7
12	Guinea	88.0	34	Pakistan	57.4
13	Liberia	87.7	35	Madagascar	57.3
14	Niger	81.4	36	Kenya	57.2
15	Cameroon	79.8	37	Tajikistan	56.4
16	Côte d'Ivoire	79.5	38	Timor-Leste	56.3
17	Zambia	78.4	39	Senegal	55.7
18	Congo-Brazzaville	77.5	40	Tanzania	55.2
19	Benin	77.1	41	Swaziland	53.2
20	Mozambique	76.9	42	Cambodia	52.8
21	Burkina Faso	75.9	43	India	49.5
22	Djibouti	75.2	44	Yemen	49.1

Lowest death rates
No. deaths per 1,000 pop., 2010–15

1	United Arab Emirates	1.5
2	Kuwait	2.1
	Qatar	2.1
4	Bahrain	2.6
5	Oman	2.8
6	Brunei	3.0
7	Syria	3.3
	West Bank & Gaza	3.3
9	Belize	3.5
10	Saudi Arabia	3.6
11	Jordan	4.0
12	Libya	4.2
13	Costa Rica	4.3
14	British Virgin Is[a]	4.5
	Maldives	4.5
16	Malaysia	4.6
	Nicaragua	4.6
18	Cape Verde	4.7
	Macau	4.7
	Philippines	4.7

Lowest infant mortality
No. deaths per 1,000 live births, 2010–15

1	Bermuda[a]	2.5
2	Iceland	2.8
3	Sweden	2.9
4	Singapore	3.0
5	Finland	3.1
	Japan	3.1
7	Norway	3.3
8	Czech Republic	3.6
	Hong Kong	3.6
	Slovenia	3.6
11	Greece	3.7
12	Andorra[a]	3.8
	France	3.8
	Italy	3.8
	Spain	3.8
16	Switzerland	3.9
17	Belgium	4.0
	Germany	4.0
	Luxembourg	4.0
20	Australia	4.1
	Austria	4.1
	Portugal	4.1

a 2011 estimate.

Death and disease

Diabetes
% of population aged 20–79,
2010 estimate

1	United Arab Emirates	18.7
2	Saudi Arabia	16.8
3	Mauritius	16.2
4	Bahrain	15.4
	Qatar	15.4
6	Réunion	15.3
7	Kuwait	14.6
8	French Polynesia	13.8
9	Oman	13.4
9	Brunei	12.6
11	French Guiana	12.0
11	Trinidad & Tobago	11.7
13	Malaysia	11.6
14	Netherlands Antilles	11.5
15	Egypt	11.4
16	Dominican Republic	11.2
17	Sri Lanka	10.9
18	Mexico	10.8
	Syria	10.8

Cardiovascular disease
Deaths per 100,000 population,
estimate, 2008

1	Ukraine	1,071
2	Bulgaria	972
3	Russia	894
4	Belarus	845
5	Latvia	815
6	Georgia	814
7	Serbia	741
8	Lithuania	708
9	Romania	702
10	Moldova	694
11	Estonia	691
12	Armenia	637
13	Hungary	629
14	Bosnia	627
15	Montenegro	626
16	Macedonia	624
17	Croatia	618
18	Kazakhstan	611
19	Slovakia	533

Cancer
Deaths per 100,000 population,
estimate, 2008

1	Hungary	318
2	Croatia	301
3	Denmark	290
4	Slovenia	282
5	Italy	277
6	Japan	275
7	Latvia	274
8	Estonia	269
9	Czech Republic	267
10	Germany	266
11	Greece	264
12	United Kingdom	262
13	Poland	261
14	Serbia	260
15	France	259
16	Netherlands	255
17	Lithuania	252
18	Portugal	250
19	Uruguay	247
20	Belgium	244
21	Bulgaria	243
22	Sweden	241
23	Austria	237

Tuberculosis
Incidence per 100,000 population,
2009

1	Swaziland	1,257
2	South Africa	971
3	Zimbabwe	742
4	Namibia	727
5	Botswana	694
6	Sierra Leone	644
7	Lesotho	634
8	Gabon	501
9	Timor-Leste	498
10	Togo	446
11	Cambodia	442
12	Zambia	433
13	Mozambique	409
14	Myanmar	404
15	Côte d'Ivoire	399
16	Congo-Brazzaville	382
17	Rwanda	376
18	Congo	372
19	Ethiopia	359
20	Burundi	348
21	North Korea	345
22	Mauritania	330
23	Central African Rep.	327

Note: Statistics are not available for all countries. The number of cases diagnosed and reported depends on the quality of medical practice and administration and can be under-reported in a number of countries.

Measles immunisation

Lowest % of children aged
12–23 months, 2009

1	Chad	23
2	Somalia	24
3	Nigeria	41
4	Guinea	51
5	Lebanon	53
6	Gabon	55
7	Papua New Guinea	58
	Yemen	58
9	Haiti	59
	Laos	59
	Mauritania	59
12	Central African Rep.	62
	South Africa	62
14	Liberia	64
	Madagascar	64
16	Ecuador	66
17	Azerbaijan	67
	Côte d'Ivoire	67
19	Uganda	68
20	Iraq	69

DPTa immunisation

Lowest % of children aged
12–23 months, 2009

1	Chad	23
2	Somalia	31
3	Nigeria	42
4	Gabon	45
5	Central African Rep.	54
6	Guinea	57
	Laos	57
8	Haiti	59
9	Liberia	64
	Mauritania	64
	Papua New Guinea	64
	Uganda	64
13	Iraq	65
14	India	66
	Yemen	66
16	Guinea-Bissau	68
17	South Africa	69
18	Niger	70
19	Timor-Leste	72

HIV/AIDS

Prevalence among population
aged 15–49, %, 2009

1	Swaziland	25.9
2	Botswana	24.8
3	Lesotho	23.6
4	South Africa	17.8
5	Zimbabwe	14.3
6	Zambia	13.5
7	Namibia	13.1
8	Mozambique	11.5
9	Malawi	11.0
10	Uganda	6.5
11	Kenya	6.3
12	Tanzania	5.6
13	Cameroon	5.3
14	Gabon	5.2
15	Equatorial Guinea	5.0
16	Central African Rep.	4.7
17	Nigeria	3.6
18	Chad	3.4
	Congo-Brazzaville	3.4
	Côte d'Ivoire	3.4
21	Burundi	3.3
22	Togo	3.2
23	Bahamas	3.1
24	Rwanda	2.9

AIDS

Estimated deaths per 100,000
pop., 2009

1	Lesotho	680
2	Zimbabwe	661
3	South Africa	627
4	Swaziland	594
5	Zambia	351
6	Malawi	337
7	Mozambique	325
8	Namibia	306
9	Botswana	296
10	Central African Rep.	248
11	Kenya	201
12	Tanzania	196
	Uganda	196
14	Cameroon	188
15	Burundi	175
16	Côte d'Ivoire	172
17	Gabon	164
18	Equatorial Guinea	141
19	Congo-Brazzaville	139
	Nigeria	139
21	Djibouti	118
22	Togo	117
23	Chad	99

a Diptheria, pertussis and tetanus

Health

Highest health spending
As % of GDP, 2009

1	United States	16.2
2	Liberia	13.2
3	Burundi	13.1
	Sierra Leone	13.1
5	Timor-Leste	12.3
6	Moldova	11.9
7	Belgium	11.8
	Cuba	11.8
9	France	11.7
10	Germany	11.3
	Portugal	11.3
	Switzerland	11.3
13	Denmark	11.2
14	Austria	11.0
15	Bosnia	10.9
	Canada	10.9
17	Netherlands	10.8
18	Greece	10.6
19	Costa Rica	10.5
20	Botswana	10.3
21	Georgia	10.1
22	Serbia	9.9
	Sweden	9.9
24	Finland	9.7
	Ireland	9.7
	New Zealand	9.7
	Norway	9.7
	Spain	9.7

Lowest health spending
As % of GDP, 2009

1	Congo-Brazzaville	2.0
	Myanmar	2.0
3	Eritrea	2.2
4	Turkmenistan	2.3
5	Indonesia	2.4
6	Mauritania	2.5
	Qatar	2.5
8	Pakistan	2.6
9	United Arab Emirates	2.8
10	Syria	2.9
11	Brunei	3.0
	Congo-Kinshasa	3.0
	Oman	3.0
14	Papua New Guinea	3.1
15	Belize	3.3
	Kuwait	3.3
17	Bangladesh	3.4
18	Gabon	3.5
19	Fiji	3.6
20	Philippines	3.8
21	Cape Verde	3.9
	Equatorial Guinea	3.9
	Iraq	3.9
	Libya	3.9
	Singapore	3.9
26	Sri Lanka	4.0
27	Laos	4.1
	Madagascar	4.1

Highest pop. per doctor
2009 or latest

1	Tanzania	145,667
2	Liberia	78,431
3	Sierra Leone	60,000
4	Malawi	59,533
4	Niger	53,125
6	Rwanda	45,249
7	Ethiopia	42,769
8	Mozambique	41,788
9	Burundi	41,500
10	Chad	32,464
11	Somalia	30,333
12	Gambia, The	27,419
13	Eritrea	23,721
14	Lesotho	23,596
15	Guinea-Bissau	20,513
16	Papua New Guinea	20,120
17	Zambia	19,877

Lowest pop. per doctor
2009 or latest

1	Greece	166
2	Cuba	168
3	Belarus	204
4	Austria	215
5	Georgia	216
6	Russia	229
7	Italy	243
8	Norway	251
9	Switzerland	256
10	Netherlands	258
	Uruguay	258
12	Lithuania	266
13	Portugal	267
14	Azerbaijan	272
	Kazakhstan	272
16	Bulgaria	273
17	Spain	276

Most hospital beds
Beds per 1,000 pop., 2009 or latest

1	Japan	13.8		Poland	6.7
2	Iceland	13.6		Taiwan	6.7
3	Belarus	11.3	23	Bulgaria	6.5
4	South Korea	10.1		Romania	6.5
5	Russia	9.6	25	Mongolia	6.1
6	Ukraine	8.6	26	Cuba	6.0
7	Germany	8.2		Moldova	6.0
	Lithuania	8.2	28	Estonia	5.6
9	Malta	8.0		Israel	5.6
10	Czech Republic	7.9		Luxembourg	5.6
11	Austria	7.8	31	Croatia	5.5
	Azerbaijan	7.8	32	Tajikistan	5.4
13	Barbados	7.6	33	Belgium	5.1
	Kazakhstan	7.6		Kyrgyzstan	5.1
	Latvia	7.6		Serbia	5.1
16	France	7.0	36	Hong Kong	5.0
	Thailand	7.0		Ireland	5.0
18	Slovakia	6.8		Nepal	5.0
19	Finland	6.7	39	Greece	4.9
	Hungary	6.7	40	Uzbekistan	4.8

Obesity[a]

Men, % of total population

1	Lebanon	36.3
2	Qatar	34.6
3	United States	33.1
4	Ireland	31.0
5	Saudi Arabia	28.3
6	Panama	27.9
7	Kuwait	27.5
8	Iraq	26.2
9	Greece	26.0
10	Australia	25.6
11	New Zealand	24.7
12	Mexico	24.4
13	Czech Republic	23.9
14	England	23.6
15	Austria	23.3
16	Canada	22.9
	Malta	22.9
18	Albania	22.8
19	Scotland	22.4
20	Croatia	21.6
21	Germany	21.0
22	Lithuania	20.6
23	Wales	20.0
24	Chile	19.6
25	Argentina	19.5

Women, % of total population

1	Qatar	45.3
2	Saudi Arabia	43.8
3	Egypt	39.5
4	Lebanon	38.3
5	Iraq	38.2
6	Panama	36.1
7	Albania	35.6
8	Mexico	34.5
9	United States	34.3
10	Fiji	32.7
11	United Arab Emirates	31.4
12	Kuwait	29.9
13	Chile	29.3
14	South Africa	27.4
15	New Zealand	26.0
	Scotland	26.0
17	England	24.4
18	Jamaica	23.9
	Turkey	23.9
20	Oman	23.8
21	Canada	23.2
22	Swaziland	23.1
23	Peru	23.0
24	Croatia	22.7
25	Czech Republic	22.3

a Defined as body mass index of 30 or more – see page 248. Latest available years.

Marriage and divorce

Highest marriage rates
Number of marriages per 1,000 population, 2009 or latest available year

#	Country	Rate	#	Country	Rate
1	Virgin Islands (US)	35.8		Macedonia	7.2
2	Antigua & Barbuda	21.7	27	Indonesia	7.1
3	British Virgin Is	19.6		United States	7.1
4	Tajikistan	13.7	29	Denmark	6.8
5	Guam	13.3		Moldova	6.8
6	Mongolia	12.4		Turkmenistan	6.8
7	Iran	11.3	32	Lithuania	6.6
8	Bermuda	11.2		South Korea	6.6
9	Jordan	10.4	34	Channel Islands[a]	6.5
10	Barbados	10.1	35	Romania	6.4
11	Lebanon	9.5	36	Hong Kong	6.3
12	Azerbaijan	9.2		Montenegro	6.3
13	Algeria	9.1		Philippines	6.3
14	Mauritius	8.8		Trinidad & Tobago	6.3
	West Bank & Gaza	8.8		Turkey	6.3
16	Kyrgyzstan	8.7	41	Egypt	6.2
17	Fiji	8.6	42	Malta	6.0
	Kazakhstan	8.6	43	Georgia	5.9
19	Cayman Islands	8.5		Kuwait	5.9
	Jamaica	8.5		Puerto Rico	5.9
21	Belarus	8.0	46	Bahamas	5.8
	Russia	8.0		Finland	5.8
23	Cyprus	7.7		Japan	5.8
24	Taiwan	7.3		Malaysia	5.8
25	Albania	7.2		Netherlands Antilles	5.8

Lowest marriage rates
Number of marriages per 1,000 population

#	Country	Rate	#	Country	Rate
1	Colombia	1.7		Bulgaria	3.9
2	Qatar	2.2		France	3.9
3	Botswana	2.5		South Africa	3.9
	Venezuela	2.5	21	Hungary	4.0
5	Peru	2.7		New Caledonia	4.0
6	St Lucia	2.8	23	Luxembourg	4.1
7	Argentina	3.0		Netherlands	4.1
8	Andorra	3.1	25	Dominican Republic	4.2
9	Chile	3.2		Suriname	4.2
10	Slovenia	3.3	27	Belgium	4.3
11	Martinique	3.4		Italy	4.3
	Panama	3.4		Thailand	4.3
13	Guadeloupe	3.6	30	Guatemala	4.4
	United Arab Emirates	3.6	31	Canada	4.5
15	Réunion	3.7		Faroe Islands	4.5
	Uruguay	3.7		French Polynesia	4.5
17	Brazil	3.9			

a Jersey only
Note: The data are based on latest available figures (no earlier than 2004) and hence will be affected by the population age structure at the time. Marriage rates refer to registered marriages only and, therefore, reflect the customs surrounding registry and efficiency of administration.

Highest divorce rates
Number of divorces per 1,000 population, 2009 or latest available year

1	Guam	11.9	26	Bulgaria	2.6
2	South Korea	4.5		Netherlands Antilles	2.6
3	Moldova	4.3	28	Costa Rica	2.5
	Uruguay	4.3		Finland	2.5
5	Aruba	4.0		Kazakhstan	2.5
6	Belarus	3.8		Portugal	2.5
	Puerto Rico	3.8	32	Austria	2.4
	Russia	3.8		Latvia	2.4
9	Taiwan	3.6	34	Australia	2.3
10	Lithuania	3.5		France	2.3
	Ukraine	3.5		Hungary	2.3
12	Cayman Islands	3.4		Luxembourg	2.3
	Czech Republic	3.4		Slovakia	2.3
14	Bermuda	3.3		Sweden	2.3
15	Cuba	3.2	40	Jordan	2.2
	Estonia	3.2		Trinidad & Tobago	2.2
	United States	3.2	42	Canada	2.1
18	Denmark	3.1		Cyprus	2.1
19	Belgium	3.0		Norway	2.1
	Germany	3.0	45	Kuwait	2.0
	United Kingdom	3.0		Netherlands	2.0
22	British Virgin Is	2.8		Réunion	2.0
	Hong Kong	2.8	48	Japan	1.9
24	New Zealand	2.7		Singapore	1.9
	Switzerland	2.7	50	Dominican Republic	1.8

Lowest divorce rates
Number of divorces per 1,000 population, 2008 or latest available year

1	Guatemala	0.1		Azerbaijan	0.9
2	Vietnam	0.2		Ecuador	0.9
3	Bahamas	0.3		Indonesia	0.9
4	Bosnia	0.4		Italy	0.9
	Jamaica	0.4		Panama	0.9
6	Chile	0.5		Venezuela	0.9
7	Egypt	0.6	26	Albania	1.0
	Macedonia	0.6		Saudi Arabia	1.0
	Qatar	0.6		South Africa	1.0
10	Georgia	0.7		United Arab Emirates	1.0
	Ireland	0.7	30	Slovenia	1.1
	Mongolia	0.7		Spain	1.1
	Montenegro	0.7		Thailand	1.1
	St Lucia	0.7		Tunisia	1.1
	Tajikistan	0.7		West Bank & Gaza	1.1
16	Brazil	0.8	35	Antigua & Barbuda	1.2
	Mexico	0.8		Macau	1.2
	Turkey	0.8		Mauritius	1.2
19	Armenia	0.9		Serbia	1.2

Households, living costs - and giving

Number of households
Biggest, m, 2009

1	China	389.0	14	Pakistan	25.1
2	India	222.2	15	Italy	24.3
3	United States	118.5	16	Ukraine	20.0
4	Indonesia	67.4	17	Iran	19.8
5	Brazil	54.5		Vietnam	19.8
6	Russia	52.8	19	Philippines	19.1
7	Japan	50.5	20	Egypt	18.9
8	Germany	39.9	21	Thailand	18.3
9	Nigeria	31.4	22	Congo-Kinshasa	18.2
10	Mexico	27.6		Turkey	18.2
11	United Kingdom	27.2	24	South Korea	17.8
12	Bangladesh	26.9	25	Spain	17.4
	France	26.9	26	Myanmar	16.0

Households with single occupation
% of total, 2009

1	Sweden	47.0		Ukraine	32.9
2	Norway	39.7	16	Lithuania	32.3
3	Denmark	39.1	17	Hungary	31.8
	Finland	39.1	18	Japan	30.8
5	Germany	38.5	19	Poland	29.0
6	Switzerland	37.6	20	Italy	28.6
7	Netherlands	35.9	21	Belarus	27.4
	Slovakia	35.9	22	Canada	27.2
9	Austria	35.7	23	United States	27.1
10	Estonia	35.1	24	Bulgaria	25.2
11	United Kingdom	34.0	25	Russia	24.6
12	France	33.9	26	Australia	24.5
13	Czech Republic	33.0		Spain	24.5
14	Belgium	32.9	28	Slovenia	24.2

Households with six or more occupants
% of total, 2009

1	Kuwait	60.5	13	Azerbaijan	28.2
2	Pakistan	58.4	14	Malaysia	27.6
3	United Arab Emirates	54.3	15	Egypt	26.8
4	Saudi Arabia	47.4	16	Bolivia	25.9
5	Algeria	45.6	17	Venezuela	24.1
6	Turkmenistan	42.5	18	Peru	21.2
7	Jordan	41.0	19	Vietnam	19.1
8	Morocco	39.5	20	Turkey	19.0
9	India	37.9	21	South Africa	18.8
10	Nigeria	37.6	22	Mexico	18.1
11	Tunisia	35.0	23	Singapore	17.3
12	Philippines	32.7	24	Ecuador	16.1

a The cost of living index shown is compiled by the Economist Intelligence Unit for use
by companies in determining expatriate compensation: it is a comparison of the cost
of maintaining a typical international lifestyle in the country rather than a
comparison of the purchasing power of a citizen of the country. The index is based on
typical urban prices an international executive and family will face abroad. The prices

Cost of living[a]
December 2010, USA = 100

Highest			Lowest		
1	Japan	158	1	Pakistan	43
2	Norway	142	2	Libya	51
3	France	137	3	Iran	52
4	Australia	129	4	India	53
	Singapore	129	5	Nepal	54
6	Switzerland	127	6	Algeria	57
7	Denmark	125	7	Paraguay	58
8	Finland	118		Philippines	58
9	Hong Kong	114	9	Panama	59
10	United Kingdom	113		Romania	59
11	Austria	111	11	Bangladesh	61
12	Israel	108	12	Cambodia	64
13	Belgium	107		Vietnam	64
	Spain	107	14	Qatar	65
15	Sweden	105		Sri Lanka	65
16	Canada	104	16	Bulgaria	66
17	New Caledonia	103		Ecuador	66
	Turkey	103		Kuwait	66
19	Germany	101		Saudi Arabia	66
	New Zealand	101	20	Argentina	67
21	Ireland	100		Bahrain	67
	South Korea	100		Uzbekistan	67
23	Brazil	99	23	Kazakhstan	68

World Giving Index[b]
Top givers, % score, 2010

1	Australia	57		Qatar	45
	New Zealand	57	18	Denmark	44
3	Canada	56		Germany	44
	Ireland	56		Guinea	44
5	Switzerland	55		Hong Kong	44
	United States	55	22	Guatemala	43
7	Netherlands	54		Myanmar	43
8	Sri Lanka	53		Trinidad & Tobago	43
	United Kingdom	53	25	Kuwait	42
10	Austria	52		Luxembourg	42
11	Laos	50		Norway	42
	Sierre Leone	50		Thailand	42
13	Malta	48	29	Angola	41
14	Iceland	47		Italy	41
	Turkmenistan	47		Kenya	41
16	Guyana	45		Malawi	41

are for products of international comparable quality found in a supermarket or
department store. Prices found in local markets and bazaars are not used unless the
available merchandise is of the specified quality and the shopping area itself is safe
for executive and family members. New York City prices are used as the base, so
United States = 100.

b   Three criteria are used to assess giving: in the previous month those surveyed either
gave money to charity, gave time to those in need or helped a stranger.

Telephones, computers and broadband

Telephone
Telephone lines per 100 people, 2009

1	Bermuda	89.0	20	Ireland	46.1
2	British Virgin Islands	87.2	21	Israel	45.3
3	Cayman Islands	64.4		Spain	45.3
4	Taiwan	63.2	23	Netherlands Antilles	44.9
5	Switzerland	61.8	24	United States	44.8
6	Hong Kong	60.9	25	Netherlands	44.1
7	Malta	59.9	26	New Zealand	43.8
8	Germany	59.3	27	Belgium	43.5
9	Iceland	57.4	28	Antigua & Barbuda	42.6
10	France	56.9	29	Australia	42.4
11	Sweden	55.7	30	Croatia	42.1
12	Luxembourg	54.2	31	Faroe Islands	41.9
13	South Korea	53.7	32	Belarus	41.2
14	Barbados	53.0	33	Singapore	40.7
15	Canada	52.5	34	Portugal	39.7
16	United Kingdom	52.2	35	Austria	38.9
17	Slovenia	51.2	36	Greenland	38.5
18	Cyprus	47.6	37	Bahamas	37.7
19	Greece	47.0		Denmark	37.7

Mobile telephone
Subscribers per 100 people, 2009

1	United Arab Emirates	232.1	30	United Kingdom	130.6
2	Montenegro	207.3	31	Argentina	130.3
3	Cayman Islands	193.6	32	Kuwait	129.8
4	Macau	192.8	33	Germany	127.8
5	Hong Kong	179.4	34	Netherlands	127.7
6	Bahrain	177.1	35	Sweden	125.9
7	Qatar	175.4	36	Israel	125.8
8	Saudi Arabia	174.4	37	Denmark	125.0
9	Panama	164.4	38	Guatemala	123.4
10	Russia	163.6	39	El Salvador	122.8
11	Antigua & Barbuda	154.0	40	Switzerland	122.3
12	Lithuania	151.0		Uruguay	122.3
13	Portugal	148.8	42	Cyprus	122.0
14	Libya	148.5	43	Ukraine	121.1
15	Luxembourg	148.1	44	Aruba	120.2
16	Maldives	147.9	45	Romania	119.4
17	Italy	147.0	46	Greece	119.1
18	Suriname	147.0	47	Hungary	118.0
19	Singapore	145.2	48	Poland	117.7
20	Finland	144.6	49	Belgium	117.5
21	Bulgaria	140.2	50	Estonia	117.2
22	Oman	139.5	51	Taiwan	116.7
23	Trinidad & Tobago	137.9	52	Faroe Islands	114.3
24	Czech Republic	137.5	53	Spain	113.8
25	Austria	136.7	54	Australia	113.7
	Croatia	136.7	55	Honduras	112.4
27	Albania	131.9	56	Vietnam	111.5
28	Barbados	131.7	57	Norway	111.4
29	Bermuda	131.0	58	New Zealand	110.2

Computer
Computers per 100 people, 2009

1	Canada	108.6	26	Italy	49.6
2	Netherlands	103.1	27	Latvia	49.5
3	Sweden	102.0	28	United Arab Emirates	47.5
4	Switzerland	96.3	29	Macau	47.1
5	United Kingdom	90.7	30	Slovenia	46.0
6	Taiwan	89.0	31	Cyprus	45.9
7	United States	84.4	32	Spain	44.7
8	France	82.9	33	Malta	37.3
9	Denmark	80.9	34	Czech Republic	36.5
10	Singapore	79.8	35	Hungary	35.8
11	Australia	78.8	36	Kuwait	34.0
12	Germany	77.7	37	Trinidad & Tobago	33.9
13	Luxembourg	75.8	38	Maldives	31.3
14	Hong Kong	74.9	39	Namibia	29.9
15	Norway	69.6	40	Costa Rica	27.1
16	Ireland	68.7	41	Malaysia	26.3
17	Austria	68.3	42	Israel	26.1
18	Iceland	67.7	43	Brazil	26.0
19	Slovakia	63.6	44	Romania	25.7
20	South Korea	63.1	45	Poland	23.0
21	New Zealand	58.9	46	Croatia	22.2
22	Estonia	56.8	47	Ecuador	19.6
23	Finland	55.9	48	Bahrain	19.5
24	Japan	52.5	49	Lithuania	19.0
25	Belgium	49.8	50	Portugal	18.8

Broadband
Subscribers per 100 people, 2009

1	Bermuda	61.7	23	Singapore	24.7
2	Denmark	37.9	24	Australia	24.4
3	Netherlands	35.6	25	Slovenia	23.7
4	Switzerland	35.5	26	Macau	23.4
5	South Korea	34.8	27	New Zealand	23.0
6	Norway	34.0	28	Estonia	22.5
7	Iceland	33.2	29	Barbados	22.4
8	Luxembourg	32.8	30	Austria	22.1
9	Sweden	31.8	31	Ireland	21.6
10	France	31.6	32	Spain	21.6
11	Faroe Islands	31.3	33	Taiwan	21.4
12	Canada	30.6	34	Greenland	21.3
13	Germany	30.4	35	Aruba	20.7
14	Gibraltar	29.9	36	Italy	20.5
15	United Kingdom	29.6	37	Cyprus	20.2
16	Belgium	29.4	38	Lithuania	19.3
17	Hong Kong	29.2	39	Hungary	18.8
18	Finland	28.8	40	Latvia	18.6
19	Malta	25.9	41	Portugal	17.4
20	Israel	25.8	42	Greece	17.2
	United States	25.8	43	Antigua & Barbuda	17.0
22	Japan	24.9	44	Croatia	15.5

The internet and music

Internet hosts

	By country, April 2011			Per 1,000 pop., April 2011	
1	United States[a]	445,388,883	1	United States[a]	1,415.3
2	Japan	59,968,541	2	Iceland	1,129.6
3	Italy	24,483,783	3	Finland	845.4
4	Brazil	21,121,168	4	Netherlands	819.0
5	Germany	20,839,544	5	Denmark	757.9
6	China	17,844,492	6	Australia	741.6
7	Australia	15,796,154	7	Norway	737.9
8	France	15,549,341	8	Switzerland	666.1
9	Mexico	13,817,502	9	New Zealand	639.6
10	Netherlands	13,596,075	10	Estonia	623.9
11	Russia	11,831,484	11	Luxembourg	518.3
12	Poland	11,299,130	12	Sweden	515.4
13	United Kingdom	8,340,756	13	Japan	471.5
14	Canada	7,705,869	14	Belgium	450.4
15	Argentina	7,139,703	15	Cayman Islands	444.0
16	Taiwan	5,970,584	16	Italy	408.7
17	India	5,708,198	17	Austria	402.0
18	Switzerland	5,062,397	18	Netherlands Antilles	389.0
19	Belgium	4,774,473	19	Czech Republic	368.4
20	Sweden	4,741,830	20	Lithuania	360.5
21	Finland	4,480,613	21	Portugal	316.3
22	South Africa	4,184,815	22	Israel	303.6
23	Denmark	4,168,431	23	Croatia	299.3
24	Turkey	4,003,186	24	Ireland	298.4
25	Spain	3,996,519	25	Poland	296.6
26	Czech Republic	3,831,296	26	Hungary	279.1
27	Norway	3,542,038	27	Greenland	270.3
28	Portugal	3,384,374	28	Cyprus	264.3

Music sales

	Total including downloads, $m, 2010			$ per head, 2009	
1	United States	6,750	1	Japan	42.0
2	Japan	5,343	2	Norway	36.4
3	Germany	1,976	3	United Kingdom	30.8
4	United Kingdom	1,899	4	Switzerland	27.0
5	France	1,252	5	Australia	26.9
6	Australia	572	6	Denmark	26.3
7	Canada	518	7	Austria	25.2
8	South Korea	362	8	Iceland	25.0
9	Brazil	332	9	Germany	24.0
10	Italy	329	10	Ireland	21.8
11	Netherlands	301	11	United States	21.4
12	Spain	242	12	Sweden	21.0
13	India	238	13	France	20.1
14	Austria	212	14	Belgium	19.5
	Mexico	212	15	Finland	18.2
16	Belgium	207	16	Netherlands	18.1
17	Switzerland	205	17	New Zealand	16.3
18	Sweden	193	18	Canada	15.4

a Includes all hosts ending ".com", ".net" and ".org", which exaggerates the numbers.

Facebook users

000s, 2011		
1	United States	150,192
2	Indonesia	38,163
3	United Kingdom	29,760
4	Turkey	29,040
5	India	27,706
6	Mexico	26,091
7	Philippines	24,792
8	France	22,578
9	Brazil	20,031
10	Italy	19,643
11	Germany	18,962
12	Canada	16,632
13	Argentina	15,291
14	Colombia	14,410
15	Spain	14,297
16	Malaysia	11,039
17	Australia	10,369
18	Thailand	10,113
19	Taiwan	9,649
20	Venezuela	8,974
21	Chile	8,418
22	Egypt	7,558
23	Poland	6,272
24	Peru	6,030
25	Russia	4,671

Users per 1,000 population, 2011		
1	Iceland	688
2	Faroe Islands	594
3	Hong Kong	526
4	Singapore	524
5	Cyprus	524
6	Brunei	517
7	Bahamas	512
	Norway	512
9	Montenegro	506
10	United Arab Emirates	499
11	Canada	495
	Chile	495
13	Denmark	492
14	Cayman Islands	489
15	Australia	487
16	United Kingdom	483
17	Sweden	477
	United States	477
19	Israel	474
20	Netherlands Antilles	470
21	Aruba	469
	Malta	469
23	New Zealand	465
24	Ireland	443
25	Macedonia	435

Internet

Users per 100 population, 2009

1	Iceland	93.5	23	Antigua & Barbuda	74.2
2	Norway	92.1	24	Austria	73.5
3	Sweden	90.8	25	Estonia	72.5
4	Netherlands	89.6	26	France	71.6
5	Luxembourg	87.3	27	Monaco	70.1
6	Denmark	86.8	28	Taiwan	69.9
7	United Kingdom	83.6	29	Hong Kong	69.4
8	Bermuda	83.3	30	Singapore	68.3
9	Finland	82.5	31	Ireland	67.4
10	South Korea	81.6	32	Latvia	66.8
11	Switzerland	81.3	33	Czech Republic	64.4
12	Canada	80.3	34	Slovenia	64.3
13	New Zealand	79.7	35	Israel	63.1
14	Germany	79.3	36	Greenland	62.8
15	Brunei	78.8	37	Spain	62.6
16	Japan	78.0	38	Hungary	61.8
	United States	78.0	39	Lithuania	59.8
18	Belgium	76.2	40	Poland	59.0
19	Faroe Islands	75.2	41	Malta	58.9
	Slovakia	75.2	42	Jamaica	58.2
21	United Arab Emirates	75.0	43	Malaysia	55.9
22	Australia	74.3	44	Bahrain	53.0

Cinema and films

Cinema attendances

Total visits, m, 2009		Visits per head, 2009	
1 India	4,331.4	1 Ireland	6.4
2 United States	1,403.5	2 Iceland	5.0
3 France	188.1	3 United States	4.5
4 United Kingdom	164.3	4 India	3.6
5 Japan	160.5	5 Singapore	3.2
6 Mexico	160.5	6 France	3.0
7 Germany	129.2	7 United Kingdom	2.7
8 Russia	128.4	8 Malta	2.5
9 Italy	112.3	9 Norway	2.5
10 Spain	110.0	10 Spain	2.4
11 Turkey	39.7	11 Denmark	2.4
12 Argentina	39.0	12 Luxembourg	2.2
13 Poland	34.9	13 Belgium	2.1
14 Malaysia	33.1	14 Italy	1.9
15 Ireland	28.8	Switzerland	1.9
16 Netherlands	23.8	16 Austria	1.9
17 Belgium	21.9	17 Sweden	1.7
18 Egypt	18.6	18 Germany	1.6
19 Portugal	16.0	19 Mexico	1.5
20 Austria	15.6	20 Portugal	1.5
21 Sweden	15.3	21 Netherlands	1.4
22 Singapore	15.1	Slovenia	1.4
23 Switzerland	14.4	United Arab Emirates	1.4
24 Denmark	13.0	24 Finland	1.3
25 Czech Republic	12.5	Japan	1.3
26 Greece	11.9	26 Czech Republic	1.2
Norway	11.9	Estonia	1.2
28 Chile	11.6	Malaysia	1.2
29 Hungary	10.6	29 Greece	1.1
30 Finland	6.8	Hungary	1.1
31 United Arab Emirates	6.6	Latvia	1.1
32 Romania	3.9	Lithuania	1.1

Top Oscar winners

	Film	Awards	Nominations
1	Ben-Hur (1959)	11	12
	Titanic (1997)	11	14
	The Lord of the Rings: The Return of the King (2003)	11	11
4	West Side Story (1961)	10	11
5	Gigi (1958)	9	9
6	The Last Emperor (1987)	9	9
	The English Patient (1996)	9	12
8	Gone with the Wind (1939)	8	13
	From Here to Eternity (1953)	8	13
	On the Waterfront (1954)	8	12
	My Fair Lady (1964)	8	12
	Cabaret[a] (1972)	8	10
	Gandhi (1982)	8	11
	Amadeus (1984)	8	11
	Slumdog Millionaire (2008)	8	10

a Did not win best picture award.

The press

Daily newspapers
Copies per '000 population, 2009

1	Iceland	620	16	Estonia	242
2	Switzerland	545	17	Germany	239
3	Denmark	533	18	Lithuania	226
4	Japan	520	19	United Arab Emirates	220
5	Hong Kong	511	20	Ireland	218
6	Luxembourg	502		Kuwait	218
7	Sweden	462	22	Czech Republic	193
8	Finland	454		Slovenia	193
9	Norway	444	24	Israel	188
10	Singapore	361	25	Spain	177
11	Austria	349	26	Taiwan	174
12	South Korea	339	27	Canada	172
13	Netherlands	314	28	France	165
14	United Kingdom	282	29	Italy	162
15	Malta	255	30	Hungary	159

Press freedom[a]
Scores, 2010

Most free			*Least free*		
1	Finland	0.00	1	Eritrea	105.00
	Iceland	0.00	2	North Korea	104.75
	Netherlands	0.00	3	Burma	94.50
	Norway	0.00	4	Syria	91.50
	Sweden	0.00	5	Sudan	85.33
	Switzerland	0.00	6	China	84.67
7	Austria	0.50	7	Yemen	82.13
8	New Zealand	1.50	8	Rwanda	81.00
9	Estonia	2.00	9	Laos	80.50
	Ireland	2.00	10	Equatorial Guinea	79.00
11	Denmark	2.50	11	Cuba	78.00
	Japan	2.50	12	Vietnam	75.75
	Lithuania	2.50	13	Tunisia	72.50
14	Belgium	4.00	14	Uzbekistan	71.50
	Luxembourg	4.00	15	Kazakhstan	68.50
	Malta	4.00	16	Somalia	66.00
17	Germany	4.25	17	Libya	63.50
18	Australia	5.38	18	Kyrgyzstan	63.00
19	United Kingdom	6.00	19	Sri Lanka	62.50
20	United States	6.75	20	Saudi Arabia	61.50
21	Canada	7.00	21	Philippines	60.00
	Namibia	7.00	22	Swaziland	57.50
23	Czech Republic	7.50	23	Belarus	57.00
	Hungary	7.50	24	Thailand	56.83
25	Jamaica	7.67	25	Azerbaijan	56.38
26	Cape Verde	8.00	26	Pakistan	56.17
	Ghana	8.00	27	Fiji	52.75
	Mali	8.00	28	Congo	51.83
29	Costa Rica	8.08	29	Afghanistan	51.67

a Based on 40 questions on topics such as threats, censorship, monopolies, pressure and new media, answered by journalists and media experts.

Nobel prize winners: 1901–2009

Peace (two or more)

1	United States	19
2	United Kingdom	11
3	France	9
4	Sweden	5
5	Belgium	4
	Germany	4
7	Austria	3
	Norway	3
	South Africa	3
	Switzerland	3
11	Argentina	2
	Egypt	2
	Israel	2
	Russia	2

Economics[a]

1	United States	34
2	United Kingdom	9
3	Norway	2
	Sweden	2
5	Denmark	1
	France	1
	Germany	1
	Israel	1
	Netherlands	1
	Russia	1

Literature (three or more)

1	France	15
2	United States	12
3	United Kingdom	11
4	Germany	8
5	Sweden	6
6	Italy	5
	Spain	5
8	Norway	3
	Poland	3
	Russia	3

Medicine (three or more)

1	United States	52
2	United Kingdom	23
3	Germany	15
4	France	7
	Sweden	7
6	Switzerland	6
7	Austria	5
	Denmark	5
9	Australia	3
	Belgium	3
	Italy	3

Physics

1	United States	50
2	United Kingdom	20
3	Germany	19
4	France	9
5	Netherlands	6
	Russia	6
7	Japan	5
8	Sweden	4
	Switzerland	4
10	Austria	3
	Italy	3
12	Canada	2
	Denmark	2
14	China	1
	India	1
	Ireland	1
	Pakistan	1
	Poland	1

Chemistry

1	United States	45
2	United Kingdom	23
3	Germany	15
4	France	7
5	Switzerland	6
6	Japan	5
	Sweden	5
8	Canada	4
9	Israel	2
10	Argentina	1
	Austria	1
	Belgium	1
	Czech Republic	1
	Denmark	1
	Finland	1
	Italy	1
	Netherlands	1
	Norway	1
	Russia	1

a Since 1969.
Notes: Prizes by country of residence at time awarded. When prizes have been shared in the same field, one credit given to each country.

Olympics[a]

Summer Olympics

1896–2008	Gold	Silver	Bronze
1 United States	931	728	640
2 Soviet Union (1952–92)	440	357	325
3 United Kingdom	208	255	252
4 Germany	192	217	238
5 France	191	212	233
6 Italy	190	157	174
7 China	163	117	106
8 Hungary	159	141	159
9 Germany (East)	153	129	127
10 Sweden	142	159	174
11 Australia	131	137	164
12 Japan	123	112	125
13 Russia	109	101	113
14 Finland	101	83	115
15 Romania	86	92	115
16 Netherlands	71	79	97
17 South Korea	68	74	73
18 Cuba	67	64	63
19 Poland	62	80	119
20 Canada	58	94	108

Winter Olympics

1956–2010	Gold	Silver	Bronze
1 Germany	139	130	100
2 Norway	105	117	88
3 United States	87	96	72
4 Austria	54	70	76
5 Canada	52	45	49
6 Sweden	51	34	38
7 Switzerland	43	37	46
8 Finland	42	58	56
9 Russia	38	31	28
10 Italy	37	32	36
11 Netherlands	29	31	26
12 France	27	27	38
13 South Korea	23	14	8
14 China	9	18	17
15 Japan	9	13	15
16 United Kingdom	9	5	15
17 Czech Republic	5	3	7
18 Australia	5	1	2
19 Croatia	4	5	1
20 Estonia	4	2	1
21 Poland	2	6	6
22 Spain	2	0	0
23 Belarus	1	2	4
24 Bulgaria	1	2	2

a Table excludes mixed teams in 1896, 1900 and 1904 and Australasia teams in 1908 and 1912. Germany 1896–1936, unified teams in 1956–64, then since 1992. Russia 1896–1912, then since 1996.

Drinking and smoking

Beer drinkers

Retail sales, litres per head of population, 2009

1	Czech Republic	79.6
2	Venezuela	75.3
3	Australia	69.9
4	Slovakia	69.1
5	Austria	68.8
6	Finland	67.9
7	Russia	67.5
8	Poland	67.2
9	Germany	66.9
10	Romania	64.1
11	United States	60.6
12	Canada	57.6
13	Denmark	56.7
14	New Zealand	52.7
15	Bulgaria	52.1
	Netherlands	52.1
17	South Africa	50.2
18	Hungary	49.3
19	Ukraine	47.9
20	Mexico	47.5
21	Japan	43.9
22	Belgium	43.0

Wine drinkers

Retail sales, litres per head of population, 2009

1	Switzerland	32.3
2	Portugal	30.3
3	Denmark	28.1
4	France	26.9
5	Italy	26.2
6	Argentina	21.8
7	Germany	21.5
8	Belgium	21.1
9	Netherlands	20.7
10	Hungary	19.6
11	Sweden	18.9
12	Austria	18.8
13	United Kingdom	18.2
14	New Zealand	17.3
15	Australia	17.1
16	Greece	13.8
17	Ireland	13.3
18	Norway	13.2
19	Chile	13.0
20	Finland	11.1
	Romania	11.1
22	Czech Republic	11.0

Alcoholic drink

Retail sales, litres per head of population, 2009

1	Australia	99.4
2	Finland	99.3
3	Germany	98.9
4	Czech Republic	95.7
5	Austria	92.8
6	Denmark	90.6
7	Russia	88.9
8	Slovakia	84.3
9	Poland	82.4
10	New Zealand	80.2
11	Venezuela	79.7
12	Romania	77.3
13	Netherlands	76.2
14	Canada	74.8
15	United States	72.9
16	Hungary	72.7
17	United Kingdom	68.9
18	Belgium	67.5
19	Sweden	66.8
20	Argentina	65.5
21	Switzerland	65.3
22	Ukraine	64.6
23	Ireland	63.5

Cigarettes

Av. ann. consumption of cigarettes per head per day, 2009

1	Serbia	7.8
2	Russia	7.5
3	Greece	7.2
4	Belarus	6.8
5	Slovenia	6.5
6	Bosnia	6.2
	Bulgaria	6.2
	Lebanon	6.2
9	Moldova	6.0
10	Ukraine	5.8
11	Czech Republic	5.6
12	Azerbaijan	5.1
	Kazakhstan	5.1
	Macedonia	5.1
	South Korea	5.1
16	Kuwait	5.0
17	China	4.8
18	Armenia	4.6
	Switzerland	4.6
20	Austria	4.5
	Japan	4.5
	Tunisia	4.5

Crime and punishment

Police
Homicides per 100,000 pop., 2008 or latest

1	Honduras	60.9
2	Jamaica	59.5
3	Venezuela	52.0
4	El Salvador	51.8
5	Guatemala	45.2
6	Trinidad & Tobago	39.7
7	Colombia	38.8
8	Lesotho	36.7
9	South Africa	36.5
10	Belize	34.3
11	Brazil	22.0
12	Dominican Republic	21.5
13	Guyana	20.7
14	Puerto Rico	20.4
15	Ecuador	18.1
16	Namibia	17.9
17	Saint Lucia	16.0
18	Russia	14.2
19	Bahamas	13.7
	Suriname	13.7

Robberies
Per 100,000 population, 2008

1	Belgium	1,837
2	Spain	1,067
3	Maldives	196
4	Chile	180
5	Russia	173
6	France	172
7	United Kingdom[a]	147
8	United States	142
9	Lithuania	104
10	Mauritius	99
11	Canada	97
	Sweden	97
13	Australia	78
14	Morocco	74
15	Kazakhstan	72
16	Zimbabwe	71
17	Belarus	69
18	Estonia	68
	Luxembourg	68
20	Latvia	64

Prisoners
Total prison pop., latest available year

1	United States	2,292,133
2	China	1,650,000
3	Russia	809,400
4	Brazil	496,251
5	India	284,753
6	Thailand	224,292
7	Mexico	220,330
8	Iran	220,000
9	South Africa	160,400
10	Ukraine	154,027
11	Turkey	122,404
12	Indonesia	117,863
13	Vietnam	108,557
14	Philippines	102,267
15	Ethiopia	85,450
16	United Kingdom	94,511
17	Poland	83,993
18	Colombia	83,667
19	Pakistan	75,586
20	Japan	74,476
21	Spain	73,459
22	Bangladesh	69,650
23	Germany	69,385
24	Italy	67,615

Per 100,000 pop., latest available year

1	United States	743
2	Rwanda	595
3	Russia	570
4	Virgin Islands (US)	539
5	Georgia	538
6	Belize	439
7	Bermuda	428
8	El Salvador	391
9	Belarus	385
10	Bahamas	382
11	Kazakhstan	367
12	French Guiana	365
13	Cayman Islands	361
14	Suriname	356
15	Barbados	354
16	Panama	349
17	Maldives	343
18	Greenland	340
19	Ukraine	338
20	Antigua & Barbuda	330
21	Thailand	328
22	Israel	319
	Netherlands Antilles	319
	South Africa	319

a England and Wales.

Stars...

Space missions
Firsts and selected events
1957 Dog in space, Laika
1961 Human in space, Yuri Gagarin
Entire day in space, Gherman Titov
1963 Woman in space, Valentina Tereshkova
1964 Space crew, one pilot and two passengers
1965 Space walk, Alexei Leonov
Eight days in space achieved (needed to travel to moon and back)
1966 Docking between space craft and target vehicle
Autopilot re-entry and landing
1968 Live television broadcast from space
Moon orbit
1969 Astronaut transfer from one craft to another in space
Moon landing
1971 Space station, Salyut
Drive on the moon
1973 Space laboratory, Skylab
1978 Non-American, non-Soviet, Vladimir Remek (Czechoslovakia)
1982 Space shuttle, Columbia (first craft to carry four crew members)
1983 Five-crew mission
1984 Space walk, untethered
Capture, repair and redeployment of satellite in space
Seven-crew mission
1985 Classified US Defence Department mission
1986 Space shuttle explosion, Challenger
Mir space station activated
1990 Hubble telescope deployed
2001 Dennis Tito, first paying space tourist
2003 Space shuttle explosion, Columbia. Shuttle programme suspended
China's first manned space flight, Yang Liwei
2004 SpaceShipOne, first successful private manned space flight
2005 Space shuttle, resumption of flights
2008 *Phoenix* lander, mission on Mars

Space vehicle launches[a]

2007			2008		
1	Russia	22	1	Russia	25
2	United States	20	2	United States	13
3	China	6	3	China	10
4	France	5	4	France	4
5	India	3	5	India	3
	Japan	3	6	Iran	2
2009			2010		
1	Russia	30	1	Russia	30
2	United States	27	2	China	15
3	France	7		United States	15
4	China	5	4	France	6
5	Japan	3	5	India	2
	India	2		Japan	2

a By host country and including
suborbital launches.

...and Wars

Defence spending
As % of GDP, 2009

#	Country	%	#	Country	%
1	Saudi Arabia	10.9	15	Colombia	4.1
2	Oman	8.7		Lebanon	4.1
3	Israel	6.9	17	Maldives	4.0
4	Chad	6.4	18	Algeria	3.8
5	Iraq	6.3		Mauritania	3.8
6	Georgia	5.6	20	Bahrain	3.6
7	Jordan	5.5		United Arab Emirates	3.6
8	Armenia	4.7	22	Azerbaijan	3.5
	United States	4.7		Djibouti	3.5
10	Kuwait	4.3		Ecuador	3.5
	Singapore	4.3		Yemen	3.5
12	Angola	4.2	26	Lesotho	3.3
	Eritrea	4.2		Morocco	3.3
	Syria	4.2		Namibia	3.3

Defence spending

$bn, 2009			Per head, $, 2009		
1	United States	661.0	1	United States	2,153
2	China[a]	70.4	2	Israel	1,816
3	United Kingdom	59.1	3	Qatar	1,774
4	France	54.4	4	United Arab Emirates	1,730
5	Japan	51.1	5	Saudi Arabia	1,626
6	Germany	47.5	6	Singapore	1,570
7	Saudi Arabia	41.3	7	Kuwait	1,497
8	India	38.3	8	Oman	1,412
	Russia	38.3	9	Norway	1,284
10	Italy	30.5	10	United Kingdom	956
11	Brazil	26.0	11	Greece	894
12	South Korea	22.4	12	Australia	892
13	Canada	19.6	13	France	870
14	Australia	19.5	14	Brunei	830
15	Spain	16.9	15	Denmark	784

Armed forces
'000, 2009

#	Country	Regulars	Reserves	#	Country	Regulars	Reserves
1	China	2,285	510	13	Brazil	318	1,340
2	United States	1,564	871	14	Thailand	306	200
3	India	1,325	1,155	15	Indonesia	302	400
4	North Korea	1,190	600	16	Syria	295	314
5	Russia	1,046	20,000	17	Taiwan	290	1,657
6	South Korea	655	4,500	18	Colombia	283	62
7	Pakistan	617	0	19	Mexico	280	87
8	Iran	523	350	20	Germany	251	40
9	Turkey	511	379	21	Japan	248	56
10	Egypt	469	479	22	Iraq	246	0
11	Vietnam	455	5,000	23	France	239	34
12	Myanmar	406	0	24	Saudi Arabia	234	0

a Official budget only at market exchange rates.

Environment

Biggest emitters of carbon dioxide
Million of tonnes, 2007

#	Country	Value	#	Country	Value
1	China	6,533.0	24	Kazakhstan	227.2
2	United States	5,832.2	25	Malaysia	194.3
3	India	1,611.0	26	Egypt	184.5
4	Russia	1,536.1	27	Argentina	183.6
5	Japan	1,253.5	28	Netherlands	173.1
6	Germany	787.3	29	Venezuela	165.4
7	Canada	556.9	30	Pakistan	156.3
8	United Kingdom	539.2	31	Algeria	140.0
9	South Korea	502.9	32	United Arab Emirates	135.4
10	Iran	495.6	33	Czech Republic	124.9
11	Mexico	471.1	34	Uzbekistan	116.0
12	Italy	456.1	35	Vietnam	111.3
13	South Africa	433.2	36	Belgium	103.0
14	Saudi Arabia	402.1	37	Iraq	100.0
15	Indonesia	396.8	38	Greece	98.0
16	Australia	373.7	39	Nigeria	95.2
17	France	371.5	40	Romania	94.1
18	Brazil	368.0	41	Kuwait	86.1
19	Spain	359.0	42	Chile	71.6
20	Ukraine	317.3	43	Philippines	70.9
21	Poland	317.1	44	North Korea	70.7
22	Turkey	288.4	45	Syria	69.8
23	Thailand	277.3	46	Austria	68.7

Largest amount of carbon dioxide emitted per person
Tonnes, 2007

#	Country	Value	#	Country	Value
1	Qatar	55.4	25	Denmark	9.1
2	Kuwait	32.3		Norway	9.1
3	United Arab Emirates	31.0	27	South Africa	9.0
4	Trinidad & Tobago	27.9	28	Greece	8.8
5	United States	19.3		United Kingdom	8.8
6	Australia	17.7	30	Austria	8.3
7	Canada	16.9		Poland	8.3
8	Saudi Arabia	16.6	32	Spain	8.0
9	Estonia	15.2	33	Bosnia	7.7
10	Kazakhstan	14.7		Italy	7.7
11	Oman	13.7		New Zealand	7.7
12	Czech Republic	12.1	36	Slovenia	7.5
	Finland	12.1	37	Malaysia	7.3
14	Singapore	11.8	38	Iran	7.0
15	Russia	10.8	39	Belarus	6.9
16	Netherlands	10.6	40	Bulgaria	6.8
17	South Korea	10.4		Slovakia	6.8
18	Ireland	10.2		Ukraine	6.8
19	Japan	9.8	43	Serbia	6.3
20	Belgium	9.7	44	France	6.0
21	Germany	9.6		Venezuela	6.0
22	Israel	9.3	46	Hong Kong	5.8
	Libya	9.3	47	Croatia	5.6
24	Turkmenistan	9.2		Hungary	5.6

Changes in carbon dioxide emissions

Biggest increase, %, 1990–2007   *Biggest decrease, %, 1990–2007*

1	Cambodia	884.6		1	Moldova	-80.1
2	Laos	554.7		2	Afghanistan	-73.3
3	Angola	459.0		3	North Korea	-71.1
4	Benin	442.1		4	Tajikistan	-69.9
5	Nepal	439.9		5	Gabon	-66.6
6	Qatar	435.5		6	Georgia	-65.1
7	Vietnam	420.3		7	Ukraine	-54.0
8	Bosnia	315.2		8	Kyrgyzstan	-51.2
9	Uganda	291.9		9	Latvia	-47.9
10	Oman	260.5		10	Albania	-43.3
11	Cameroon	254.9		11	Burundi	-41.0
12	Malaysia	243.6		12	Romania	-40.7
13	Honduras	240.7		13	Congo-Kinshasa	-40.2
14	Sierra Leone	237.7		14	Belarus	-39.9
15	Sri Lanka	226.3		15	Lithuania	-38.9
16	Myanmar	208.5		16	Zimbabwe	-37.9
17	Thailand	189.6		17	Azerbaijan	-36.2
18	Burkina Faso	188.8		18	Russia	-34.3
19	Bangladesh	181.7		19	Slovakia	-32.8
20	Costa Rica	174.7		20	Bulgaria	-32.5

Biggest emitters of carbon dioxide per $ of GDP

Kg of carbon dioxide emitted in 2007 per $ of GDP (PPP) in 2005

1	Uzbekistan	1.9		Tajikistan	0.6
2	Turkmenistan	1.6		Thailand	0.6
3	Kazakhstan	1.4		United Arab Emirates	0.6
4	Mongolia	1.3	31	Australia	0.5
5	Trinidad & Tobago	1.2		Azerbaijan	0.5
6	Bosnia	1.1		Canada	0.5
	Iraq	1.1		Czech Republic	0.5
8	South Africa	1.0		Egypt	0.5
	Ukraine	1.0		India	0.5
10	China	0.9		Indonesia	0.5
11	Estonia	0.8		Liberia	0.5
	Jordan	0.8		Moldova	0.5
	Russia	0.8		Poland	0.5
	Saudi Arabia	0.8		Venezuela	0.5
	Syria	0.8		Vietnam	0.5
16	Belarus	0.7	43	Argentina	0.4
	Iran	0.7		Bolivia	0.4
	Jamaica	0.7		Finland	0.4
	Kuwait	0.7		Israel	0.4
	Macedonia	0.7		Morocco	0.4
	Qatar	0.7		Pakistan	0.4
22	Algeria	0.6		Romania	0.4
	Bulgaria	0.6		Slovakia	0.4
	Kyrgyzstan	0.6		South Korea	0.4
	Libya	0.6		United States	0.4
	Malaysia	0.6		Yemen	0.4
	Oman	0.6			

Largest forested areas
Millions of hectares, 2010

1	Russia	809.1	25	Central African Rep.	22.6
2	Brazil	519.5	26	Congo-Brazzaville	22.4
3	Canada	310.1	27	Finland	22.2
4	United States	304.0	28	Gabon	22.0
5	China	206.9	29	Malaysia	20.5
6	Congo-Kinshasa	154.1	30	Cameroon	19.9
7	Australia	149.3	31	Thailand	19.0
8	Indonesia	94.4	32	Spain	18.2
9	Sudan	69.9	33	Paraguay	17.6
10	India	68.4	34	Chile	16.2
11	Peru	68.0	35	France	16.0
12	Mexico	64.8	36	Laos	15.8
13	Colombia	60.5	37	Zimbabwe	15.6
14	Angola	58.5	38	Guyana	15.2
15	Bolivia	57.2	39	Suriname	14.8
16	Zambia	49.5	40	Vietnam	13.8
17	Venezuela	46.3	41	Madagascar	12.6
18	Mozambique	39.0	42	Mali	12.5
19	Tanzania	33.4	43	Ethiopia	12.3
20	Myanmar	31.8	44	Chad	11.5
21	Argentina	29.4	45	Botswana	11.4
22	Papua New Guinea	28.7	46	Turkey	11.3
23	Sweden	28.2	47	Germany	11.1
24	Japan	25.0		Iran	11.1

Most forested
Forests as % of land area, 2010

1	French Guiana	98		Virgin Islands (US)	58
2	Suriname	95	25	Cambodia	57
3	Gabon	85	26	Fiji	56
4	Guyana	77	27	Colombia	55
	St Lucia	77	28	Latvia	54
6	Finland	73	29	Bolivia	53
7	Brunei	72		Peru	53
	Guinea-Bissau	72	31	Estonia	52
9	Bhutan	69		Indonesia	52
	Japan	69		Venezuela	52
	Sweden	69	34	Bahamas	51
12	Congo-Kinshasa	68		Costa Rica	51
	Laos	68	36	Cayman Islands	50
14	Zambia	67		Mozambique	50
15	Congo-Brazzaville	66		Timor-Leste	50
16	Papua New Guinea	63	39	Russia	49
	South Korea	63	40	Gambia, The	48
18	Brazil	62		Myanmar	48
	Malaysia	62	42	Angola	47
	Puerto Rico	62		Austria	47
	Slovenia	62		Guam	47
22	Belize	61		North Korea	47
23	Equatorial Guinea	58			

Deforestation
Average annual rate of deforestation, %, 2000–10

1	Togo	-5.1		Namibia	-1.0
2	Nigeria	-3.7		Paraguay	-1.0
3	Mauritania	-2.7	29	Myanmar	-0.9
4	Uganda	-2.6	30	Argentina	-0.8
5	Pakistan	-2.2		Haiti	-0.8
6	Ghana	-2.1		Virgin Islands (US)	-0.8
	Honduras	-2.1	33	Belize	-0.7
8	Nicaragua	-2.0		Chad	-0.7
	North Korea	-2.0		Equatorial Guinea	-0.7
10	Zimbabwe	-1.9		Liberia	-0.7
11	Ecuador	-1.8		Mongolia	-0.7
12	Armenia	-1.5		Nepal	-0.7
13	Burundi	-1.4		Sierra Leone	-0.7
	El Salvador	-1.4	40	Algeria	-0.6
	Guatemala	-1.4		Mali	-0.6
	Timor-Leste	-1.4		Venezuela	-0.6
17	Cambodia	-1.3	43	Bolivia	-0.5
18	Ethiopia	-1.1		Brazil	-0.5
	Somalia	-1.1		Guinea	-0.5
	Sri Lanka	-1.1		Guinea-Bissau	-0.5
	Tanzania	-1.1		Indonesia	-0.5
22	Benin	-1.0		Laos	-0.5
	Burkina Faso	-1.0		Malaysia	-0.5
	Cameroon	-1.0		Mozambique	-0.5
	Malawi	-1.0		Papua New Guinea	-0.5
	Mauritius	-1.0		Senegal	-0.5

Forestation
Average annual rate of forestation, %, 2000–10

1	Iceland	5.0	20	Serbia	1.0
2	French Polynesia	4.0	21	Costa Rica	0.9
3	Bahrain	3.6		Italy	0.9
4	Kuwait	2.6	23	Greece	0.8
5	Rwanda	2.4		Norway	0.8
6	Uruguay	2.1		Swaziland	0.8
7	Tunisia	1.9	26	Lithuania	0.7
8	Moldova	1.8		Philippines	0.7
	Puerto Rico	1.8		Spain	0.7
10	Cuba	1.7	29	Hungary	0.6
	Egypt	1.7	30	India	0.5
12	China	1.6		Lesotho	0.5
	Vietnam	1.6	32	Belarus	0.4
14	Bulgaria	1.5		Cape Verde	0.4
	Ireland	1.5		France	0.4
16	Syria	1.3		Gambia, The	0.4
17	Denmark	1.1		Lebanon	0.4
	Kyrgyzstan	1.1		Macedonia	0.4
	Turkey	1.1		Switzerland	0.4

Happy Planet Index[a]

Highest, 2009

1	Costa Rica	76.1
2	Dominican Republic	71.8
3	Jamaica	70.1
4	Guatemala	68.4
5	Vietnam	66.5
6	Colombia	66.1
7	Cuba	65.7
8	El Salvador	61.5
9	Brazil	61.0
	Honduras	61.0
11	Nicaragua	60.5
12	Egypt	60.3
13	Saudi Arabia	59.7
14	Argentina	59.0
	Philippines	59.0
16	Indonesia	58.9
17	Bhutan	58.5
18	Panama	57.4
19	Laos	57.3
20	China	57.1
21	Morocco	56.8
22	Sri Lanka	56.5
23	Mexico	55.6
	Pakistan	55.6

Lowest, 2009

1	Zimbabwe	16.6
2	Tanzania	17.8
3	Botswana	20.9
4	Namibia	21.1
5	Burundi	21.8
6	Burkina Faso	22.4
7	Central African Rep.	22.9
8	Sierra Leone	23.1
9	Togo	23.3
10	Benin	24.6
	Mozambique	24.6
12	Mali	25.8
13	Estonia	26.4
14	Angola	26.8
15	Niger	26.9
16	Kuwait	27.0
17	Cameroon	27.2
	Zambia	27.2
19	Kenya	27.8
20	Ethiopia	28.1
21	United Arab Emirates	28.2
22	Luxembourg	28.5
	Sudan	28.5
24	Congo-Kinshasa	29.0

Ecological footprint[b]

Hectares, highest

1	Luxembourg	10.2
2	United Arab Emirates	9.5
3	United States	9.4
4	Kuwait	8.9
5	Denmark	8.0
6	Australia	7.8
7	New Zealand	7.7
8	Iceland	7.4
9	Canada	7.1
10	Norway	6.9
11	Estonia	6.4
12	Ireland	6.3
13	Greece	5.9
14	Hong Kong	5.7
	Spain	5.7
16	Uruguay	5.5
17	Czech Republic	5.4
18	United Kingdom	5.3
19	Finland	5.2

20	Belgium	5.1
	Sweden	5.1
22	Austria	5.0
	Switzerland	5.0
24	France	4.9
	Japan	4.9
26	Israel	4.8
	Italy	4.8
28	Macedonia	4.6
29	Cyprus	4.5
	Slovenia	4.5
31	Netherlands	4.4
	Portugal	4.4
33	Germany	4.2
	Singapore	4.2
35	Poland	4.0
36	Belarus	3.9
37	Malta	3.8

a A measure which comprises life satisfaction, life expectancy and an individual's ecological footprint.
b Amount of land measured in hectares required to provide for an individual's requirements and to absorb their carbon emissions

Country
profiles

ALGERIA

Area	2,381,741 sq km	Capital	Algiers
Arable as % of total land	3	Currency	Algerian dinar (AD)

People

Population	34.9m	Life expectancy: men	71.9 yrs
Pop. per sq km	14.9	women	75.0 yrs
Av. ann. growth		Adult literacy	72.6%
in pop. 2010–15	1.51%	Fertility rate (per woman)	2.4
Pop. under 15	27.0%	Urban population	66.5%
Pop. over 60	6.9%		per 1,000 pop.
No. of men per 100 women	101.9	Crude birth rate	20.8
Human Development Index	67.7	Crude death rate	4.9

The economy

GDP	AD10,212bn	GDP per head	$4,030
GDP	$141bn	GDP per head in purchasing	
Av. ann. growth in real		power parity (USA=100)	17.8
GDP 2004–09	3.0%	Economic freedom index	52.4

Origins of GDP

	% of total
Agriculture	12
Industry, of which:	55
manufacturing	6
Services	34

Components of GDP

	% of total
Private consumption	41
Public consumption	14
Investment	41
Exports	40
Imports	-36

Structure of employment

	% of total		% of labour force
Agriculture	21	Unemployed 2008	11.3
Industry	27	Av. ann. rate 1995–2008	22.6
Services	52		

Energy

	m TOE		
Total output	162.0	Net energy imports as %	
Total consumption	37.1	of energy use	-337
Consumption per head,			
kg oil equivalent	1,078		

Inflation and finance

		av. ann. increase 2004–09	
Consumer price			
inflation 2010	3.5%	Narrow money (M1)	18.0%
Av. ann. inflation 2005–10	4.1%	Broad money	14.5%
Treasury bill rate, 2010	0.31%		

Exchange rates

	end 2010		2010
AD per $	74.94	Effective rates	2005 = 100
AD per SDR	115.42	– nominal	94.1
AD per €	94.09	– real	102.0

Trade

Principal exports		Principal imports	
	$bn fob		$bn cif
Hydrocarbons	44.4	Capital goods	15.1
Semi-finished goods	0.4	Semi-finished goods	10.3
Raw materials	0.2	Food	5.8
Total incl. others	**45.2**	Total incl. others	**39.3**

Main export destinations		Main origins of imports	
	% of total		% of total
United States	22.9	France	15.7
Italy	12.6	China	12.1
Spain	11.9	Italy	9.4
France	9.8	Spain	7.6

Balance of payments, reserves and debt, $bn

Visible exports fob	45.2	Change in reserves	7.0
Visible imports fob	-37.4	Level of reserves	
Trade balance	7.8	end Dec.	155.1
Invisibles inflows	7.7	No. months of import cover	33.7
Invisibles outflows	-17.8	Official gold holdings, m oz	5.6
Net transfers	2.6	Foreign debt	5.3
Current account balance	0.4	– as % of GDP	3.0
– as % of GDP	0.1	– as % of total exports	5.0
Capital balance	3.5	Debt service ratio[a]	9
Overall balance	3.9		

Health and education

Health spending, % of GDP	5.6	Education spending, % of GDP	4.3
Doctors per 1,000 pop.	1.2	Enrolment, %: primary	108
Hospital beds per 1,000 pop.	1.6	secondary	83
Improved-water source access,		tertiary	31
% of pop.	83		

Society

No. of households	5.9m	Colour TVs per 100 households	91.5
Av. no. per household	5.8	Telephone lines per 100 pop.	7.4
Marriages per 1,000 pop.	9.1	Mobile telephone subscribers	
Divorces per 1,000 pop.	...	per 100 pop.	93.8
Cost of living, Dec. 2010		Broadband subs per 100 pop.	2.3
New York = 100	57	Internet hosts per 1,000 pop.	...

a 2008

ARGENTINA

Area	2,766,889 sq km	Capital	Buenos Aires
Arable as % of total land	12	Currency	Peso (P)

People

Population	40.3m	Life expectancy: men		72.5 yrs
Pop. per sq km	14.5		women	80.0 yrs
Av. ann. growth		Adult literacy		97.7%
in pop. 2010–15	0.88%	Fertility rate (per woman)		2.3
Pop. under 15	24.9%	Urban population		92.4%
Pop. over 60	14.7%			per 1,000 pop.
No. of men per 100 women	95.8	Crude birth rate		17.5
Human Development Index	77.5	Crude death rate		7.7

The economy

GDP	P1,145bn	GDP per head	$7,630
GDP	$307bn	GDP per head in purchasing	
Av. ann. growth in real		power parity (USA=100)	31.6
GDP 2004–09	6.7%	Economic freedom index	51.7

Origins of GDP		Components of GDP	
	% of total		% of total
Agriculture	8	Private consumption	59
Industry, of which:	32	Public consumption	15
manufacturing	21	Investment	21
Services	61	Exports	21
		Imports	-16

Structure of employment

	% of total		% of labour force
Agriculture	1	Unemployed 2009	8.6
Industry	24	Av. ann. rate 1995–2009	13.6
Services	75		

Energy

	m TOE		
Total output	82.9	Net energy imports as %	
Total consumption	76.4	of energy use	-9
Consumption per head			
kg oil equivalent	1,915		

Inflation and finance

Consumer price			av. ann. increase 2004–09
inflation 2010	10.8%	Narrow money (M1)	18.6%
Av. ann. inflation 2005–10	9.1%	Broad money	18.1%
Money market rate, 2010	9.09%		

Exchange rates

	end 2010		2010
P per $	3.96	Effective rates	2005 = 100
P per SDR	6.09	– nominal	...
P per €	5.29	– real	...

Trade

Principal exports		Principal imports	
	$bn fob		*$bn cif*
Agricultural products	21.3	Intermediate goods	12.6
Manufactures	18.7	Capital goods	8.7
Primary products	9.3	Consumer goods	5.1
Fuels	6.4	Fuels	2.6
Total incl. others	**55.7**	Total incl. others	**39.1**

Main export destinations		Main origins of imports	
	% of total		*% of total*
Brazil	20.4	Brazil	30.8
Chile	7.9	United States	13.2
China	6.6	China	12.3
United States	6.6	Germany	5.1

Balance of payments, reserves and debt, $bn

Visible exports fob	55.7	Change in reserves	1.6
Visible imports fob	-37.1	Level of reserves	
Trade balance	18.5	end Dec.	48.0
Invisibles inflows	14.4	No. months of import cover	9.4
Invisibles outflows	-24.3	Official gold holdings, m oz	1.8
Net transfers	0	Foreign debt	120.2
Current account balance	8.6	– as % of GDP	41.0
– as % of GDP	2.8	– as % of total exports	156.0
Capital balance	-8.2	Debt service ratio	17
Overall balance	-0.4		

Health and education

Health spending, % of GDP	9.5	Education spending, % of GDP	4.9
Doctors per 1,000 pop.	3.0	Enrolment, %: primary	116
Hospital beds per 1,000 pop.	4.0	secondary	85
Improved-water source access,		tertiary	68
% of pop.	97		

Society

No. of households	11.0m	Colour TVs per 100 households	96.3
Av. no. per household	3.7	Telephone lines per 100 pop.	24.3
Marriages per 1,000 pop.	3.0	Mobile telephone subscribers	
Divorces per 1,000 pop.	...	per 100 pop.	130.3
Cost of living, Dec. 2010		Broadband subs per 100 pop.	10.6
New York = 100	67	Internet hosts per 1,000 pop.	177.2

AUSTRALIA

Area	7,682,300 sq km	Capital	Canberra
Arable as % of total land	6	Currency	Australian dollar (A$)

People

Population	21.3m	Life expectancy:	men	80.0 yrs
Pop. per sq km	2.9		women	84.4 yrs
Av. ann. growth		Adult literacy		...
in pop. 2010–15	1.75%	Fertility rate (per woman)		1.9
Pop. under 15	18.9%	Urban population		89.1%
Pop. over 60	19.5%			per 1,000 pop.
No. of men per 100 women	99.3	Crude birth rate		13.6
Human Development Index	93.7	Crude death rate		7.1

The economy

GDP	A$1,256bn	GDP per head	$42,280
GDP	$925bn	GDP per head in purchasing	
Av. ann. growth in real		power parity (USA=100)	86.0
GDP 2004–09	2.8%	Economic freedom index	82.5

Origins of GDP		Components of GDP	
	% of total		% of total
Agriculture	3	Private consumption	57
Industry, of which:	29	Public consumption	17
manufacturing	10	Investment	28
Services	68	Exports	20
		Imports	-22

Structure of employment

	% of total		% of labour force
Agriculture	3	Unemployed 2009	5.6
Industry	21	Av. ann. rate 1995–2009	6.3
Services	76		

Energy

	m TOE		
Total output	302.1	Net energy imports as %	
Total consumption	130.1	of energy use	-132
Consumption per head,			
kg oil equivalent	6,071		

Inflation and finance

Consumer price		av. ann. increase 2004–09	
inflation 2010	2.8%	Narrow money (M1)	8.9%
Av. ann. inflation 2005–10	3.0%	Broad money	13.2%
Money market rate, 2010	4.35%	Household saving rate, 2010	9.3%

Exchange rates

	end 2010		2010
A$ per $	0.98	Effective rates	2005 = 100
A$ per SDR	1.52	– nominal	118.4
A$ per €	1.31	– real	121.7

Trade

Principal exports		Principal imports	
	$bn fob		*$bn cif*
Coal	30.8	Intermediate & other goods	71.2
Meat & meat products	6.8	Capital goods	48.0
Wheat	3.7	Consumption goods	40.0
Total incl. others	**154.5**	Total incl. others	**159.3**

Main export destinations		Main origins of imports	
	% of total		*% of total*
China	21.7	China	19.7
Japan	19.1	United States	12.4
South Korea	7.8	Japan	9.2
India	7.5	Singapore	6.4
United States	4.9	Thailand	6.4

Balance of payments, reserves and aid, $bn

Visible exports fob	154.8	Overall balance	5.9
Visible imports fob	-159.2	Change in reserves	8.8
Trade balance	-4.4	Level of reserves	
Invisibles inflows	69.7	end Dec.	41.7
Invisibles outflows	-108.1	No. months of import cover	1.2
Net transfers	-1.1	Official gold holdings, m oz	2.6
Current account balance	-43.8	Aid given	2.76
– as % of GDP	-4.7	– as % of GDP	0.29
Capital balance	54.6		

Health and education

Health spending, % of GDP	8.5	Education spending, % of GDP	4.5
Doctors per 1,000 pop.	2.9	Enrolment, %: primary	106
Hospital beds per 1,000 pop.	3.7	secondary	149
Improved-water source access,		tertiary	77
% of pop.	100		

Society

No. of households	8.0m	Colour TVs per 100 households	99.2
Av. no. per household	2.7	Telephone lines per 100 pop.	42.4
Marriages per 1,000 pop.	5.2	Mobile telephone subscribers	
Divorces per 1,000 pop.	2.3	per 100 pop.	113.8
Cost of living, Dec. 2010		Broadband subs per 100 pop.	24.4
New York = 100	129	Internet hosts per 1,000 pop.	741.6

AUSTRIA

Area	83,855 sq km	Capital	Vienna
Arable as % of total land	17	Currency	Euro (€)

People

Population	8.4m	Life expectancy: men	78.2 yrs
Pop. per sq km	100.1	women	83.2 yrs
Av. ann. growth		Adult literacy	...
in pop. 2010–15	0.39%	Fertility rate (per woman)	1.4
Pop. under 15	14.7%	Urban population	67.6%
Pop. over 60	23.1%		per 1,000 pop.
No. of men per 100 women	95.3	Crude birth rate	9.1
Human Development Index	85.1	Crude death rate	9.5

The economy

GDP	€274bn	GDP per head	$45,560
GDP	$381bn	GDP per head in purchasing	
Av. ann. growth in real		power parity (USA=100)	84.4
GDP 2004–09	1.6%	Economic freedom index	71.9

Origins of GDP

	% of total
Agriculture	2
Industry, of which:	29
manufacturing	19
Services	69

Components of GDP

	% of total
Private consumption	54
Public consumption	20
Investment	21
Exports	51
Imports	-46

Structure of employment

	% of total		% of labour force
Agriculture	6	Unemployed 2009	4.8
Industry	26	Av. ann. rate 1995–2009	4.2
Services	68		

Energy

	m TOE		
Total output	11.0	Net energy imports as %	
Total consumption	33.2	of energy use	67
Consumption per head,			
kg oil equivalent	3,988		

Inflation and finance

Consumer price		av. ann. increase 2004–09	
inflation 2010	1.8%	Euro area:	
Av. ann. inflation 2005–10	1.8%	Narrow money (M1)	9.0%
Deposit rate, h'holds, 2010	1.24%	Broad money	7.3%
		Household saving rate, 2010	9.1%

Exchange rates

	end 2010		December 2010
€ per $	0.75	Effective rates	2005 = 100
€ per SDR	1.15	– nominal	99.8
		– real	97.9

Trade

Principal exports		Principal imports	
	$bn fob		*$bn cif*
Machinery & transport equip.	50.5	Machinery & transport equip.	46.9
Chemicals & related products	16.7	Chemicals & related products	17.1
Food, drink & tobacco	10.0	Mineral fuels & lubricants	13.8
Mineral fuels & lubricants	4.5	Food, drink & tobacco	10.4
Raw materials	4.3	Raw materials	5.6
Total incl. others	**130.8**	Total incl. others	**136.1**

Main export destinations		Main origins of imports	
	% of total		*% of total*
Germany	32.5	Germany	47.5
Italy	8.4	Italy	7.1
Switzerland	5.3	Switzerland	7.1
United States	4.2	Netherlands	4.2
EU27	71.8	EU27	78.0

Balance of payments, reserves and aid, $bn

Visible exports fob	135.3	Overall balance	-1.1
Visible imports fob	-138.5	Change in reserves	1.2
Trade balance	-3.3	Level of reserves	
Invisibles inflows	89.7	end Dec.	17.9
Invisibles outflows	-73.2	No. months of import cover	1.0
Net transfers	-2.3	Official gold holdings, m oz	9.0
Current account balance	11.0	Aid given	1.14
– as % of GDP	2.9	– as % of GDP	0.30
Capital balance	-6.6		

Health and education

Health spending, % of GDP	11.0	Education spending, % of GDP	5.4
Doctors per 1,000 pop.	4.7	Enrolment, %: primary	100
Hospital beds per 1,000 pop.	7.8	secondary	100
Improved-water source access,		tertiary	55
% of pop.	100		

Society

No. of households	3.6m	Colour TVs per 100 households	98.9
Av. no. per household	2.3	Telephone lines per 100 pop.	38.9
Marriages per 1,000 pop.	4.9	Mobile telephone subscribers	
Divorces per 1,000 pop.	2.4	per 100 pop.	136.7
Cost of living, Dec. 2010		Broadband subs per 100 pop.	22.1
New York = 100	111	Internet hosts per 1,000 pop.	402.0

BANGLADESH

Area	143,998 sq km	Capital	Dhaka
Arable as % of total land	61	Currency	Taka (Tk)

People

Population	162.2m	Life expectancy: men	66.5 yrs
Pop. per sq km	1,032.6	women	69.0 yrs
Av. ann. growth		Adult literacy	55.9%
in pop. 2010–15	1.12%	Fertility rate (per woman)	2.4
Pop. under 15	30.9%	Urban population	28.1%
Pop. over 60	6.2%		per 1,000 pop.
No. of men per 100 women	102.6	Crude birth rate	21.5
Human Development Index	46.9	Crude death rate	6.3

The economy

GDP	Tk6,148bn	GDP per head	$550
GDP	$89.4bn	GDP per head in purchasing	
Av. ann. growth in real		power parity (USA=100)	3.1
GDP 2004–09	6.2%	Economic freedom index	53.0

Origins of GDP		Components of GDP	
	% of total		% of total
Agriculture	19	Private consumption	77
Industry, of which:	29	Public consumption	5
manufacturing	18	Investment	24
Services	53	Exports	19
		Imports	-27

Structure of employment

	% of total		% of labour force
Agriculture	52	Unemployed 2005	4.3
Industry	14	Av. ann. rate 1995–2005	2.9
Services	35		

Energy

			m TOE
Total output	23.4	Net energy imports as %	
Total consumption	27.9	of energy use	16
Consumption per head,			
kg oil equivalent	175		

Inflation and finance

Consumer price		av. ann. increase 2004–09	
inflation 2010	8.1%	Narrow money (M1)	18.5%
Av. ann. inflation 2005–10	7.7%	Broad money	17.2%
Deposit rate, 2010	7.14%		

Exchange rates

	end 2010		2010
Tk per $	70.75	Effective rates	2005 = 100
Tk per SDR	108.96	– nominal	...
Tk per €	94.54	– real	...

Trade

Principal exports[a]		Principal imports[a]	
	$bn fob		*$bn cif*
Clothing	9.8	Capital goods	4.7
Fish & fish products	0.5	Textiles & yarns	4.3
Jute goods	0.3	Fuels	2.6
Leather	0.3	Iron & steel	1.5
Total incl. others	**14.2**	Total incl. others	**22.5**

Main export destinations		Main origins of imports	
	% of total		*% of total*
United States	20.2	China	16.2
Germany	12.7	India	12.6
United Kingdom	8.6	Kuwait	7.6
France	6.5	Singapore	4.6
Netherlands	5.9	Hong Kong	4.5

Balance of payments, reserves and debt, $bn

Visible exports fob	15.1	Change in reserves	4.6
Visible imports fob	-19.8	Level of reserves	
Trade balance	-4.7	end Dec.	10.3
Invisibles inflows	2.0	No. months of import cover	5.0
Invisibles outflows	-4.8	Official gold holdings, m oz	0.1
Net transfers	10.9	Foreign debt	23.8
Current account balance	3.3	– as % of GDP	17
– as % of GDP	3.7	– as % of total exports	90
Capital balance	1.0	Debt service ratio	6
Overall balance	4.4		

Health and education

Health spending, % of GDP	3.4	Education spending, % of GDP	2.4
Doctors per 1,000 pop.	0.3	Enrolment, %: primary	95
Hospital beds per 1,000 pop.	0.4	secondary	42
Improved-water source access,		tertiary	8
% of pop.	80		

Society

No. of households	26.9m	Colour TVs per 100 households	...
Av. no. per household	6.0	Telephone lines per 100 pop.	0.9
Marriages per 1,000 pop.	...	Mobile telephone subscribers	
Divorces per 1,000 pop.	...	per 100 pop.	32.3
Cost of living, Dec. 2010		Broadband subs per 100 pop.	...
New York = 100	61	Internet hosts per 1,000 pop.	0.4

a Fiscal year ending June 30 2009 .

BELGIUM

Area	30,520 sq km	Capital	Brussels
Arable as % of total land	28	Currency	Euro (€)

People

Population	10.6m	Life expectancy: men	77.7 yrs
Pop. per sq km	350.9	women	83.9 yrs
Av. ann. growth		Adult literacy	...
in pop. 2010–15	0.56%	Fertility rate (per woman)	1.8
Pop. under 15	16.7%	Urban population	97.4%
Pop. over 60	23.4%		per 1,000 pop.
No. of men per 100 women	96	Crude birth rate	11.5
Human Development Index	86.7	Crude death rate	9.7

The economy

GDP	€339bn	GDP per head	$43,670
GDP	$471bn	GDP per head in purchasing	
Av. ann. growth in real		power parity (USA=100)	79.0
GDP 2004–09	1.1%	Economic freedom index	70.2

Origins of GDP		**Components of GDP**	
	% of total		% of total
Agriculture	1	Private consumption	52
Industry, of which:	22	Public consumption	25
manufacturing	14	Investment	20
Services	78	Exports	73
		Imports	-70

Structure of employment

	% of total		% of labour force
Agriculture	2	Unemployed 2009	7.9
Industry	25	Av. ann. rate 1995–2009	8.1
Services	73		

Energy

	m TOE		
Total output	14.5	Net energy imports as %	
Total consumption	58.6	of energy use	75
Consumption per head,			
kg oil equivalent	5,471		

Inflation and finance

Consumer price			av. ann. increase 2004–09
inflation 2010	2.2%	Euro area:	
Av. ann. inflation 2005–10	2.0%	Narrow money (M1)	9.0%
Treasury bill rate, 2010	0.32%	Broad money	7.3%
		Household saving rate, 2010	12.2%

Exchange rates

	end 2010		2010
€ per $	0.75	Effective rates	2005 = 100
€ per SDR	1.15	– nominal	101.2
		– real	100.2

Trade

Principal exports		Principal imports	
	$bn fob		*$bn cif*
Chemicals & related products	117.4	Chemicals & related products	91.3
Machinery & transport equip.	77.9	Minerals, fuels & lubricants	83.1
Food, drink & tobacco	34.1	Machinery & transport equip.	40.6
Minerals, fuels & lubricants	25.5	Food, drink & tobacco	29.0
Raw materials	9.5	Raw materials	13.8
Total incl. others	**370.3**	Total incl. others	**353.4**

Main export destinations		Main origins of imports	
	% of total		*% of total*
Germany	19.6	Netherlands	17.9
France	17.7	Germany	17.1
Netherlands	11.8	France	11.6
United Kingdom	7.2	United Kingdom	6.2
EU27	75.9	EU27	71.1

Balance of payments, reserves and aid, $bn

Visible exports fob	252.2	Overall balance	7.0
Visible imports fob	-255.1	Change in reserves	8.2
Trade balance	-2.9	Level of reserves	
Invisibles inflows	152.5	end Dec.	23.9
Invisibles outflows	-137.1	No. months of import cover	0.7
Net transfers	-8.9	Official gold holdings, m oz	7.3
Current account balance	3.5	Aid given	2.61
– as % of GDP	0.7	– as % of GDP	0.55
Capital balance	0.4		

Health and education

Health spending, % of GDP	11.8	Education spending, % of GDP	6.0
Doctors per 1,000 pop.	3.0	Enrolment, %: primary	103
Hospital beds per 1,000 pop.	5.1	secondary	108
Improved-water source access,		tertiary	63
% of pop.	100		

Society

No. of households	4.6m	Colour TVs per 100 households	96.2
Av. no. per household	2.3	Telephone lines per 100 pop.	43.5
Marriages per 1,000 pop.	4.3	Mobile telephone subscribers	
Divorces per 1,000 pop.	3.0	per 100 pop.	117.5
Cost of living, Dec. 2010		Broadband subs per 100 pop.	29.4
New York = 100	107	Internet hosts per 1,000 pop.	450.2

BRAZIL

Area	8,511,965 sq km	Capital	Brasilia
Arable as % of total land	7	Currency	Real (R)

People

Population	193.7m	Life expectancy: men	69.9 yrs
Pop. per sq km	22.9	women	77.2 yrs
Av. ann. growth		Adult literacy	90.0%
in pop. 2010–15	0.94%	Fertility rate (per woman)	1.9
Pop. under 15	25.5%	Urban population	86.5%
Pop. over 60	10.2%		per 1,000 pop.
No. of men per 100 women	96.9	Crude birth rate	16.4
Human Development Index	69.9	Crude death rate	6.5

The economy

GDP	R3,185bn	GDP per head	$8,230
GDP	$1,595bn	GDP per head in purchasing	
Av. ann. growth in real		power parity (USA=100)	22.5
GDP 2004–09	3.5%	Economic freedom index	56.3

Origins of GDP		Components of GDP	
	% of total		% of total
Agriculture	6	Private consumption	62
Industry, of which:	25	Public consumption	22
manufacturing	16	Investment	17
Services	69	Exports	11
		Imports	-11

Structure of employment

	% of total		% of labour force
Agriculture	19	Unemployed 2009	8.3
Industry	21	Av. ann. rate 1995–2009	8.4
Services	60		

Energy

			m TOE
Total output	228.1	Net energy imports as %	
Total consumption	248.5	of energy use	8
Consumption per head,			
kg oil equivalent	1,295		

Inflation and finance

Consumer price		av. ann. increase 2004–09	
inflation 2010	5.0%	Narrow money (M1)	14.2%
Av. ann. inflation 2005–10	4.7%	Broad money	17.4%
Money market rate, 2010	9.80%		

Exchange rates

	end 2010		2010
R per $	1.69	Effective rates	2005 = 100
R per sdr	2.60	– nominal	135.8
R per €	2.26	– real	152.3

Trade

Principal exports	$bn fob	Principal imports	$bn cif
Primary products	67.3	Intermediate products and raw	
Semi-manufactured products	62.0	materials	59.8
Manufactured products	20.5	Capital goods	29.7
		Consumer goods	21.5
		Fuels and lubricants	16.7
Total	153.0	Total	127.6

Main export destinations	% of total	Main origins of imports	% of total
China	12.3	United States	17.5
United States	10.3	China	13.7
Argentina	8.3	Argentina	9.5
Netherlands	5.3	Germany	8.3

Balance of payments, reserves and debt, $bn

Visible exports fob	153.0	Change in reserves	44.8
Visible imports fob	-127.7	Level of reserves	
Trade balance	25.3	end Dec.	238.5
Invisibles inflows	36.6	No. months of import cover	13.2
Invisibles outflows	-89.5	Official gold holdings, m oz	1.1
Net transfers	3.3	Foreign debt	276.9
Current account balance	-24.3	– as % of GDP	17
– as % of GDP	-1.8	– as % of total exports	125
Capital balance	71.3	Debt service ratio	23
Overall balance	47.6		

Health and education

Health spending, % of GDP	9.0	Education spending, % of GDP	5.1
Doctors per 1,000 pop.	1.7	Enrolment, %: primary	127
Hospital beds per 1,000 pop.	2.4	secondary	101
Improved-water source access,		tertiary	34
% of pop.	97		

Society

No. of households	54.5m	Colour TVs per 100 households	95.6
Av. no. per household	3.7	Telephone lines per 100 pop.	21.4
Marriages per 1,000 pop.	3.9	Mobile telephone subscribers	
Divorces per 1,000 pop.	0.8	per 100 pop.	89.8
Cost of living, Dec. 2010		Broadband subs per 100 pop.	5.9
New York = 100	99	Internet hosts per 1,000 pop.	109.0

BULGARIA

Area	110,994 sq km	Capital	Sofia
Arable as % of total land	28	Currency	Lev (BGL)

People

Population	7.5m	Life expectancy: men	70.9 yrs
Pop. per sq km	67.6	women	77.7 yrs
Av. ann. growth		Adult literacy	98.3%
in pop. 2010–15	-0.64%	Fertility rate (per woman)	1.5
Pop. under 15	13.5%	Urban population	71.5%
Pop. over 60	24.5%		per 1,000 pop.
No. of men per 100 women	93.6	Crude birth rate	9.9
Human Development Index	74.3	Crude death rate	14.6

The economy

GDP	BGL68.5bn	GDP per head	$6,420
GDP	$48.7bn	GDP per head in purchasing	
Av. ann. growth in real		power parity (USA=100)	30.2
GDP 2004–09	3.9%	Economic freedom index	64.9

Origins of GDP		Components of GDP	
	% of total		% of total
Agriculture	6	Private consumption	66
Industry, of which:	30	Public consumption	16
manufacturing	15	Investment	26
Services	64	Exports	48
		Imports	-56

Structure of employment

	% of total		% of labour force
Agriculture	8	Unemployed 2009	6.8
Industry	36	Av. ann. rate 1995–2009	12.5
Services	56		

Energy

		m TOE	
Total output	10.2	Net energy imports as %	
Total consumption	19.8	of energy use	48
Consumption per head,			
kg oil equivalent	2,595		

Inflation and finance

Consumer price		av. ann. change 2004–09	
inflation 2010	2.4%	Narrow money (M1)	12.0%
Av. ann. inflation 2005–10	6.6%	Broad money	18.6%
Money market rate, 2010	0.18%		

Exchange rates

	end 2010		2010
BGL per $	1.47	Effective rates	2005 = 100
BGL per SDR	2.27	– nominal	103.4
BGL per €	1.96	– real	121.3

Trade

Principal exports		Principal imports	
	$bn fob		*$bn cif*
Clothing & footwear	1.7	Crude oil & natural gas	3.6
Other metals	1.7	Machinery & equipment	2.1
Chemicals, plastics & rubber	0.7	Chemicals, plastics & rubber	1.5
Iron & steel	0.6	Textiles	1.3
Total incl. others	**16.4**	Total incl. others	**22.2**

Main export destinations		Main origins of imports	
	% of total		*% of total*
Greece	11.3	Russia	14.3
Germany	9.5	Germany	13.0
Italy	9.3	Italy	8.2
Romania	8.6	Greece	6.5
EU27	64.4	EU27	60.3

Balance of payments, reserves and debt, $bn

Visible exports fob	16.4	Change in reserves	0.6
Visible imports fob	-22.2	Level of reserves	
Trade balance	-5.8	end Dec.	18.5
Invisibles inflows	8.0	No. months of import cover	7.3
Invisibles outflows	-8.3	Official gold holdings, m oz	1.3
Net transfers	1.3	Foreign debt	40.6
Current account balance	-4.8	– as % of GDP	85
– as % of GDP	-9.8	– as % of total exports	132
Capital balance	3.7	Debt service ratio	21
Overall balance	0.0		

Health and education

Health spending, % of GDP	7.4	Education spending, % of GDP	3.5
Doctors per 1,000 pop.	3.7	Enrolment, %: primary	101
Hospital beds per 1,000 pop.	6.5	secondary	89
Improved-water source access,		tertiary	51
% of pop.	100		

Society

No. of households	2.9m	Colour TVs per 100 households	90.9
Av. no. per household	2.6	Telephone lines per 100 pop.	29.2
Marriages per 1,000 pop.	3.9	Mobile telephone subscribers	
Divorces per 1,000 pop.	2.6	per 100 pop.	140.2
Cost of living, Dec. 2010		Broadband subs per 100 pop.	12.9
New York = 100	66	Internet hosts per 1,000 pop.	119.0

CAMEROON

Area	475,442 sq km	Capital	Yaoundé
Arable as % of total land	13	Currency	CFA franc (CFAfr)

People

Population	19.5m	Life expectancy: men	52.0 yrs
Pop. per sq km	41.2	women	53.4 yrs
Av. ann. growth		Adult literacy	75.9%
in pop. 2010–15	2.20%	Fertility rate (per woman)	4.7
Pop. under 15	40.8%	Urban population	58.4%
Pop. over 60	5.4%		per 1,000 pop.
No. of men per 100 women	99.7	Crude birth rate	37.2
Human Development Index	46.0	Crude death rate	13.2

The economy

GDP	CFAfr10,474bn	GDP per head	$1,140
GDP	$22.2bn	GDP per head in purchasing	
Av. ann. growth in real		power parity (USA=100)	4.8
GDP 2004–09	2.7%	Economic freedom index	51.8

Origins of GDP		**Components of GDP**	
	% of total		% of total
Agriculture	19	Private consumption	72
Industry, of which:	31	Public consumption	9
manufacturing	17	Investment	18
Services	50	Exports	27
		Imports	-31

Structure of employment

	% of total		% of labour force
Agriculture	70	Unemployed 2007	2.9
Industry	13	Av. ann. rate 1995–2007	5.2
Services	17		

Energy

	m TOE		
Total output	10.1	Net energy imports as %	
Total consumption	7.1	of energy use	-42
Consumption per head,			
kg oil equivalent	372		

Inflation and finance

Consumer price		av. ann. change 2004–09	
inflation 2010	1.3%	Narrow money (M1)	11.8%
Av. ann. inflation 2005–10	3.1%	Broad money	9.9%
Deposit rate, Nov. 2010	3.25%		

Exchange rates

	end 2010		2010
CFAfr per $	490.91	Effective rates	2005 = 100
CFAfr per SDR	756.02	– nominal	100.3
CFAfr per €	655.95	– real	99.7

Trade

Principal exports[a]		Principal imports[a]	
	$bn fob		*$bn cif*
Crude oil	2.7	Minerals & raw materials	1.7
Timber	0.5	Intermediate goods	0.8
Cocoa	0.4	Food, drink & tobacco	0.6
Cotton	0.1	Industrial equipment	0.6
Total incl. others	**5.9**	Total incl. others	**5.1**

Main export destinations		Main origins of imports	
	% of total		*% of total*
Netherlands	14.4	France	21.0
Spain	12.6	China	11.7
Italy	12.2	Belgium	6.6
China	9.4	United States	4.3

Balance of payments, reserves and debt, $bn

Visible exports fob	4.1	Change in reserves	0.6
Visible imports fob	-4.4	Level of reserves	
Trade balance	-0.3	end Dec.	3.7
Invisible inflows	1.3	No. months of import cover	6.5
Invisible outflows	-2.5	Official gold holdings, m oz	0
Net transfers	0.4	Foreign debt	2.9
Current account balance	-1.1	– as % of GDP	4
– as % of GDP	-5.1	– as % of total exports	12
Capital balance	1.8	Debt service ratio	7
Overall balance	0.2		

Health and education

Health spending, % of GDP	5.6	Education spending, % of GDP	3.7
Doctors per 1,000 pop.	0.2	Enrolment, %: primary	114
Hospital beds per 1,000 pop.	1.5	secondary	37
Improved-water source access,		tertiary	9
% of pop.	74		

Society

No. of households	3.9m	Colour TVs per 100 households	69.1
Av. no. per household	5.0	Telephone lines per 100 pop.	2.2
Marriages per 1,000 pop.	...	Mobile telephone subscribers	
Divorces per 1,000 pop.	...	per 100 pop.	41.0
Cost of living, Dec. 2010		Broadband subs per 100 pop.	...
New York = 100	...	Internet hosts per 1,000 pop.	...

a 2008

CANADA

Area[a]	9,970,610 sq km	Capital	Ottawa
Arable as % of total land	5	Currency	Canadian dollar (C$)

People

Population	33.6m	Life expectancy: men	79.2 yrs
Pop. per sq km	3.4	women	83.6 yrs
Av. ann. growth		Adult literacy	...
in pop. 2010–15	1.05%	Fertility rate (per woman)	1.7
Pop. under 15	16.3%	Urban population	80.6%
Pop. over 60	20.0%		per 1,000 pop.
No. of men per 100 women	98.4	Crude birth rate	11.2
Human Development Index	88.8	Crude death rate	7.6

The economy

GDP	C$1,527bn	GDP per head	$39,600
GDP	$1,336bn	GDP per head in purchasing	
Av. ann. growth in real		power parity (USA=100)	82.2
GDP 2004–09	1.2%	Economic freedom index	80.8

Origins of GDP

Components of GDP

	% of total		% of total
Agriculture	2	Private consumption	59
Industry, of which:	26	Public consumption	22
manufacturing & mining	...	Investment	21
Services	72	Exports	29
		Imports	-30

Structure of employment

	% of total		% of labour force
Agriculture	3	Unemployed 2009	8.3
Industry	22	Av. ann. rate 1995–2009	7.6
Services	75		

Energy

	m TOE		
Total output	407.4	Net energy imports as %	
Total consumption	266.8	of energy use	-53
Consumption per head,			
kg oil equivalent	8,008		

Inflation and finance

Consumer price		av. ann. increase 2004–09	
inflation 2010	1.8%	Narrow money (M1)	10.0%
Av. ann. inflation 2004–09	1.7%	Broad money	7.9%
Money market rate, 2010	0.60%	Household saving rate, 2010	4.4%

Exchange rates

	end 2010		December 2010
C$ per $	1.00	Effective rates	2005 = 100
C$ per SDR	1.54	– nominal	112.8
C$ per €	1.34	– real	109.8

Trade

Principal exports		Principal imports	
	$bn fob		*$bn fob*
Machinery & equipment	70.4	Machinery & equipment	94.4
Energy products	69.9	Industrial goods & materials	65.7
Industrial goods & materials	69.3	Consumer goods	50.3
Motor vehicles & parts	38.3	Motor vehicles & parts	48.4
Agricultural & fishing products	32.6	Energy products	29.7
Total incl. others	**323.3**	Total incl. others	**327.3**

Main export destinations		Main origins of imports	
	% of total		*% of total*
United States	75.1	United States	51.1
United Kingdom	3.4	China	10.9
China	3.1	Mexico	4.6
Japan	2.3	Japan	3.4
EU 27	8.3	EU 27	12.4

Balance of payments, reserves and aid, $bn

Visible exports fob	324.7	Overall balance	-8.2
Visible imports fob	-328.9	Change in reserves	10.5
Trade balance	-4.2	Level of reserves	
Invisibles inflows	109.6	end Dec.	54.4
Invisibles outflows	-141.8	No. months of import cover	1.4
Net transfers	-1.9	Official gold holdings, m oz	0.1
Current account balance	-38.4	Aid given	4.00
– as % of GDP	-2.9	– as % of GDP	0.30
Capital balance	50.1		

Health and education

Health spending, % of GDP	10.9	Education spending, % of GDP	4.9
Doctors per 1,000 pop.	1.9	Enrolment, %: primary	98
Hospital beds per 1,000 pop.	3.4	secondary	101
Improved-water source access,		tertiary	62
% of pop.	100		

Society

No. of households	12.9m	Colour TVs per 100 households	98.8
Av. no. per household	2.6	Telephone lines per 100 pop.	52.5
Marriages per 1,000 pop.	4.5	Mobile telephone subscribers	
Divorces per 1,000 pop.	2.1	per 100 pop.	70.9
Cost of living, Dec. 2010		Broadband subs per 100 pop.	30.6
New York = 100	104	Internet hosts per 1,000 pop.	229.3

a Including freshwater.

CHILE

Area	756,945 sq km	Capital	Santiago
Arable as % of total land	2	Currency	Chilean peso (Ps)

People

Population	17.0m	Life expectancy:	men	76.2 yrs
Pop. per sq km	22.6		women	82.3 yrs
Av. ann. growth		Adult literacy		98.6%
in pop. 2010–15	0.97%	Fertility rate (per woman)		1.9
Pop. under 15	22.3%	Urban population		89.0%
Pop. over 60	13.2%			per 1,000 pop.
No. of men per 100 women	97.8	Crude birth rate		14.7
Human Development Index	78.3	Crude death rate		5.8

The economy

GDP	91.6trn pesos	GDP per head	$9,640
GDP	$164bn	GDP per head in purchasing	
Av. ann. growth in real		power parity (USA=100)	31.1
GDP 2004–09	3.3%	Economic freedom index	77.4

Origins of GDP

	% of total
Agriculture	3
Industry, of which:	42
manufacturing	13
Services	55

Components of GDP

	% of total
Private consumption	60
Public consumption	13
Investment	19
Exports	38
Imports	-30

Structure of employment

	% of total		% of labour force
Agriculture	12	Unemployed 2009	9.7
Industry	23	Av. ann. rate 1995–2009	7.8
Services	65		

Energy

	m TOE		
Total output	9.0	Net energy imports as %	
Total consumption	31.4	of energy use	71
Consumption per head,			
kg oil equivalent	1,871		

Inflation and finance

		av. ann. increase 2004–09	
Consumer price			
inflation 2010	1.4%	Narrow money (M1)	14.7%
Av. ann. inflation 2005–10	3.8%	Broad money	12.0%
Money market rate, 2010	1.40%		

Exchange rates

	end 2010		2010
Ps per $	468.37	Effective rates	2005 = 100
Ps per SDR	721.30	– nominal	110.9
Ps per €	625.84	– real	111.1

Trade

Principal exports		Principal imports	
	$bn fob		*$bn cif*
Copper	27.5	Intermediate goods	23.0
Fresh fruit	3.0	Consumer goods	8.7
Paper products	2.6	Capital goods	6.9
Total incl. others	**54.0**	Total incl. others	**42.6**

Main export destinations		Main origins of imports	
	% of total		*% of total*
China	23.1	United States	16.7
United States	11.2	China	11.7
Japan	9.2	Argentina	10.8
South Korea	5.8	Brazil	6.7
Brazil	5.0	South Korea	5.0

Balance of payments, reserves and debt, $bn

Visible exports fob	53.7	Change in reserves	2.2
Visible imports fob	-39.8	Level of reserves	
Trade balance	14.0	end Dec.	25.3
Invisibles inflows	13.9	No. months of import cover	4.7
Invisibles outflows	-25.2	Official gold holdings, m oz	0.0
Net transfers	1.6	Foreign debt	71.6
Current account balance	4.2	– as % of GDP	43
– as % of GDP	2.6	– as % of total exports	84
Capital balance	-2.5	Debt service ratio	23
Overall balance	1.6		

Health and education

Health spending, % of GDP	8.2	Education spending, % of GDP	4.0
Doctors per 1,000 pop.	1.0	Enrolment, %: primary	106
Hospital beds per 1,000 pop.	2.3	secondary	90
Improved-water source access,		tertiary	55
% of pop.	96		

Society

No. of households	4.7m	Colour TVs per 100 households	95.3
Av. no. per household	3.6	Telephone lines per 100 pop.	21.1
Marriages per 1,000 pop.	3.2	Mobile telephone subscribers	
Divorces per 1,000 pop.	0.5	per 100 pop.	96.9
Cost of living, Dec. 2010		Broadband subs per 100 pop.	9.6
New York = 100	80	Internet hosts per 1,000 pop.	86.1

CHINA

Area	9,560,900 sq km	Capital	Beijing
Arable as % of total land	15	Currency	Yuan

People

Population	1,345.8m	Life expectancy: men		72.3 yrs
Pop. per sq km	139.8	women		75.9 yrs
Av. ann. growth		Adult literacy		93.7%
in pop. 2010–15	0.51%	Fertility rate (per woman)		1.6
Pop. under 15	19.9%	Urban population		47.0%
Pop. over 60	12.3%		per 1,000 pop.	
No. of men per 100 women	108.0	Crude birth rate		12.6
Human Development Index	66.3	Crude death rate		7.3

The economy

GDP	Yuan34.1trn	GDP per head	$3,740
GDP	$4,986bn	GDP per head in purchasing	
Av. ann. growth in real		power parity (USA=100)	14.9
GDP 2004–09	11.4%	Economic freedom index	52.0

Origins of GDP

	% of total
Agriculture	10
Industry, of which:	46
manufacturing	34
Services	43

Components of GDP

	% of total
Private consumption	34
Public consumption	13
Investment	48
Exports	27
Imports	-22

Structure of employment

	% of total		% of labour force
Agriculture	41	Unemployed 2009	4.3
Industry	25	Av. ann. rate 1995–2009	3.7
Services	34		

Energy

	m TOE		
Total output	1,993.3	Net energy imports as %	
Total consumption	2,116.4	of energy use	6
Consumption per head,			
kg oil equivalent	1,598		

Inflation and finance

		av. ann. increase 2004–09	
Consumer price			
inflation 2010	3.3%	Narrow money (M1)	18.2%
Av. ann. inflation 2005–10	2.9%	Broad money	20.3%
Deposit rate, 2010	2.75%		

Exchange rates

	end 2010		2010
Yuan per $	6.62	Effective rates	2005 = 100
Yuan per SDR	10.20	– nominal	113.8
Yuan per €	8.85	– real	121.4

Trade

Principal exports		Principal imports	
	$bn fob		$bn cif
Telecoms equipment	159.1	Electrical machinery	198.8
Office machinery	147.0	Petroleum & products	108.6
Electrical goods	134.1	Metal ores & scrap	85.0
Clothing & apparel	107.3	Professional instruments	55.2
Total incl. others	**1,201.6**	Total incl. others	**1,006.1**

Main export destinations		Main origins of imports	
	% of total		% of total
United States	18.4	Japan	13.0
Hong Kong	13.8	South Korea	10.2
Japan	8.2	Taiwan	8.5
South Korea	4.5	United States	7.7
EU27	19.7	EU27	12.7

Balance of payments, reserves and debt, $bn

Visible exports fob	1,204	Change in reserves	487
Visible imports fob	-954	Level of reserves	
Trade balance	250	end Dec.	2,453
Invisibles inflows	233	No. months of import cover	25.0
Invisibles outflows	-224	Official gold holdings, m oz	33.9
Net transfers	34	Foreign debt	428.4
Current account balance	297	– as % of GDP	9
– as % of GDP	6.0	– as % of total exports	25
Capital balance	147	Debt service ratio	3
Overall balance	401		

Health and education

Health spending, % of GDP	4.6	Education spending, % of GDP	2.1
Doctors per 1,000 pop.	1.0	Enrolment, %: primary	113
Hospital beds per 1,000 pop.	2.9	secondary	78
Improved-water source access,		tertiary	25
% of pop.	89		

Society

No. of households	389m	Colour TVs per 100 households	96.5
Av. no. per household	3.4	Telephone lines per 100 pop.	23.3
Marriages per 1,000 pop.	5.7	Mobile telephone subscribers	
Divorces per 1,000 pop.	1.6	per 100 pop.	55.5
Cost of living, Dec. 2010		Broadband subs per 100 pop.	7.7
New York = 100	88	Internet hosts per 1,000 pop.	13.3

Note: Data excludes Special Administrative Regions ie, Hong Kong and Macau.

COLOMBIA

Area	1,141,748 sq km	Capital	Bogota
Arable as % of total land	2	Currency	Colombian peso (peso)

People

Population	45.7m	Life expectancy: men	70.4 yrs
Pop. per sq km	40.6	women	77.7 yrs
Av. ann. growth		Adult literacy	93.2%
in pop. 2010–15	1.46%	Fertility rate (per woman)	2.5
Pop. under 15	28.6%	Urban population	75.1%
Pop. over 60	8.6%		per 1,000 pop.
No. of men per 100 women	96.8	Crude birth rate	20.6
Human Development Index	68.9	Crude death rate	5.6

The economy

GDP	505trn pesos	GDP per head	$5,130
GDP	$234bn	GDP per head in purchasing	
Av. ann. growth in real		power parity (USA=100)	19.5
GDP 2004–09	4.6%	Economic freedom index	68.0

Origins of GDP		Components of GDP	
	% of total		% of total
Agriculture	7	Private consumption	64
Industry, of which:	34	Public consumption	16
manufacturing	14	Investment	23
Services	58	Exports	16
		Imports	-18

Structure of employment

	% of total		% of labour force
Agriculture	18	Unemployed 2009	12
Industry	20	Av. ann. rate 1995–2009	13
Services	62		

Energy

	m TOE		
Total output	93.6	Net energy imports as %	
Total consumption	30.8	of energy use	-204
Consumption per head,			
kg oil equivalent	684		

Inflation and finance

Consumer price		av. ann. increase 2004–09	
inflation 2010	2.3%	Narrow money (M1)	12.6%
Av. ann. inflation 2005–10	4.7%	Broad money	15.8%
Money market rate, 2010	3.15%		

Exchange rates

	end 2010		2010
Peso per $	1,990	Effective rates	2005 = 100
Peso per SDR	3,065	– nominal	112.0
Peso per €	2,659	– real	122.2

Trade

Principal exports		Principal imports	
	$bn fob		*$bn cif*
Petroleum & products	10.3	Intermediate goods &	
Coal	5.4	raw materials	13.2
Coffee	1.5	Capital goods	13.0
Nickel	0.7	Consumer goods	6.7
Total incl. others	**32.9**	Total	**32.9**

Main export destinations		Main origins of imports	
	% of total		*% of total*
United States	40.2	United States	28.9
Venezuela	12.3	China	11.3
Netherlands	4.1	Mexico	7.0
Ecuador	3.8	Brazil	6.5

Balance of payments, reserves and debt, $bn

Visible exports fob	34.0	Change in reserves	1.3
Visible imports fob	-31.5	Level of reserves	
Trade balance	2.5	end Dec.	25.0
Invisibles inflows	5.5	No. months of import cover	6.1
Invisibles outflows	-17.7	Official gold holdings, m oz	0.2
Net transfers	4.6	Foreign debt	52.2
Current account balance	-5.0	– as % of GDP	20
– as % of GDP	-2.1	– as % of total exports	111
Capital balance	6.4	Debt service ratio	23
Overall balance	1.4		

Health and education

Health spending, % of GDP	6.4	Education spending, % of GDP	4.8
Doctors per 1,000 pop.	1.3	Enrolment, %: primary	120
Hospital beds per 1,000 pop.	1.0	secondary	95
Improved-water source access,		tertiary	37
% of pop.	92		

Society

No. of households	12.0m	Colour TVs per 100 households	81.4
Av. no. per household	3.8	Telephone lines per 100 pop.	16.4
Marriages per 1,000 pop.	1.7	Mobile telephone subscribers	
Divorces per 1,000 pop.	...	per 100 pop.	92.3
Cost of living, Dec. 2010		Broadband subs per 100 pop.	4.4
New York = 100	95	Internet hosts per 1,000 pop.	65.9

CÔTE D'IVOIRE

Area	322,463 sq km	Capital	Abidjan/Yamoussoukro
Arable as % of total land	9	Currency	CFA franc (CFAfr)

People

Population	21.1m	Life expectancy:	men	58.4 yrs
Pop. per sq km	61.2		women	61.0 yrs
Av. ann. growth		Adult literacy		55.3%
in pop. 2010–15	1.82%	Fertility rate (per woman)		4.7
Pop. under 15	40.4%	Urban population		50.6%
Pop. over 60	6.1%			per 1,000 pop.
No. of men per 100 women	103.9	Crude birth rate		35.0
Human Development Index	39.7	Crude death rate		9.8

The economy

GDP	CFAfr11,004bn	GDP per head	$1,110
GDP	$23.3bn	GDP per head in purchasing	
Av. ann. growth in real		power parity (USA=100)	3.7
GDP 2004–09	2.1%	Economic freedom index	55.4

Origins of GDP		Components of GDP	
	% of total		% of total
Agriculture	24	Private consumption	72
Industry, of which:	25	Public consumption	9
manufacturing	18	Investment	11
Services	50	Exports	42
		Imports	-34

Structure of employment

	% of total		% of labour force
Agriculture	...	Unemployed 2008	...
Industry	...	Av. ann. rate 1995–2008	...
Services	...		

Energy

	m TOE		
Total output	11.4	Net energy imports as %	
Total consumption	10.3	of energy use	-11
Consumption per head,			
kg oil equivalent	499		

Inflation and finance

Consumer price			av. ann. change 2004–09
inflation 2009	1.0%	Narrow money (M1)	12.5%
Av. ann. inflation 2005–09	2.9%	Broad money	12.7%
Money market rate, 2010	3.31%		

Exchange rates

	end 2010		2010
CFAfr per $	490.91	Effective rates	2005 = 100
CFAfr per SDR	756.02	– nominal	99.0
CFAfr per €	655.95	– real	99.2

Trade

Principal exports[a]	$bn fob	Principal imports[a]	$bn cif
Petroleum products	4.0	Fuel & lubricants	2.7
Cocoa beans & products	2.8	Capital equipment	
Timber	0.4	& raw materials	2.4
Coffee & products	0.2	Foodstuffs	1.3
Total incl. others	**10.4**	Total incl. others	**7.7**

Main export destinations	% of total	Main origins of imports	% of total
Netherlands	13.9	Nigeria	20.7
France	10.7	France	14.2
United States	7.8	China	7.2
Germany	7.2	Thailand	5.1
Nigeria	7.0	United States	3.3

Balance of payments, reserves and debt, $bn

Visible exports fob	10.5	Change in reserves	1.0
Visible imports fob	-6.3	Level of reserves	
Trade balance	4.2	end Dec.	3.3
Invisibles inflows	1.2	No. months of import cover	4.0
Invisibles outflows	-3.6	Official gold holdings, m oz	0.0
Net transfers	-0.1	Foreign debt	11.7
Current account balance	1.7	– as % of GDP	46
– as % of GDP	7.2	– as % of total exports	88
Capital balance	-0.7	Debt service ratio	10
Overall balance	1.0		

Health and education

Health spending, % of GDP	5.1	Education spending, % of GDP	4.6
Doctors per 1,000 pop.	0.1	Enrolment, %: primary	74
Hospital beds per 1,000 pop.	0.4	secondary	25
Improved-water source access,		tertiary	8
% of pop.	80		

Society

No. of households	3.9m	Colour TVs per 100 households	...
Av. no. per household	5.4	Telephone lines per 100 pop.	1.3
Marriages per 1,000 pop.	...	Mobile telephone subscribers	
Divorces per 1,000 pop.	...	per 100 pop.	62.6
Cost of living, Dec. 2010		Broadband subs per 100 pop.	0.1
New York = 100	74	Internet hosts per 1,000 pop.	0.4

a 2008

CZECH REPUBLIC

Area	78,864 sq km	Capital	Prague
Arable as % of total land	39	Currency	Koruna (Kc)

People

Population	10.4m	Life expectancy: men	74.3 yrs
Pop. per sq km	133.0	women	80.3 yrs
Av. ann. growth		Adult literacy	...
in pop. 2010–15	0.53%	Fertility rate (per woman)	1.4
Pop. under 15	14.1%	Urban population	73.5%
Pop. over 60	22.2%		per 1,000 pop.
No. of men per 100 women	96.3	Crude birth rate	10.7
Human Development Index	84.1	Crude death rate	10.9

The economy

GDP	Kc3,627bn	GDP per head	$18,140
GDP	$190bn	GDP per head in purchasing	
Av. ann. growth in real		power parity (USA=100)	55.6
GDP 2004–09	3.4%	Economic freedom index	70.4

Origins of GDP

Components of GDP

	% of total		% of total
Agriculture	2	Private consumption	51
Industry, of which:	37	Public consumption	22
manufacturing	23	Investment	22
Services	61	Exports	70
		Imports	-64

Structure of employment

	% of total		% of labour force
Agriculture	3	Unemployed 2009	6.7
Industry	41	Av. ann. rate 1995–2009	6.6
Services	56		

Energy

	m TOE		
Total output	32.8	Net energy imports as %	
Total consumption	44.6	of energy use	26
Consumption per head,			
kg oil equivalent	4,282		

Inflation and finance

Consumer price		av. ann. increase 2004–09	
inflation 2010	1.4%	Narrow money (M1)	11.5%
Av. ann. inflation 2005–10	2.8%	Broad money	10.6%
Money market rate, 2010	1.22%	Household saving rate, 2010	1.6%

Exchange rates

	end 2010		2010
Kc per $	18.75	Effective rates	2005 = 100
Kc per SDR	28.88	– nominal	118.6
Kc per €	25.05	– real	121.4

Trade

Principal exports		Principal imports	
	$bn fob		*$bn cif*
Machinery & transport equipment	59.9	Machinery & transport equipment	35.3
Semi-manufactures	20.4	Semi-manufactures	15.5
Chemicals	7.1	Raw materials & fuels	10.0
Raw materials & fuels	7.1	Chemicals	9.7
Total incl. others	**113.2**	Total incl. others	**105.3**

Main export destinations		Main origins of imports	
	% of total		*% of total*
Germany	32.4	Germany	30.6
Slovakia	8.8	Poland	6.9
Poland	5.8	Slovakia	6.7
France	5.7	Netherlands	6.0
EU27	84.7	EU27	78.0

Balance of payments, reserves and debt, $bn

Visible exports fob	112.6	Change in reserves	4.6
Visible imports fob	-103.1	Level of reserves	
Trade balance	9.5	end Dec.	41.6
Invisibles inflows	25.2	No. months of import cover	3.6
Invisibles outflows	-36.1	Official gold holdings, m oz	0.4
Net transfers	-0.8	Foreign debt	57.0
Current account balance	-2.1	– as % of GDP	43
– as % of GDP	-1.1	– as % of total exports	62
Capital balance	8.7	Debt service ratio	14
Overall balance	4.3	Aid given	0.21
		– as % of GDP	0.12

Health and education

Health spending, % of GDP	7.6	Education spending, % of GDP	4.4
Doctors per 1,000 pop.	3.6	Enrolment, %: primary	103
Hospital beds per 1,000 pop.	7.9	secondary	95
Improved-water source access,		tertiary	58
% of pop.	100		

Society

No. of households	4.5m	Colour TVs per 100 households	98.4
Av. no. per household	2.3	Telephone lines per 100 pop.	20.4
Marriages per 1,000 pop.	5.0	Mobile telephone subscribers	
Divorces per 1,000 pop.	3.4	per 100 pop.	137.5
Cost of living, Dec. 2010		Broadband subs per 100 pop.	13.2
New York = 100	93	Internet hosts per 1,000 pop.	368.4

DENMARK

Area	43,075 sq km	Capital	Copenhagen
Arable as % of total land	54	Currency	Danish krone (DKr)

People

Population	5.5m	Life expectancy: men	76.7 yrs
Pop. per sq km	128.8	women	81.4 yrs
Av. ann. growth		Adult literacy	...
in pop. 2010–15	0.48%	Fertility rate (per woman)	1.9
Pop. under 15	18.0%	Urban population	86.9%
Pop. over 60	23.4%		per 1,000 pop.
No. of men per 100 women	98.3	Crude birth rate	11.8
Human Development Index	86.6	Crude death rate	10.4

The economy

GDP	DKr1,660bn	GDP per head	$55,990
GDP	$310bn	GDP per head in purchasing	
Av. ann. growth in real		power parity (USA=100)	82.0
GDP 2004–09	0.2%	Economic freedom index	78.6

Origins of GDP

	% of total
Agriculture	1
Industry, of which:	22
manufacturing	13
Services	77

Components of GDP

	% of total
Private consumption	49
Public consumption	30
Investment	17
Exports	48
Imports	-44

Structure of employment

	% of total		% of labour force
Agriculture	3	Unemployed 2009	6
Industry	23	Av. ann. rate 1995–2009	5.1
Services	74		

Energy

	m TOE		
Total output	26.6	Net energy imports as %	
Total consumption	19.0	of energy use	-40
Consumption per head,			
kg oil equivalent	3,460		

Inflation and finance

Consumer price		av. ann. increase 2004–09	
inflation 2010	2.3%	Narrow money (M1)	8.9%
Av. ann. inflation 2005–10	2.1%	Broad money	11.0%
Money market rate, 2010	0.70%	Household saving rate, 2010	-1.2%

Exchange rates

	end 2010		2010
DKr per $	5.61	Effective rates	2005 = 100
DKr per SDR	8.65	– nominal	100.7
DKr per €	7.50	– real	100.7

Trade

Principal exports		Principal imports	
	$bn fob		*$bn cif*
Machinery & transport equip.	22.9	Machinery & transport equip.	27.1
Food, drinks & tobacco	17.4	Food, drinks & tobacco	10.6
Chemicals & related products	13.7	Chemicals & related products	9.4
Minerals, fuels & lubricants	8.2	Minerals, fuels & lubricants	5.2
Total incl. others	**92.8**	Total incl. others	**81.9**

Main export destinations		Main origins of imports	
	% of total		*% of total*
Germany	17.7	Germany	21.2
Sweden	12.9	Sweden	13.2
United Kingdom	8.6	Norway	7.1
United States	6.1	Netherlands	7.0
Norway	6.0	China	6.3
EU27	67.5	EU27	69.7

Balance of payments, reserves and aid, $bn

Visible exports fob	91.9	Overall balance	33.7
Visible imports fob	-83.8	Change in reserves	34.3
Trade balance	8.1	Level of reserves	
Invisibles inflows	81.4	end Dec.	76.6
Invisibles outflows	-73.1	No. months of import cover	5.9
Net transfers	-5.2	Official gold holdings, m oz	2.1
Current account balance	11.2	Aid given	2.81
– as % of GDP	3.6	– as % of GDP	0.88
Capital balance	25.9		

Health and education

Health spending, % of GDP	11.2	Education spending, % of GDP	7.8
Doctors per 1,000 pop.	3.4	Enrolment, %: primary	99
Hospital beds per 1,000 pop.	3.4	secondary	119
Improved-water source access,		tertiary	78
% of pop.	100		

Society

No. of households	2.6m	Colour TVs per 100 households	98.2
Av. no. per household	2.2	Telephone lines per 100 pop.	37.7
Marriages per 1,000 pop.	6.8	Mobile telephone subscribers	
Divorces per 1,000 pop.	3.1	per 100 pop.	125.0
Cost of living, Dec. 2010		Broadband subs per 100 pop.	37.9
New York = 100	125	Internet hosts per 1,000 pop.	757.9

EGYPT

Area	1,000,250 sq km	Capital	Cairo
Arable as % of total land	3	Currency	Egyptian pound (£E)

People

Population	83.0m	Life expectancy: men	69.3 yrs
Pop. per sq km	81.0	women	73.0 yrs
Av. ann. growth		Adult literacy	66.4%
in pop. 2010–15	1.78%	Fertility rate (per woman)	2.9
Pop. under 15	32.1%	Urban population	43.4%
Pop. over 60	7.5%		per 1,000 pop.
No. of men per 100 women	100.9	Crude birth rate	23.9
Human Development Index	62.0	Crude death rate	5.7

The economy

GDP	£E1,039bn	GDP per head	$2,270
GDP	$188bn	GDP per head in purchasing	
Av. ann. growth in real		power parity (USA=100)	12.3
GDP 2004–09	6.0%	Economic freedom index	59.1

Origins of GDP		Components of GDPa	
	% of total		% of total
Agriculture	14	Private consumption	76
Industry, of which:	37	Public consumption	11
manufacturing	16	Investment	19
Services	49	Exports	25
		Imports	-32

Structure of employment

	% of total		% of labour force
Agriculture	31	Unemployed 2009	9.4
Industry	22	Av. ann. rate 1995–2009	9.7
Services	47		

Energy

	m TOE		
Total output	87.5	Net energy imports as %	
Total consumption	70.7	of energy use	-24
Consumption per head,			
kg oil equivalent	867		

Inflation and finance

Consumer price		av. ann. increase 2004–09	
inflation 2010	11.3%	Narrow money (M1)	18.7%
Av. ann. inflation 2005–10	11.6%	Broad money	13.1%
Treasury bill rate, 2010	9.28%		

Exchange rates

	end 2010		2010
£E per $	5.79	Effective rates	2005 = 100
£E per SDR	8.92	– nominal	...
£E per €	7.74	– real	...

Trade

Principal exports[a]		Principal imports[a]	
	$bn fob		$bn fob
Petroleum & products	11.4	Intermediate goods	16.7
Finished goods incl. textiles	10.6	Capital goods	10.3
Semi-finished products	1.9	Consumer goods	9.6
Raw materials	0.9	Fuels	4.9
Total incl. others	**25.2**	Total incl. others	**50.3**

Main export destinations		Main origins of imports	
	% of total		% of total
Spain	6.8	United States	10.6
Italy	6.7	China	8.7
United States	6.3	Germany	8.0
India	6.1	Italy	5.9

Balance of payments, reserves and debt, $bn

Visible exports fob	23.1	Change in reserves	0.6
Visible imports fob	-39.9	Level of reserves	
Trade balance	-16.8	end Dec.	34.9
Invisibles inflows	22.5	No. months of import cover	7.4
Invisibles outflows	-17.0	Official gold holdings, m oz	2.4
Net transfers	8.0	Foreign debt	33.3
Current account balance	-3.3	– as % of GDP	16
– as % of GDP	-1.8	– as % of total exports	53
Capital balance	1.3	Debt service ratio	7
Overall balance	-1.6		

Health and education

Health spending, % of GDP	5.0	Education spending, % of GDP	3.8
Doctors per 1,000 pop.	2.7	Enrolment, %: primary	100
Hospital beds per 1,000 pop.	2.1	secondary	79
Improved-water source access, % of pop.	99	tertiary	28

Society

No. of households	18.9m	Colour TVs per 100 households	90.1
Av. no. per household	4.1	Telephone lines per 100 pop.	12.4
Marriages per 1,000 pop.	6.2	Mobile telephone subscribers	
Divorces per 1,000 pop.	0.6	per 100 pop.	66.7
Cost of living, Dec. 2010		Broadband subs per 100 pop.	1.3
New York – 100	73	Internet hosts per 1,000 pop.	9.7

a Year ending June 30, 2009.

ESTONIA

Area	45,200 sq km	Capital	Tallinn
Arable as % of total land	14	Currency	Kroon (EEK)/Euro (€)[a]

People

Population	1.3m	Life expectancy: men	68.9 yrs
Pop. per sq km	29.7	women	79.3 yrs
Av. ann. growth		Adult literacy	99.8%
in pop. 2010–15	-0.07%	Fertility rate (per woman)	1.6
Pop. under 15	15.4%	Urban population	69.5%
Pop. over 60	22.6%		per 1,000 pop.
No. of men per 100 women	85.5	Crude birth rate	11.7
Human Development Index	81.2	Crude death rate	13.0

The economy

GDP	EEK215bn	GDP per head	$14,240
GDP	$19.1bn	GDP per head in purchasing	
Av. ann. growth in real		power parity (USA=100)	42.8
GDP 2004–09	1.1%	Economic freedom index	75.2

Origins of GDP		**Components of GDP**	
	% of total		% of total
Agriculture	3	Private consumption	53
Industry, of which:	29	Public consumption	22
manufacturing	17	Investment	19
Services	68	Exports	71
		Imports	-65

Structure of employment

	% of total		% of labour force
Agriculture	4	Unemployed 2009	13.7
Industry	36	Av. ann. rate 1995–2009	9.7
Services	60		

Energy

	m TOE		
Total output	4.2	Net energy imports as %	
Total consumption	5.4	of energy use	22
Consumption per head,			
kg oil equivalent	4,026		

Inflation and finance

Consumer price		av. ann. increase 2004–09	
inflation 2010	3.0%	Narrow money (M1)	9.2%
Av. ann. inflation 2005–10	4.8%	Broad money	16.6%
Money market rate, 2010	1.57%	Household saving rate, 2010	6.4%

Exchange rates

	end 2010		2010
EEK per $	11.71	Effective rates	2005 = 100
EEK per SDR	18.03	– nominal	...
EEK per €	15.65	– real	...

Trade

Principal exports		Principal imports	
	$bn fob		$bn cif
Machinery & equipment	1.8	Machinery & equipment	1.9
Mineral products	1.5	Mineral products	2.0
Wood & paper	1.1	Chemicals	1.5
Non-precious metals & products	0.8	Transport equipment	0.6
Total incl. others	**9.0**	Total incl. others	**10.1**

Main export destinations		Main origins of imports	
	% of total		% of total
Finland	18.4	Finland	14.4
Sweden	12.5	Lithuania	10.9
Latvia	9.7	Germany	10.4
Russia	9.3	Latvia	10.2
Germany	6.0	Russia	8.8
EU27	69.5	EU27	80.3

Balance of payments, reserves and debt, $bn

Visible exports fob	9.1	Change in reserves	0.0
Visible imports fob	-9.9	Level of reserves	
Trade balance	-0.8	end Dec.	4.0
Invisibles inflows	5.4	No. months of import cover	3.4
Invisibles outflows	-4.0	Official gold holdings, m oz	0.0
Net transfers	0.3	Foreign debt	17.0
Current account balance	0.9	– as % of GDP	128
– as % of GDP	4.7	– as % of total exports	171
Capital balance	-0.7	Debt service ratio	23
Overall balance	0.0		

Health and education

Health spending, % of GDP	7.0	Education spending, % of GDP	4.8
Doctors per 1,000 pop.	3.5	Enrolment, %: primary	100
Hospital beds per 1,000 pop.	5.6	secondary	99
Improved-water source access,		tertiary	65
% of pop.	98		

Society

No. of households	0.6m	Colour TVs per 100 households	97.4
Av. no. per household	2.3	Telephone lines per 100 pop.	36.8
Marriages per 1,000 pop.	4.6	Mobile telephone subscribers	
Divorces per 1,000 pop.	3.2	per 100 pop.	117.2
Cost of living, Dec. 2010		Broadband subs per 100 pop.	22.5
New York = 100	...	Internet hosts per 1,000 pop.	623.9

---

a Estonia joined the Euro area on January 1, 2011.

FINLAND

Area	338,145 sq km	Capital	Helsinki
Arable as % of total land	7	Currency	Euro (€)

People

Population	5.3m	Life expectancy: men	77.2 yrs
Pop. per sq km	15.9	women	83.6 yrs
Av. ann. growth		Adult literacy	...
in pop. 2010–15	0.45%	Fertility rate (per woman)	1.8
Pop. under 15	16.6%	Urban population	85.1%
Pop. over 60	24.7%		per 1,000 pop.
No. of men per 100 women	96.3	Crude birth rate	11.2
Human Development Index	87.1	Crude death rate	9.7

The economy

GDP	€171bn	GDP per head	$44,580
GDP	$238bn	GDP per head in purchasing	
Av. ann. growth in real		power parity (USA=100)	76.7
GDP 2004–09	1.0%	Economic freedom index	74.0

Origins of GDP		Components of GDP	
	% of total		% of total
Agriculture	3	Private consumption	54
Industry, of which:	28	Public consumption	25
manuf., mining & utilities	18	Investment	18
Services	69	Exports	37
		Imports	-35

Structure of employment

	% of total		% of labour force
Agriculture	5	Unemployed 2009	8.2
Industry	25	Av. ann. rate 1995–2009	9.8
Services	70		

Energy

	m TOE		
Total output	16.6	Net energy imports as %	
Total consumption	35.3	of energy use	53
Consumption per head,			
kg oil equivalent	6,635		

Inflation and finance

Consumer price		av. ann. increase 2004–09	
inflation 2010	1.2%	Euro area:	
Av. ann. inflation 2005–10	1.9%	Narrow money (M1)	9.0%
Money market rate, 2010	0.81%	Broad money	7.3%
		Household saving rate, 2010	4.3%

Exchange rates

	end 2010		2010
€ per $	0.75	Effective rates	2005 = 100
€ per SDR	1.15	– nominal	100.0
		– real	97.2

Trade

Principal exports		Principal imports	
	$bn fob		*$bn cif*
Machinery & transport equipment	25.1	Machinery & transport equipment	20.2
Chemicals & related products	4.8	Minerals & fuels	9.9
Mineral fuels & lubricants	4.0	Chemicals & related products	6.7
Raw materials	2.9	Food, drink & tobacco	4.2
Total incl. others	62.9	Total incl. others	60.8

Main export destinations		Main origins of imports	
	% of total		*% of total*
Germany	10.3	Russia	16.2
Sweden	9.8	Germany	15.8
Russia	8.9	Sweden	14.7
United States	7.9	Netherlands	7.0
Netherlands	5.9	China	5.3
United Kingdom	5.2	France	4.2
EU27	55.6	EU27	65.0

Balance of payments, reserves and aid, $bn

Visible exports fob	62.9	Overall balance	2.5
Visible imports fob	-58.1	Change in reserves	3.1
Trade balance	4.8	Level of reserves	
Invisibles inflows	43.0	end Dec.	11.4
Invisibles outflows	-38.7	No. months of import cover	1.4
Net transfers	-2.3	Official gold holdings, m oz	1.6
Current account balance	6.8	Aid given	1.29
– as % of GDP	2.9	– as % of GDP	0.54
Capital balance	17.9		

Health and education

Health spending, % of GDP	9.7	Education spending, % of GDP	5.9
Doctors per 1,000 pop.	2.7	Enrolment, %: primary	97
Hospital beds per 1,000 pop.	6.7	secondary	110
Improved-water source access,		tertiary	94
% of pop.	100		

Society

No. of households	2.5m	Colour TVs per 100 households	95.2
Av. no. per household	2.1	Telephone lines per 100 pop.	26.9
Marriages per 1,000 pop.	5.8	Mobile telephone subscribers	
Divorces per 1,000 pop.	2.5	per 100 pop.	144.6
Cost of living, Dec. 2010		Broadband subs per 100 pop.	28.8
New York = 100	118	Internet hosts per 1,000 pop.	845.4

FRANCE

Area	543,965 sq km	Capital	Paris
Arable as % of total land	34	Currency	Euro (€)

People

Population	62.3m	Life expectancy: men	78.6 yrs
Pop. per sq km	113.8	women	85.1 yrs
Av. ann. growth		Adult literacy	...
in pop. 2010–15	0.58%	Fertility rate (per woman)	2.0
Pop. under 15	18.4%	Urban population	85.3%
Pop. over 60	23.2%		per 1,000 pop.
No. of men per 100 women	94.8	Crude birth rate	12.8
Human Development Index	87.2	Crude death rate	9.0

The economy

GDP	€1,907bn	GDP per head	$41,050
GDP	$2,649bn	GDP per head in purchasing	
Av. ann. growth in real		power parity (USA=100)	73.2
GDP 2004–09	0.8%	Economic freedom index	64.6

Origins of GDP		Components of GDP	
	% of total		% of total
Agriculture	2	Private consumption	58
Industry, of which:	19	Public consumption	25
manufacturing	11	Investment	19
Services	79	Exports	23
		Imports	-25

Structure of employment

	% of total		% of labour force
Agriculture	3	Unemployed 2009	9.1
Industry	23	Av. ann. rate 1995–2009	9.8
Services	74		

Energy

	m TOE		
Total output	136.6	Net energy imports as %	
Total consumption	266.5	of energy use	49
Consumption per head,			
kg oil equivalent	4,279		

Inflation and finance

		av. ann. increase 2004–09	
Consumer price			
inflation 2010	1.5%	Euro area:	
Av. ann. inflation 2005–10	1.5%	Narrow money (M1)	9.0%
Treasury bill rate, 2010	0.38%	Broad money	7.3%
		Household saving rate[a], 2010	16.0%

Exchange rates

	end 2010		2010
€ per $	0.75	Effective rates	2005 = 100
€ per SDR	1.15	– nominal	100.8
		– real	97.3

Trade

Principal exports		Principal imports	
	$bn fob		*$bn cif*
Machinery & transport equip.	178.9	Machinery & transport equip.	188.5
Chemicals & related products	91.1	Mineral fuels & lubricants	77.2
Food, drink & tobacco	55.4	Chemicals & related products	70.5
Mineral fuels & lubricants	18.5	Food, drink & tobacco	46.6
Raw materials	10.6	Raw materials	13.8
Total incl. others	**474.8**	Total incl. others	**556.6**

Main export destinations		Main origins of imports	
	% of total		*% of total*
Germany	16.2	Germany	19.5
Italy	8.3	Belgium	11.7
Spain	7.9	Italy	8.0
Belgium	7.6	Netherlands	7.2
United Kingdom	7.2	Spain	6.7
United States	5.8	United Kingdom	4.9
EU27	62.1	EU27	69.2

Balance of payments, reserves and aid, $bn

Visible exports fob	473.9	Overall balance	9.4
Visible imports fob	-535.8	Change in reserves	28.5
Trade balance	-62.0	Level of reserves	
Invisibles inflows	341.3	end Dec.	131.8
Invisibles outflows	-293.4	No. months of import cover	1.9
Net transfers	-37.8	Official gold holdings, m oz	78.3
Current account balance	-51.9	Aid given	12.60
– as % of GDP	-2.0	– as % of GDP	0.47
Capital balance	93.6		

Health and education

Health spending, % of GDP	11.7	Education spending, % of GDP	5.6
Doctors per 1,000 pop.	3.4	Enrolment, %: primary	110
Hospital beds per 1,000 pop.	7.0	secondary	113
Improved-water source access,		tertiary	55
% of pop.	100		

Society

No. of households	26.9m	Colour TVs per 100 households	97.7
Av. no. per household	2.3	Telephone lines per 100 pop.	56.9
Marriages per 1,000 pop.	3.9	Mobile telephone subscribers	
Divorces per 1,000 pop.	2.3	per 100 pop.	95.5
Cost of living, Dec. 2010		Broadband subs per 100 pop.	31.6
New York = 100	137	Internet hosts per 1,000 pop.	249.6

a Gross.

GERMANY

Area	357,868 sq km	Capital	Berlin
Arable as % of total land	34	Currency	Euro (€)

People

Population	82.2m	Life expectancy: men	77.8 yrs
Pop. per sq km	230.5	women	83.1 yrs
Av. ann. growth		Adult literacy	...
in pop. 2010–15	-0.06%	Fertility rate (per woman)	1.4
Pop. under 15	13.4%	Urban population	73.8%
Pop. over 60	26.0%		per 1,000 pop.
No. of men per 100 women	96.1	Crude birth rate	8.4
Human Development Index	88.5	Crude death rate	11.0

The economy

GDP	€2,397bn	GDP per head	$40,670
GDP	$3,330bn	GDP per head in purchasing	
Av. ann. growth in real		power parity (USA=100)	79.0
GDP 2004–09	0.6%	Economic freedom index	71.8

Origins of GDP		Components of GDP	
	% of total		% of total
Agriculture	1	Private consumption	59
Industry, of which:	26	Public consumption	20
manufacturing	19	Investment	16
Services	73	Exports	41
		Imports	-36

Structure of employment

	% of total		% of labour force
Agriculture	2	Unemployed 2009	7.7
Industry	30	Av. ann. rate 1995–2009	9.7
Services	68		

Energy

	m TOE		
Total output	134.1	Net energy imports as %	
Total consumption	335.3	of energy use	60
Consumption per head,			
kg oil equivalent	4,083		

Inflation and finance

Consumer price		av. ann. increase 2004–09	
inflation 2010	1.1%	Euro area:	
Av. ann. inflation 2005–10	1.6%	Narrow money (M1)	9.0%
Money market rate, 2010	0.38%	Broad money	7.3%
		Household saving rate, 2010	11.4%

Exchange rates

	end 2010		2010
€ per $	0.75	Effective rates	2005 = 100
€ per SDR	1.15	– nominal	100.0
		– real	95.9

Trade

Principal exports		Principal imports	
	$bn fob		*$bn cif*
Machinery & transport equip.	513.3	Machinery & transport equip.	323.7
Chemicals & related products	178.4	Chemicals & related products	125.9
Food, drink & tobacco	62.5	Mineral fuels & lubricants	105.2
Mineral fuels & lubricants	25.1	Food, drink & tobacco	71.7
Raw materials	21.1	Raw materials	21.1
Total incl. others	**1,116.9**	Total incl. others	**925.0**

Main export destinations		Main origins of imports	
	% of total		*% of total*
France	10.1	Netherlands	13.0
United States	6.8	France	8.3
Netherlands	6.6	Belgium	7.2
United Kingdom	6.6	China	6.8
Italy	6.3	Italy	5.6
Austria	5.7	United Kingdom	4.7
Belgium	5.2	Austria	4.4
EU27	63.0	EU27	65.1

Balance of payments, reserves and aid, $bn

Visible exports fob	1,146	Overall balance	21.3
Visible imports fob	-957	Change in reserves	41.0
Trade balance	188	Level of reserves	
Invisibles inflows	464	end Dec.	179.5
Invisibles outflows	-440	No. months of import cover	1.5
Net transfers	-47	Official gold holdings, m oz	109.5
Current account balance	166	Aid given	12.08
– as % of GDP	5.0	– as % of GDP	0.35
Capital balance	-174		

Health and education

Health spending, % of GDP	11.3	Education spending, % of GDP	4.5
Doctors per 1,000 pop.	3.6	Enrolment, %: primary	105
Hospital beds per 1,000 pop.	8.2	secondary	102
Improved-water source access,		tertiary	46
% of pop.	100		

Society

No. of households	39.9m	Colour TVs per 100 households	98.1
Av. no. per household	2.1	Telephone lines per 100 pop.	59.3
Marriages per 1,000 pop.	4.9	Mobile telephone subscribers	
Divorces per 1,000 pop.	3.0	per 100 pop.	127.8
Cost of living, Dec. 2010		Broadband subs per 100 pop.	30.4
New York = 100	101	Internet hosts per 1,000 pop.	253.5

GREECE

Area	131,957 sq km	Capital	Athens
Arable as % of total land	16	Currency	Euro (€)

People

Population	11.2m	Life expectancy: men	77.7 yrs
Pop. per sq km	86.1	women	82.5 yrs
Av. ann. growth		Adult literacy	97.2%
in pop. 2010–15	0.31%	Fertility rate (per woman)	1.5
Pop. under 15	14.2%	Urban population	61.4%
Pop. over 60	24.3%		per 1,000 pop.
No. of men per 100 women	97.9	Crude birth rate	10.4
Human Development Index	85.5	Crude death rate	10.4

The economy

GDP	€237bn	GDP per head	$29,240
GDP	$330bn	GDP per head in purchasing	
Av. ann. growth in real		power parity (USA=100)	64.4
GDP 2004–09	2.1%	Economic freedom index	60.3

Origins of GDP

Components of GDP

	% of total		% of total
Agriculture	3	Private consumption	75
Industry, of which:	18	Public consumption	19
mining & manufacturing	10	Investment	16
Services	79	Exports	19
		Imports	-29

Structure of employment

	% of total		% of labour force
Agriculture	11	Unemployed 2009	9.5
Industry	22	Av. ann. rate 1995–2009	9.9
Services	67		

Energy

	m TOE		
Total output	9.9	Net energy imports as %	
Total consumption	30.4	of energy use	68
Consumption per head,			
kg oil equivalent	2,707		

Inflation and finance

Consumer price		av. ann. increase 2004–09	
inflation 2010	4.7%	Euro area:	
Av. ann. inflation 2005–10	3.2%	Narrow money (M1)	9.0%
Treasury bill rate, 2010	1.35%	Broad money	7.3%

Exchange rates

	end 2010		2010
€ per $	0.75	Effective rates	2005 = 100
€ per SDR	1.15	– nominal	101.5
		– real	106.6

Trade

Principal exports		Principal imports	
	$bn fob		*$bn cif*
Food, drink & tobacco	4.5	Machinery & transport equip.	20.0
Chemicals & related products	2.8	Chemicals & related products	10.5
Machinery & transport equip.	2.7	Food, drink & tobacco	7.6
Mineral fuels & lubricants	1.8	Mineral fuels & lubricants	2.8
Raw materials	1.4	Raw materials	1.6
Total incl. others	**20.2**	Total incl. others	**63.3**

Main export destinations		Main origins of imports	
	% of total		*% of total*
Germany	11.5	Germany	12.3
Italy	11.5	Italy	11.5
Bulgaria	7.2	China	6.3
Cyprus	6.7	France	5.5
United States	4.8	Netherlands	5.4
EU27	62.7	EU27	64.3

Balance of payments, reserves and debt, $bn

Visible exports fob	21.4	Overall balance	1.2
Visible imports fob	-64.2	Change in reserves	2.0
Trade balance	-42.8	Level of reserves	
Invisibles inflows	43.7	end Dec.	5.5
Invisibles outflows	-38.5	No. months of import cover	0.6
Net transfers	1.7	Official gold holdings, m oz	3.6
Current account balance	-35.9	Aid given	0.61
– as % of GDP	-10.9	– as % of GDP	0.19
Capital balance	37.9		

Health and education

Health spending, % of GDP	10.6	Education spending, % of GDP	3.9
Doctors per 1,000 pop.	6.0	Enrolment, %: primary	101
Hospital beds per 1,000 pop.	4.9	secondary	102
Improved-water source access,		tertiary	91
% of pop.	100		

Society

No. of households	4.0m	Colour TVs per 100 households	99.8
Av. no. per household	2.8	Telephone lines per 100 pop.	47.0
Marriages per 1,000 pop.	5.2	Mobile telephone subscribers	
Divorces per 1,000 pop.	1.3	per 100 pop.	119.1
Cost of living, Dec. 2010		Broadband subs per 100 pop.	17.2
New York = 100	86	Internet hosts per 1,000 pop.	262.9

HONG KONG

Area	1,075 sq km	Capital	Victoria
Arable as % of total land	5	Currency	Hong Kong dollar (HK$)

People

Population	7.0m	Life expectancy: men	79.9 yrs
Pop. per sq km	6,417.8	women	85.7 yrs
Av. ann. growth		Adult literacy	...
in pop. 2010–15	0.70%	Fertility rate (per woman)	1.0
Pop. under 15	11.5%	Urban population	100.0%
Pop. over 60	18.4%		per 1,000 pop.
No. of men per 100 women	90	Crude birth rate	8.2
Human Development Index	86.2	Crude death rate	6.7

The economy

GDP	HK$1,632bn	GDP per head	$30,070
GDP	$211bn	GDP per head in purchasing	
Av. ann. growth in real		power parity (USA=100)	94.0
GDP 2004–09	4.0%	Economic freedom index	89.7

Origins of GDP		Components of GDP	
	% of total		% of total
Agriculture	0	Private consumption	62
Industry, of which:	8	Public consumption	9
manufacturing	2	Investment	23
Services	92	Exports	194
		Imports	-187

Structure of employment

	% of total		% of labour force
Agriculture	0	Unemployed 2009	5.2
Industry	14	Av. ann. rate 1995–2009	5.0
Services	86		

Energy

	m TOE		
Total output	0.1	Net energy imports as %	
Total consumption	14.1	of energy use	100
Consumption per head,			
kg oil equivalent	2,026		

Inflation and finance

		av. ann. increase 2004–09	
Consumer price inflation 2010	2.4%	Narrow money (M1)	9.5%
Av. ann. inflation 2005–10	2.2%	Broad money	9.4%
Money market rate, 2010	0.13%		

Exchange rates

	end 2010		2010
HK$ per $	7.78	Effective rates	2005 = 100
HK$ per SDR	11.97	– nominal	...
HK$ per €	10.40	– real	...

Trade

Principal exports[a]		Principal imports[a]	
	$bn fob		$bn cif
Electrical goods	2.4	Raw materials &	
Telecoms equipment	1.0	semi-manufactures	31.9
Jewellery etc	0.8	Consumer goods	17.8
Clothing & apparel	0.6	Capital goods	17.7
Textiles & related products	0.3	Fuels	11.2
		Foodstuffs	10.1
Total incl. others	7.4	Total	88.7

Main export destinations		Main origins of imports	
	% of total		% of total
China	46.3	China	46.4
United States	12.7	Japan	8.8
Singapore	3.8	Singapore	6.5
Taiwan	3.3	Taiwan	6.5

Balance of payments, reserves and debt, $bn

Visible exports fob	321.8	Change in reserves	73.3
Visible imports fob	-348.7	Level of reserves	
Trade balance	-26.9	end Dec.	255.8
Invisibles inflows	188.4	No. months of import cover	6.3
Invisibles outflows	-140.1	Official gold holdings, m oz	0.1
Net transfers	-3.2	Foreign debt	28.0
Current account balance	18.3	– as % of GDP	19
– as % of GDP	8.7	– as % of total exports	8
Capital balance	49.6	Debt service ratio	1
Overall balance	70.9		

Health and education

Health spending, % of GDP	...	Education spending, % of GDP	4.5
Doctors per 1,000 pop.	1.3	Enrolment, %: primary	104
Hospital beds per 1,000 pop.	5.0	secondary	82
Improved-water source access, % of pop.	...	tertiary	34

Society

No. of households	2.3m	Colour TVs per 100 households	99.5
Av. no. per household	3.0	Telephone lines per 100 pop.	60.9
Marriages per 1,000 pop.	6.3	Mobile telephone subscribers	
Divorces per 1,000 pop.	2.8	per 100 pop.	179.4
Cost of living, Dec. 2010		Broadband subs per 100 pop.	29.2
New York = 100	114	Internet hosts per 1,000 pop.	118.3

a Domestic, excluding re-exports.
Note: Hong Kong became a Special Administrative Region of China on July 1 1997.

HUNGARY

Area	93,030 sq km	Capital	Budapest
Arable as % of total land	51	Currency	Forint (Ft)

People

Population	10.0m	Life expectancy: men	70.4 yrs
Pop. per sq km	107.3	women	78.3 yrs
Av. ann. growth		Adult literacy	99.0
in pop. 2010–15	-0.21%	Fertility rate (per woman)	1.3
Pop. under 15	14.7%	Urban population	68.1%
Pop. over 60	22.4%		per 1,000 pop.
No. of men per 100 women	90.4	Crude birth rate	9.8
Human Development Index	80.5	Crude death rate	13.4

The economy

GDP	Ft26,095bn	GDP per head	$12,870
GDP	$129bn	GDP per head in purchasing	
Av. ann. growth in real		power parity (USA=100)	44.2
GDP 2004–09	0.3%	Economic freedom index	66.6

Origins of GDP

	% of total
Agriculture	4
Industry, of which:	29
manufacturing	22
Services	66

Components of GDP

	% of total
Private consumption	67
Public consumption	9
Investment	22
Exports	81
Imports	-80

Structure of employment

	% of total		% of labour force
Agriculture	5	Unemployed 2009	10
Industry	32	Av. ann. rate 1995–2009	7.6
Services	63		

Energy

	m TOE		
Total output	10.5	Net energy imports as %	
Total consumption	26.5	of energy use	60
Consumption per head,			
kg oil equivalent	2,636		

Inflation and finance

		av. ann. increase 2004–09	
Consumer price			
inflation 2010	4.9%	Narrow money (M1)	8.0%
Av. ann. inflation 2005–10	5.4%	Broad money	10.2%
Treasury bill rate, 2010	5.37%	Household saving rate, 2010	8.9%

Exchange rates

	end 2010		2010
Ft per $	208.65	Effective rates	2005 = 100
Ft per SDR	321.33	– nominal	90.2
Ft per €	278.80	– real	105.6

Trade

Principal exports		Principal imports	
	$bn fob		*$bn cif*
Machinery & equipment	50.6	Machinery & equipment	38.6
Other manufactures	22.4	Other manufactures	24.6
Food, drink & tobacco	6.0	Fuels	8.6
Raw materials	1.8	Food, drink & tobacco	4.3
Total incl. others	**81.9**	Total incl. others	**76.7**

Main export destinations		Main origins of imports	
	% of total		*% of total*
Germany	25.8	Germany	25.1
Italy	5.8	China	8.8
France	5.5	Russia	7.5
United Kingdom	5.4	Austria	6.6
EU27	78.9	EU27	68.8

Balance of payments, reserves and debt, $bn

Visible exports fob	81.5	Change in reserves	10.3
Visible imports fob	-76.8	Level of reserves	
Trade balance	4.8	end Dec.	44.2
Invisibles inflows	34.8	No. months of import cover	4.5
Invisibles outflows	-40.8	Official gold holdings, m oz	0.1
Net transfers	0.5	Foreign debt	112.0
Current account balance	-0.7	– as % of GDP	124
– as % of GDP	-0.5	– as % of total exports	137
Capital balance	4.7	Debt service ratio	39
Overall balance	4.0	Aid given	0.12
		% of GDP	0.10

Health and education

Health spending, % of GDP	7.3	Education spending, % of GDP	5.2
Doctors per 1,000 pop.	3.1	Enrolment, %: primary	99
Hospital beds per 1,000 pop.	6.7	secondary	97
Improved-water source access,		tertiary	65
% of pop.	100		

Society

No. of households	4.2m	Colour TVs per 100 households	97.4
Av. no. per household	2.4	Telephone lines per 100 pop.	30.7
Marriages per 1,000 pop.	4.0	Mobile telephone subscribers	
Divorces per 1,000 pop.	2.3	per 100 pop.	118.0
Cost of living, Dec. 2010		Broadband subs per 100 pop.	18.8
New York = 100	73	Internet hosts per 1,000 pop.	279.1

INDIA

Area	3,287,263 sq km	Capital	New Delhi
Arable as % of total land	53	Currency	Indian rupee (Rs)

People

Population	1,198.0m	Life expectancy:	men	63.7 yrs
Pop. per sq km	372.5		women	66.9 yrs
Av. ann. growth		Adult literacy		62.8%
in pop. 2010–15	1.43%	Fertility rate (per woman)		2.7
Pop. under 15	30.8%	Urban population		30.0%
Pop. over 60	7.5%			per 1,000 pop.
No. of men per 100 women	106.8	Crude birth rate		23.1
Human Development Index	51.9	Crude death rate		8.1

The economy

GDP	Rs65.5trn	GDP per head	$1,190
GDP	$1,377bn	GDP per head in purchasing	
Av. ann. growth in real		power parity (USA=100)	7.2
GDP 2004–09	8.3%	Economic freedom index	54.6

Origins of GDP		Components of GDP	
	% of total		% of total
Agriculture	18	Private consumption	56
Industry, of which:	27	Public consumption	12
manufacturing	15	Investment	36
Services	55	Exports	20
		Imports	-24

Structure of employment

	% of total		% of labour force
Agriculture	...	Unemployed 2005	4.4
Industry	...	Av. ann. rate 1995–2005	3.5
Services	...		

Energy

	m TOE		
Total output	468.3	Net energy imports as %	
Total consumption	621.0	of energy use	25
Consumption per head,			
kg oil equivalent	545		

Inflation and finance

Consumer price		av. ann. increase 2004–09	
inflation 2010	12.0%	Narrow money (M1)	16.4%
Av. ann. inflation 2005–10	8.7%	Broad money	19.6%
Lending rate, Dec. 2010	9.00%		

Exchange rates

	end 2010		2010
Rs per $	44.81	Effective rates	2005 = 100
Rs per SDR	69.01	– nominal	...
Rs per €	59.88	– real	...

Trade

Principal exports[a]		Principal imports[a]	
	$bn fob		*$bn cif*
Engineering goods	47.3	Petroleum & products	93.7
Gems & jewellery	28.0	Electronic goods	23.3
Petroleum & products	27.5	Gold & silver	22.8
Textiles	20.0	Machinery	21.6
Agricultural goods	17.5	Gems	16.6
Total incl. others	**185.3**	Total incl. others	**303.7**

Main export destinations		Main origins of imports	
	% of total		*% of total*
United Arab Emirates	11.7	China	10.3
United States	10.4	United States	6.0
China	5.8	United Arab Emirates	5.5
Hong Kong	3.9	Saudi Arabia	5.2

Balance of payments, reserves and debt, $bn

Visible exports fob	168.2	Change in reserves	27.3
Visible imports fob	-247.0	Level of reserves	
Trade balance	-78.8	end Dec.	284.7
Invisibles inflows	104.4	No. months of import cover	9.8
Invisibles outflows	-101.2	Official gold holdings, m oz	17.9
Net transfers	49.1	Foreign debt	237.7
Current account balance	-26.4	– as % of GDP	17
– as % of GDP	-1.9	– as % of total exports	71
Capital balance	44.1	Debt service ratio	6
Overall balance	16.8		

Health and education

Health spending, % of GDP	4.2	Education spending, % of GDP	3.1
Doctors per 1,000 pop.	0.6	Enrolment, %: primary	117
Hospital beds per 1,000 pop.	0.9	secondary	60
Improved-water source access,		tertiary	13
% of pop.	88		

Society

No. of households	222.2m	Colour TVs per 100 households	33.8
Av. no. per household	5.3	Telephone lines per 100 pop.	3.1
Marriages per 1,000 pop.	...	Mobile telephone subscribers	
Divorces per 1,000 pop.	...	per 100 pop.	43.8
Cost of living, Dec. 2010		Broadband subs per 100 pop.	0.7
New York = 100	53	Internet hosts per 1,000 pop.	4.8

a Year ending March 31, 2009.

INDONESIA

Area	1,904,443 sq km	Capital	Jakarta
Arable as % of total land	12	Currency	Rupiah (Rp)

People

Population	230.0m	Life expectancy: men	70.2 yrs
Pop. per sq km	125.9	women	74.3 yrs
Av. ann. growth		Adult literacy	92.0%
in pop. 2010–15	1.08%	Fertility rate (per woman)	2.2
Pop. under 15	26.7%	Urban population	44.3%
Pop. over 60	8.9%		per 1,000 pop.
No. of men per 100 women	99.5	Crude birth rate	19.1
Human Development Index	60.0	Crude death rate	6.3

The economy

GDP	Rp5,613trn	GDP per head	$2,350
GDP	$540bn	GDP per head in purchasing	
Av. ann. growth in real		power parity (USA=100)	9.1
GDP 2004–09	5.6%	Economic freedom index	56.0

Origins of GDP		Components of GDP	
	% of total		% of total
Agriculture	16	Private consumption	57
Industry, of which:	49	Public consumption	10
manufacturing	27	Investment	31
Services	35	Exports	24
		Imports	-21

Structure of employment

	% of total		% of labour force
Agriculture	41	Unemployed 2008	7.9
Industry	19	Av. ann. rate 1995–2008	7.6
Services	40		

Energy

	m TOE		
Total output	347.0	Net energy imports as %	
Total consumption	198.7	of energy use	-75
Consumption per head,			
kg oil equivalent	874		

Inflation and finance

Consumer price		av. ann. increase 2004–09	
inflation 2010	7.0%	Narrow money (M1)	16.0%
Av. ann. inflation 2005–10	8.5%	Broad money	15.7%
Money market rate, 2010	6.06%		

Exchange rates

	end 2010		2010
Rp per $	8,991	Effective rates	2005 = 100
Rp per SDR	13,846	– nominal	...
Rp per €	12,014	– real	...

Trade

Principal exports		Principal imports	
	$bn fob		*$bn cif*
Mineral products	20.2	Intermediate goods	69.7
Fats, oils & waxes	12.1	Capital goods	14.0
Liquefied natural gas	8.9	Consumer goods	6.8
Petroleum & products	7.8		
Total incl. others	**116.5**	**Total incl. others**	**96.8**

Main export destinations		Main origins of imports	
	% of total		*% of total*
Japan	15.9	Singapore	16.1
China	9.9	China	14.5
United States	9.4	Japan	10.2
Singapore	8.8	United States	7.3

Balance of payments, reserves and debt, $bn

Visible exports fob	119.5	Change in reserves	14.5
Visible imports fob	-84.3	Level of reserves	
Trade balance	35.1	end Dec.	66.1
Invisibles inflows	15.7	No. months of import cover	6.1
Invisibles outflows	-44.9	Official gold holdings, m oz	2.4
Net transfers	4.8	Foreign debt	157.5
Current account balance	10.7	– as % of GDP	30
– as % of GDP	2.0	– as % of total exports	99
Capital balance	3.5	Debt service ratio	18
Overall balance	12.5		

Health and education

Health spending, % of GDP	2.4	Education spending, % of GDP	2.8
Doctors per 1,000 pop.	0.3	Enrolment, %: primary	121
Hospital beds per 1,000 pop.	0.6	secondary	79
Improved-water source access,		tertiary	24
% of pop.	80		

Society

No. of households	67.4m	Colour TVs per 100 households	86.5
Av. no. per household	3.4	Telephone lines per 100 pop.	14.8
Marriages per 1,000 pop.	7.1	Mobile telephone subscribers	
Divorces per 1,000 pop.	0.9	per 100 pop.	69.3
Cost of living, Dec. 2010		Broadband subs per 100 pop.	0.7
New York = 100	82	Internet hosts per 1,000 pop.	5.6

IRAN

Area	1,648,000 sq km	Capital	Tehran
Arable as % of total land	11	Currency	Rial (IR)

People

Population	74.2m	Life expectancy: men	71.1 yrs
Pop. per sq km	44.9	women	74.1 yrs
Av. ann. growth		Adult literacy	82.3%
in pop. 2010–15	1.18%	Fertility rate (per woman)	1.8
Pop. under 15	23.8%	Urban population	70.8%
Pop. over 60	7.1%		per 1,000 pop.
No. of men per 100 women	103.0	Crude birth rate	17.7
Human Development Index	70.2	Crude death rate	5.5

The economy

GDP	IR3,265trn	GDP per head	$4,540
GDP	$331bn	GDP per head in purchasing	
Av. ann. growth in real		power parity (USA=100)	25.1
GDP 2004–09	3.8%	Economic freedom index	42.1

Origins of GDP[a]

	% of total
Agriculture	10
Industry, of which:	44
manufacturing	11
Services	45

Components of GDP[a]

	% of total
Private consumption	45
Public consumption	11
Investment	33
Exports	32
Imports	-22

Structure of employment

	% of total		% of labour force
Agriculture	23	Unemployed 2008	10.5
Industry	32	Av. ann. rate 2000-2008	12.1
Services	45		

Energy

	m TOE		
Total output	326.9	Net energy imports as %	
Total consumption	202.1	of energy use	-62
Consumption per head,			
kg oil equivalent	2,808		

Inflation and finance

			av. ann. increase 2004–09
Consumer price			
inflation 2010	10.1%	Narrow money (M1)	17.8%
Av. ann. inflation 2005–10	15.5%	Broad money	23.3%
Deposit rate, end 2009	13.10%		

Exchange rates

	end 2010		2010
IR per $	10,353	Effective rates	2005 = 100
IR per SDR	15,944	– nominal	83.1
IR per €	13,834	– real	150.0

Trade

Principal exports[b]		Principal imports[b]	
	$bn fob		*$bn cif*
Oil & gas	86.6	Machinery &	
Industrial goods excl.		transport equipment	19.2
oil & gas products	10.8	Iron & steel	9.3
Agricultural & traditional goods	3.3	Foodstuffs & live animals	6.4
Metallic mineral ores	0.3	Chemicals	6.3
		Mineral products & fuels	4.7
Total incl. others	**101.3**	Total incl. others	**56.0**

Main export destinations		Main origins of imports	
	% of total		*% of total*
China	16.1	United Arab Emirates	15.0
India	12.9	China	14.5
Japan	11.3	Germany	9.7
South Korea	7.0	South Korea	7.3
Turkey	4.1	Italy	5.2

Balance of payments[c], reserves and debt, $bn

Visible exports fob	87.5	Change in reserves	4.7
Visible imports fob	-66.6	Level of reserves	
Trade balance	20.9	end Dec.	84.3
Net invisibles	-11.1	No. months of import cover	15.2
Net transfers	0.4	Official gold holdings, m oz	...
Current account balance	10.3	Foreign debt	13.4
– as % of GDP	3.1	– as % of GDP	4
Capital balance	-13.5	– as % of total exports[a]	12
Overall balance	4.7	Debt service ratio[a]	3

Health and education

Health spending, % of GDP	5.5	Education spending, % of GDP	4.7
Doctors per 1,000 pop.	0.8	Enrolment, %: primary	103
Hospital beds per 1,000 pop.	1.4	secondary	83
Improved-water source access,		tertiary	36
% of pop.	94		

Society

No. of households	19.8m	Colour TVs per 100 households	88.9
Av. no. per household	3.8	Telephone lines per 100 pop.	34.8
Marriages per 1,000 pop.	11.3	Mobile telephone subscribers	
Divorces per 1,000 pop.	1.5	per 100 pop.	70.8
Cost of living, Dec. 2010		Broadband subs per 100 pop.	0.5
New York = 100	52	Internet hosts per 1,000 pop.	1.8

a 2008
b 2007
c Iranian year ending March 20, 2010.

IRELAND

Area	70,282 sq km	Capital	Dublin
Arable as % of total land	16	Currency	Euro (€)

People

Population	4.5m	Life expectancy: men	78.1 yrs
Pop. per sq km	63.6	women	82.9 yrs
Av. ann. growth		Adult literacy	...
in pop. 2010–15	1.45%	Fertility rate (per woman)	2.1
Pop. under 15	20.8%	Urban population	61.9%
Pop. over 60	16.1%		per 1,000 pop.
No. of men per 100 women	100.1	Crude birth rate	16.4
Human Development Index	89.5	Crude death rate	6.5

The economy

GDP	€164bn	GDP per head	$51,050
GDP	$227bn	GDP per head in purchasing	
Av. ann. growth in real		power parity (USA=100)	88.5
GDP 2004–09	1.0%	Economic freedom index	78.7

Origins of GDP		Components of GDP	
	% of total		% of total
Agriculture	1	Private consumption	52
Industry, of which:	31	Public consumption	19
manufacturing	24	Investment	14
Services	68	Exports	89
		Imports	-74

Structure of employment

	% of total		% of labour force
Agriculture	6	Unemployed 2009	11.7
Industry	26	Av. ann. rate 1995–2009	6.7
Services	68		

Energy

	m TOE		
Total output	1.5	Net energy imports as %	
Total consumption	15.0	of energy use	90
Consumption per head,			
kg oil equivalent	3,385		

Inflation and finance

Consumer price		av. ann. increase 2004–09	
inflation 2010	-0.9%	Euro area:	
Av. ann. inflation 2005–10	1.4%	Narrow money (M1)	9.0%
Money market rate, 2010	0.81%	Broad money	7.3%
		Household saving rate, 2010	19.3%

Exchange rates

	end 2010		2010
€ per $	0.75	Effective rates	2005 = 100
€ per SDR	1.15	– nominal	102.0
		– real	98.4

Trade

Principal exports		Principal imports	
	$bn fob		$bn cif
Chemicals & related products	63.9	Machinery & transport	
Machinery & transport		equipment	19.4
equipment	18.2	Chemicals	10.0
Food, drink & tobacco	9.6	Food, drink & tobacco	7.0
Raw materials	1.3	Minerals, fuels & lubricants	6.0
Total incl. others	**117.1**	Total incl. others	**62.6**

Main export destinations		Main origins of imports	
	% of total		% of total
United States	20.7	United Kingdom	35.3
Belgium	16.7	United States	16.7
United Kingdom	15.9	Germany	6.8
Germany	6.9	Netherlands	5.9
France	5.3	France	4.8
Spain	3.8	China	3.8
EU27	61.4	EU27	65.5

Balance of payments, reserves and aid, $bn

Visible exports fob	107.0	Overall balance	1.0
Visible imports fob	-62.0	Change in reserves	1.1
Trade balance	45.0	Level of reserves	
Invisibles inflows	168.6	end Dec.	2.1
Invisibles outflows	-218.9	No. months of import cover	0.1
Net transfers	-1.1	Official gold holdings, m oz	0.2
Current account balance	-6.5	Aid given	1.01
– as % of GDP	-2.9	– as % of GDP	0.54
Capital balance	-5.8		

Health and education

Health spending, % of GDP	9.7	Education spending, % of GDP	4.9
Doctors per 1,000 pop.	3.1	Enrolment, %: primary	105
Hospital beds per 1,000 pop.	5.0	secondary	118
Improved-water source access,		tertiary	58
% of pop.	100		

Society

No. of households	1.6m	Colour TVs per 100 households	99.7
Av. no. per household	2.8	Telephone lines per 100 pop.	46.1
Marriages per 1,000 pop.	4.7	Mobile telephone subscribers	
Divorces per 1,000 pop.	0.7	per 100 pop.	107.9
Cost of living, Dec. 2010		Broadband subs per 100 pop.	21.6
New York = 100	100	Internet hosts per 1,000 pop.	298.4

ISRAEL

Area	20,770 sq km	Capital	Jerusalem[a]
Arable as % of total land	14	Currency	New Shekel (NIS)

People

Population	7.2m	Life expectancy: men	79.4 yrs
Pop. per sq km	335.0	women	83.4 yrs
Av. ann. growth		Adult literacy	...
in pop. 2010–15	2.32%	Fertility rate (per woman)	2.9
Pop. under 15	27.6%	Urban population	91.9%
Pop. over 60	14.6%		per 1,000 pop.
No. of men per 100 women	97.4	Crude birth rate	21.1
Human Development Index	87.2	Crude death rate	5.6

The economy

GDP	NIS768bn	GDP per head	$26,260
GDP	$195bn	GDP per head in purchasing	
Av. ann. growth in real		power parity (USA=100)	60.1
GDP 2004–09	4.2%	Economic freedom index	68.5

Origins of GDP[b]

	% of total
Agriculture	3
Industry, of which:	31
manufacturing	22
Services	65

Components of GDP

	% of total
Private consumption	57
Public consumption	24
Investment	16
Exports	35
Imports	-32

Structure of employment

	% of total		% of labour force
Agriculture	2	Unemployed 2009	7.6
Industry	22	Av. ann. rate 1995–2009	8.4
Services	76		

Energy

	m TOE		
Total output	3.3	Net energy imports as %	
Total consumption	22.0	of energy use	85
Consumption per head,			
kg oil equivalent	3,011		

Inflation and finance

Consumer price		av. ann. increase 2004–09	
inflation 2010	2.7%	Narrow money (M1)	19.2%
Av. ann. inflation 2005–10	2.6%	Broad money	8.2%
Treasury bill rate, 2010	2.19%		

Exchange rates

	end 2010		2010
NIS per $	3.55	Effective rates	2005 = 100
NIS per SDR	5.47	– nominal	118.4
NIS per €	4.74	– real	119.3

Trade

Principal exports		Principal imports	
	$bn fob		*$bn fob*
Chemicals	10.4	Fuel	8.1
Diamonds	9.4	Diamonds	5.3
Communications, medical &		Machinery & equipment	5.3
scientific equipment	6.7	Chemicals	3.6
Electronics	4.8		
Total incl. others	**42.1**	Total incl. others	**46.9**

Main export destinations		Main origins of imports	
	% of total		*% of total*
United States	39.8	United States	12.5
Belgium	6.8	China	7.5
Hong Kong	5.6	Germany	7.2
India	4.3	Switzerland	7.0
Netherlands	3.7	Belgium	5.5

Balance of payments, reserves and debt, $bn

Visible exports fob	45.9	Change in reserves	18.1
Visible imports fob	-46.0	Level of reserves	
Trade balance	-0.1	end Dec.	60.6
Invisibles inflows	27.7	No. months of import cover	9.9
Invisibles outflows	-27.4	Official gold holdings, m oz	0.0
Net transfers	7.4	Foreign debt	61.0
Current account balance	7.6	– as % of GDP	44
– as % of GDP	3.9	– as % of total exports	114
Capital balance	5.5	Debt service ratio	12
Overall balance	17.3	Aid given	0.12
		% of GDP	0.06

Health and education

Health spending, % of GDP	7.6	Education spending, % of GDP	5.9
Doctors per 1,000 pop.	3.5	Enrolment, %: primary	111
Hospital beds per 1,000 pop.	5.6	secondary	90
Improved-water source access,		tertiary	60
% of pop.	100		

Society

No. of households	2.1m	Colour TVs per 100 households	95.3
Av. no. per household	3.5	Telephone lines per 100 pop.	45.3
Marriages per 1,000 pop.	4.9	Mobile telephone subscribers	
Divorces per 1,000 pop.	1.6	per 100 pop.	125.8
Cost of living, Dec. 2010		Broadband subs per 100 pop.	25.8
New York = 100	108	Internet hosts per 1,000 pop.	303.6

a Sovereignty over the city is disputed.
b 2006

ITALY

Area	301,245 sq km	Capital	Rome
Arable as % of total land	24	Currency	Euro (€)

People

Population	59.9m	Life expectancy:	men	78.6 yrs
Pop. per sq km	201.0		women	84.6 yrs
Av. ann. growth		Adult literacy		98.9%
in pop. 2010–15	0.63%	Fertility rate (per woman)		1.4
Pop. under 15	14.2%	Urban population		68.4%
Pop. over 60	26.7%			per 1,000 pop.
No. of men per 100 women	95.7	Crude birth rate		9.4
Human Development Index	85.4	Crude death rate		10.5

The economy

GDP	€1,521bn	GDP per head	$35,080
GDP	$2,113bn	GDP per head in purchasing	
Av. ann. growth in real		power parity (USA=100)	70.5
GDP 2004–09	-0.5%	Economic freedom index	60.3

Origins of GDP		**Components of GDP**	
	% of total		% of total
Agriculture	2	Private consumption	60
Industry, of which:	25	Public consumption	22
manufacturing	16	Investment	19
Services	73	Exports	24
		Imports	-24

Structure of employment

	% of total		% of labour force
Agriculture	4	Unemployed 2009	7.8
Industry	30	Av. ann. rate 1995–2009	9.3
Services	66		

Energy

	m TOE		
Total output	26.9	Net energy imports as %	
Total consumption	176.0	of energy use	85
Consumption per head,			
kg oil equivalent	2,942		

Inflation and finance

Consumer price		*av. ann. increase 2004–09*	
inflation 2010	1.5%	Euro area:	
Av. ann. inflation 2005–10	1.9%	Narrow money (M1)	9.0%
Money market rate, 2010	1.02%	Broad money	7.3%
		Household saving rate, 2010	6.1%

Exchange rates

	end 2010		2010
€ per $	0.75	Effective rates	2005 = 100
€ per SDR	1.15	– nominal	100.5
		– real	98.1

Trade

Principal exports	$bn fob	Principal imports	$bn cif
Machinery & transport equip.	146.9	Machinery & transport equip.	112.5
Chemicals & related products	44.3	Mineral fuels & lubricants	70.9
Food, drink & tobacco	30.5	Chemicals & related products	58.0
Mineral fuels & lubricants	15.0	Food, drink & tobacco	37.7
Total incl. others	**406.7**	Total incl. others	**414.7**

Main export destinations	% of total	Main origins of imports	% of total
Germany	12.7	Germany	16.7
France	11.6	France	8.8
United States	5.9	Netherlands	5.6
United Kingdom	5.1	United Kingdom	3.3
EU27	57.4	EU27	57.2

Balance of payments, reserves and aid, $bn

Visible exports fob	407.2	Overall balance	9.0
Visible imports fob	-403.9	Change in reserves	25.8
Trade balance	3.3	Level of reserves	
Invisibles inflows	164.9	end Dec.	131.5
Invisibles outflows	-217.4	No. months of import cover	2.5
Net transfers	-17.0	Official gold holdings, m oz	78.8
Current account balance	-66.2	Aid given	3.30
– as % of GDP	-3.1	– as % of GDP	0.16
Capital balance	30.0		

Health and education

Health spending, % of GDP	9.5	Education spending, % of GDP	4.3
Doctors per 1,000 pop.	4.1	Enrolment, %: primary	103
Hospital beds per 1,000 pop.	3.7	secondary	101
Improved-water source access,		tertiary	67
% of pop.	100		

Society

No. of households	24.3m	Colour TVs per 100 households	96.8
Av. no. per household	2.5	Telephone lines per 100 pop.	36.2
Marriages per 1,000 pop.	4.3	Mobile telephone subscribers	
Divorces per 1,000 pop.	0.9	per 100 pop.	147.0
Cost of living, Dec. 2010		Broadband subs per 100 pop.	20.5
New York = 100	98	Internet hosts per 1,000 pop.	408.7

JAPAN

Area	377,727 sq km	Capital	Tokyo
Arable as % of total land	12	Currency	Yen (¥)

People

Population	127.2m	Life expectancy:	men	80.1 yrs
Pop. per sq km	334.9		women	87.2 yrs
Av. ann. growth		Adult literacy		...
in pop. 2010–15	0.02%	Fertility rate (per woman)		1.3
Pop. under 15	13.2%	Urban population		66.8%
Pop. over 60	30.5%			per 1,000 pop.
No. of men per 100 women	95.0	Crude birth rate		8.6
Human Development Index	88.4	Crude death rate		9.8

The economy

GDP	¥474trn	GDP per head	$39,740
GDP	$5,069bn	GDP per head in purchasing	
Av. ann. growth in real		power parity (USA=100)	70.5
GDP 2004–09	-0.3%	Economic freedom index	72.8

Origins of GDP		Components of GDP	
	% of total		% of total
Agriculture	1	Private consumption	60
Industry, of which:	28	Public consumption	20
manufacturing	20	Investment	20
Services	71	Exports	13
		Imports	-12

Structure of employment

	% of total		% of labour force
Agriculture	4	Unemployed 2009	5.0
Industry	28	Av. ann. rate 1995–2009	4.3
Services	68		

Energy

	m TOE		
Total output	88.7	Net energy imports as %	
Total consumption	495.8	of energy use	82
Consumption per head,			
kg oil equivalent	3,883		

Inflation and finance

Consumer price		av. ann. increase 2004–09	
inflation 2010	-0.7%	Narrow money (M1)	1.2%
Av. ann. inflation 2005–10	-0.1%	Broad money	0.7%
Money market rate, 2010	0.09%	Household saving rate, 2010	6.5%

Exchange rates

	end 2010		2010
¥ per $	81.45	Effective rates	2005 = 100
¥ per SDR	125.44	– nominal	121.3
¥ per €	108.83	– real	104.7

Trade

Principal exports	$bn fob	Principal imports	$bn cif
Capital equipment	299.9	Industrial supplies	272.7
Industrial supplies	148.0	Capital equipment	128.3
Consumer durable goods	83.3	Food & direct consumer goods	52.7
Consumer nondurable goods	4.5	Consumer durable goods	39.6
Total incl. others	**580.5**	Total incl. others	**551.8**

Main export destinations	% of total	Main origins of imports	% of total
China	18.9	China	22.2
United States	16.4	United States	11.0
South Korea	8.1	Australia	6.3
Hong Kong	5.5	Saudi Arabia	5.3
Thailand	3.8	United Arab Emirates	4.1

Balance of payments, reserves and aid, $bn

Visible exports fob	545.3	Overall balance	26.9
Visible imports fob	-501.7	Change in reserves	18.2
Trade balance	43.6	Level of reserves	
Invisibles inflows	303.6	end Dec.	1,049.0
Invisibles outflows	-192.6	No. months of import cover	18.1
Net transfers	-12.4	Official gold holdings, m oz	24.6
Current account balance	142.2	Aid given	9.47
– as % of GDP	2.8	– as % of GDP	0.18
Capital balance	-135.1		

Health and education

Health spending, % of GDP	8.3	Education spending, % of GDP	3.5
Doctors per 1,000 pop.	2.1	Enrolment, %: primary	102
Hospital beds per 1,000 pop.	13.8	secondary	101
Improved-water source access,		tertiary	58
% of pop.	100		

Society

No. of households	50.5m	Colour TVs per 100 households	99.6
Av. no. per household	2.5	Telephone lines per 100 pop.	34.1
Marriages per 1,000 pop.	5.8	Mobile telephone subscribers	
Divorces per 1,000 pop.	1.9	per 100 pop.	91.5
Cost of living, Dec. 2010		Broadband subs per 100 pop.	24.9
New York = 100	158	Internet hosts per 1,000 pop.	4/1.5

KENYA

Area	582,646 sq km	Capital	Nairobi
Arable as % of total land	9	Currency	Kenyan shilling (KSh)

People

Population	39.8m	Life expectancy: men	56.3 yrs
Pop. per sq km	69.8	women	57.5 yrs
Av. ann. growth		Adult literacy	86.5%
in pop. 2010–15	2.58%	Fertility rate (per woman)	4.8
Pop. under 15	42.8%	Urban population	22.2%
Pop. over 60	4.1%		per 1,000 pop.
No. of men per 100 women	99.8	Crude birth rate	38.0
Human Development Index	47.0	Crude death rate	10.3

The economy

GDP	KSh2,273bn	GDP per head	$740
GDP	$29.4bn	GDP per head in purchasing	
Av. ann. growth in real		power parity (USA=100)	3.4
GDP 2004–09	4.7%	Economic freedom index	57.4

Origins of GDP

	% of total
Agriculture	23
Industry, of which:	15
manufacturing	9
Other	62

Components of GDP

	% of total
Private consumption	76
Public consumption	16
Investment	21
Exports	25
Imports	-38

Structure of employment

	% of total		% of labour force
Agriculture	...	Unemployed 2008	...
Industry	...	Av. ann. rate 1995–2008	...
Services	...		

Energy

	m TOE		
Total output	15.1	Net energy imports as %	
Total consumption	18.0	of energy use	16
Consumption per head,			
kg oil equivalent	465		

Inflation and finance

Consumer price		av. ann. increase 2004–09	
inflation 2010	4.0%	Narrow money (M1)	16.0%
Av. ann. inflation 2005–10	12.5%	Broad money	15.3%
Treasury bill rate, 2010	3.60%		

Exchange rates

	end 2010		2010
KSh per $	80.75	Effective rates	2005 = 100
KSh per SDR	124.36	– nominal	...
KSh per €	107.90	– real	...

Trade

Principal exports[a]		Principal imports[a]	
	$bn fob		*$bn cif*
Horticultural products	1.0	Machinery & other capital equip.	3.6
Tea	0.9	Food & drink	1.8
Coffee	0.1	Industrial supplies	0.8
Fish products	0.1	Transport equipment	0.8
Total incl. others	**5.0**	Total incl. others	**10.7**

Main export destinations		Main origins of imports	
	% of total		*% of total*
United Kingdom	10.0	India	13.3
Netherlands	9.2	United Arab Emirates	11.5
Uganda	8.9	China	10.0
Tanzania	8.7	Saudi Arabia	8.1

Balance of payments, reserves and debt, $bn

Visible exports fob	4.5	Change in reserves	1.0
Visible imports fob	-9.5	Level of reserves	
Trade balance	-5.0	end Dec.	3.9
Invisibles inflows	3.1	No. months of import cover	4.0
Invisibles outflows	-2.1	Official gold holdings, m oz	0.0
Net transfers	2.3	Foreign debt	8.0
Current account balance	-1.7	– as % of GDP	19
– as % of GDP	-5.7	– as % of total exports	72
Capital balance	2.9	Debt service ratio	5
Overall balance	1.1		

Health and education

Health spending, % of GDP	4.3	Education spending, % of GDP	7.0
Doctors per 1,000 pop.	0.1	Enrolment, %: primary	113
Hospital beds per 1,000 pop.	1.4	secondary	59
Improved-water source access,		tertiary	4
% of pop.	59		

Society

No. of households	9.1m	Colour TVs per 100 households	63.5
Av. no. per household	4.4	Telephone lines per 100 pop.	1.7
Marriages per 1,000 pop.	...	Mobile telephone subscribers	
Divorces per 1,000 pop.	...	per 100 pop.	48.7
Cost of living, Dec. 2010		Broadband subs per 100 pop.	...
New York = 100	73	Internet hosts per 1,000 pop.	1.4

a 2008

LATVIA

Area	63,700 sq km	Capital	Riga
Arable as % of total land	19	Currency	Lats (LVL)

People

Population	2.2m	Life expectancy:	men	68.7 yrs
Pop. per sq km	34.9		women	78.1 yrs
Av. ann. growth		Adult literacy		99.8%
in pop. 2010–15	-0.47%	Fertility rate (per woman)		1.4
Pop. under 15	13.8%	Urban population		67.7%
Pop. over 60	22.5%			per 1,000 pop.
No. of men per 100 women	85.2	Crude birth rate		10.2
Human Development Index	76.9	Crude death rate		13.9

The economy

GDP	LVL13.2bn	GDP per head	$11,620
GDP	$26.2bn	GDP per head in purchasing	
Av. ann. growth in real		power parity (USA=100)	35.7
GDP 2004–09	1.4%	Economic freedom index	65.8

Origins of GDP		Components of GDP	
	% of total		% of total
Agriculture	3	Private consumption	61
Industry, of which:	20	Public consumption	21
manufacturing	10	Investment	19
Services	77	Exports	42
		Imports	-43

Structure of employment

	% of total		% of labour force
Agriculture	8	Unemployed 2009	17.1
Industry	29	Av. ann. rate 1995–2009	12.3
Services	63		

Energy

			m TOE
Total output	1.8	Net energy imports as %	
Total consumption	4.5	of energy use	60
Consumption per head,			
kg oil equivalent	1,979		

Inflation and finance

Consumer price		av. ann. increase 2004–09	
inflation 2010	-1.1%	Narrow money (M1)	8.3%
Av. ann. inflation 2005–10	6.7%	Broad money	15.8%
Money market rate, 2010	0.93%		

Exchange rates

	end 2010		2010
LVL per $	0.54	Effective rates	2005 = 100
LVL per SDR	0.82	– nominal	...
LVL per €	0.72	– real	...

Trade

Principal exports		Principal imports	
	$bn fob		*$bn cif*
Wood & wood products	1.2	Mineral products	1.6
Machinery & equipment	1.0	Machinery & equipment	1.5
Metals	0.9	Chemicals	1.1
Chemicals	0.6	Foodstuffs	0.8
Total incl. others	**7.1**	Total incl. others	**9.3**

Main export destinations		Main origins of imports	
	% of total		*% of total*
Lithuania	16.4	Lithuania	17.0
Estonia	14.4	Germany	11.5
Russia	8.8	Russia	10.7
Germany	8.7	Poland	8.4
Sweden	6.1	Estonia	8.0
EU27	67.6	EU27	75.5

Balance of payments, reserves and debt, $bn

Visible exports fob	7.4	Change in reserves	1.7
Visible imports fob	-9.2	Level of reserves	
Trade balance	-1.8	end Dec.	6.9
Invisibles inflows	5.2	No. months of import cover	7.4
Invisibles outflows	-2.0	Official gold holdings, m oz	0.2
Net transfers	0.9	Foreign debt	29.0
Current account balance	2.3	– as % of GDP	161
– as % of GDP	8.7	– as % of total exports	318
Capital balance	-1.2	Debt service ratio	60
Overall balance	1.3		

Health and education

Health spending, % of GDP	6.5	Education spending, % of GDP	5.0
Doctors per 1,000 pop.	3.1	Enrolment, %: primary	98
Hospital beds per 1,000 pop.	7.6	secondary	98
Improved-water source access,		tertiary	69
% of pop.	99		

Society

No. of households	0.8m	Colour TVs per 100 households	96.2
Av. no. per household	2.8	Telephone lines per 100 pop.	28.6
Marriages per 1,000 pop.	5.0	Mobile telephone subscribers	
Divorces per 1,000 pop.	2.4	per 100 pop.	105.4
Cost of living, Dec. 2010		Broadband subs per 100 pop.	18.6
New York = 100	...	Internet hosts per 1,000 pop.	151.0

LITHUANIA

Area	65,200 sq km	Capital	Vilnius
Arable as % of total land	30	Currency	Litas (LTL)

People

Population	3.3m	Life expectancy:	men	67.0 yrs
Pop. per sq km	50.9		women	78.3 yrs
Av. ann. growth		Adult literacy		99.7%
in pop. 2010–15	-0.55%	Fertility rate (per woman)		1.4
Pop. under 15	14.6%	Urban population		67.0%
Pop. over 60	21.5%			per 1,000 pop.
No. of men per 100 women	86.8	Crude birth rate		10.1
Human Development Index	78.3	Crude death rate		13.8

The economy

GDP	LTL92.5bn	GDP per head	$11,140
GDP	$37.2bn	GDP per head in purchasing	
Av. ann. growth in real		power parity (USA=100)	37.6
GDP 2004–09	2.3%	Economic freedom index	71.3

Origins of GDP		Components of GDP	
	% of total		% of total
Agriculture	4	Private consumption	65
Industry, of which:	31	Public consumption	19
manufacturing	18	Investment	27
Services	64	Exports	60
		Imports	-72

Structure of employment

	% of total		% of labour force
Agriculture	8	Unemployed 2009	13.7
Industry	30	Av. ann. rate 1995–2009	12.2
Services	62		

Energy

		m TOE	
Total output	3.9	Net energy imports as %	
Total consumption	9.2	of energy use	58
Consumption per head,			
kg oil equivalent	2,733		

Inflation and finance

Consumer price		av. ann. increase 2005–09	
inflation 2010	1.3%	Narrow money (M1)	7.8%
Av. ann. inflation 2005–10	5.2%	Broad money	14.4%
Money market rate, 2010	0.22%		

Exchange rates

	end 2010		2010
		Effective rates	2005 = 100
LTL per $	2.61		
LTL per SDR	4.02	– nominal	...
LTL per €	3.49	– real	...

Trade

Principal exports		Principal imports	
	$bn fob		$bn cif
Mineral products	3.5	Mineral products	5.3
Machinery & equipment	1.6	Machinery & equipment	2.4
Chemicals	1.5	Transport equipment	2.2
Transport equipment	1.2	Chemicals	1.2
Total incl. others	**16.4**	Total incl. others	**18.3**

Main export destinations		Main origins of imports	
	% of total		% of total
Russia	13.2	Russia	30.0
Latvia	10.0	Germany	11.1
Germany	9.7	Poland	9.9
Estonia	7.2	Latvia	6.3
Poland	7.2	Netherlands	4.1
EU27	64.3	EU25	59.1

Balance of payments, reserves and debt, $bn

Visible exports fob	16.5	Change in reserves	0.2
Visible imports fob	-17.6	Level of reserves	
Trade balance	-1.1	end Dec.	6.7
Invisibles inflows	4.6	No. months of import cover	3.8
Invisibles outflows	-3.5	Official gold holdings, m oz	0.2
Net transfers	1.6	Foreign debt	31.7
Current account balance	1.6	– as % of GDP	72
– as % of GDP	4.4	– as % of total exports	120
Capital balance	-1.5	Debt service ratio	31
Overall balance	0.1		

Health and education

Health spending, % of GDP	6.6	Education spending, % of GDP	4.7
Doctors per 1,000 pop.	3.8	Enrolment, %: primary	96
Hospital beds per 1,000 pop.	8.2	secondary	99
Improved-water source access,		tertiary	77
% of pop.	...		

Society

No. of households	1.4m	Colour TVs per 100 households	98.3
Av. no. per household	2.4	Telephone lines per 100 pop.	22.7
Marriages per 1,000 pop.	6.6	Mobile telephone subscribers	
Divorces per 1,000 pop.	3.5	per 100 pop.	151.0
Cost of living, Dec. 2010		Broadband subs per 100 pop.	19.3
New York = 100	...	Internet hosts per 1,000 pop.	360.5

MALAYSIA

Area	332,665 sq km	Capital	Kuala Lumpur
Arable as % of total land	6	Currency	Malaysian dollar/ringgit (M$)

People

Population	27.5m	Life expectancy: men	72.9 yrs
Pop. per sq km	86.1	women	77.6 yrs
Av. ann. growth		Adult literacy	92.1%
in pop. 2010–15	1.69%	Fertility rate (per woman)	2.7
Pop. under 15	29.1%	Urban population	72.2%
Pop. over 60	7.8%		per 1,000 pop.
No. of men per 100 women	103.0	Crude birth rate	20.9
Human Development Index	74.4	Crude death rate	4.6

The economy

GDP	M$680bn	GDP per head	$7,030
GDP	$193bn	GDP per head in purchasing	
Av. ann. growth in real		power parity (USA=100)	30.5
GDP 2004–09	4.1%	Economic freedom index	66.3

Origins of GDP		Components of GDP	
	% of total		% of total
Agriculture	10	Private consumption	50
Industry, of which:	44	Public consumption	14
manufacturing	25	Investment	14
Services	46	Exports	96
		Imports	-75

Structure of employment

	% of total		% of labour force
Agriculture	15	Unemployed 2009	3.7
Industry	29	Av. ann. rate 1995–2009	3.3
Services	56		

Energy

	m TOE		
Total output	93.1	Net energy imports as %	
Total consumption	72.7	of energy use	-28
Consumption per head,			
kg oil equivalent	2,693		

Inflation and finance

Consumer price		av. ann. increase 2004–09	
inflation 2010	1.7%	Narrow money (M1)	11.9%
Av. ann. inflation 2005–10	2.7%	Broad money	10.5%
Money market rate, 2010	2.45%		

Exchange rates

	end 2010		2010
M$ per $	3.08	Effective rates	2005 = 100
M$ per SDR	4.75	– nominal	108.2
M$ per €	4.12	– real	109.6

Trade

Principal exports		**Principal imports**	
	$bn fob		*$bn cif*
Machinery & transport equip.	73.0	Machinery & transport equip.	63.1
Mineral fuels	23.2	Manufactured goods	15.0
Manufactured goods	14.0	Chemicals	11.2
Chemicals	9.5	Mineral fuels	10.1
Total incl. others	**157.4**	Total incl. others	**123.8**

Main export destinations		**Main origins of imports**	
	% of total		*% of total*
Singapore	14.0	China	14.0
China	12.2	Japan	12.5
United States	11.0	United States	11.2
Japan	9.8	Singapore	11.1
Thailand	5.4	Thailand	6.0

Balance of payments, reserves and debt, $bn

Visible exports fob	157.7	Change in reserves	4.5
Visible imports fob	-117.4	Level of reserves	
Trade balance	40.3	end Dec.	96.7
Invisibles inflows	40.0	No. months of import cover	7.2
Invisibles outflows	-42.9	Official gold holdings, m oz	1.2
Net transfers	-5.6	Foreign debt	66.4
Current account balance	31.8	– as % of GDP	31
– as % of GDP	16.5	– as % of total exports	27
Capital balance	-22.7	Debt service ratio	5
Overall balance	3.9		

Health and education

Health spending, % of GDP	4.8	Education spending, % of GDP	4.1
Doctors per 1,000 pop.	0.9	Enrolment, %: primary	95
Hospital beds per 1,000 pop.	1.2	secondary	69
Improved-water source access,		tertiary	36
% of pop.	100		

Society

No. of households	6.4m	Colour TVs per 100 households	96.5
Av. no. per household	4.4	Telephone lines per 100 pop.	15.7
Marriages per 1,000 pop.	5.8	Mobile telephone subscribers	
Divorces per 1,000 pop.	...	per 100 pop.	109.7
Cost of living, Dec. 2010		Broadband subs per 100 pop.	6.1
New York = 100	79	Internet hosts per 1,000 pop.	12.6

MEXICO

Area	1,972,545 sq km	Capital	Mexico city
Arable as % of total land	13	Currency	Mexican peso (PS)

People

Population	109.6m	Life expectancy:	men	74.9 yrs
Pop. per sq km	57.9		women	79.7 yrs
Av. ann. growth		Adult literacy		93.4%
in pop. 2010–15	1.26%	Fertility rate (per woman)		2.4
Pop. under 15	27.9%	Urban population		77.8%
Pop. over 60	9.4%			per 1,000 pop.
No. of men per 100 women	97.3	Crude birth rate		20.6
Human Development Index	75.0	Crude death rate		4.9

The economy

GDP	PS11,822bn	GDP per head	$8,140
GDP	$875bn	GDP per head in purchasing	
Av. ann. growth in real		power parity (USA=100)	31.0
GDP 2004–09	1.3%	Economic freedom index	67.8

Origins of GDP

	% of total
Agriculture	4
Industry, of which:	35
manufacturing & mining	17
Services	61

Components of GDP

	% of total
Private consumption	67
Public consumption	12
Investment	22
Exports	28
Imports	-29

Structure of employment

	% of total		% of labour force
Agriculture	14	Unemployed 2009	5.2
Industry	26	Av. ann. rate 1995–2009	3.2
Services	60		

Energy

	m TOE		
Total output	233.6	Net energy imports as %	
Total consumption	180.6	of energy use	-29
Consumption per head,			
kg oil equivalent	1,698		

Inflation and finance

		av. ann. increase 2004–09	
Consumer price inflation 2010	4.2%	Narrow money (M1)	11.3%
Av. ann. inflation 2005–10	4.4%	Broad money	12.2%
Money market rate, 2010	4.91%		

Exchange rates

	end 2010		2010
PS per $	12.36	Effective rates	2005 = 100
PS per SDR	19.03	– nominal	...
PS per €	16.52	– real	...

Trade

Principal exports		Principal imports	
	$bn fob		*$bn fob*
Manufactured products	189.7	Intermediate goods	170.9
Crude oil & products	30.9	Consumer goods	32.8
Agricultural products	7.7	Capital goods	30.6
Mining products	1.4		
Total	**229.8**	Total	**234.4**

Main export destinations		Main origins of imports	
	% of total		*% of total*
United States	80.6	United States	52.8
Canada	3.6	China	15.3
Germany	1.4	Japan	5.3
Spain	1.1	South Korea	5.1

Balance of payments, reserves and debt, $bn

Visible exports fob	229.8	Change in reserves	4.6
Visible imports fob	-234.4	Level of reserves	
Trade balance	-4.6	end Dec.	99.9
Invisibles inflows	20.1	No. months of import cover	4.3
Invisibles outflows	-43.2	Official gold holdings, m oz	0.3
Net transfers	21.5	Foreign debt	192.0
Current account balance	-6.2	– as % of GDP	18
– as % of GDP	-0.7	– as % of total exports	61
Capital balance	21.5	Debt service ratio	16
Overall balance	5.7		

Health and education

Health spending, % of GDP	6.5	Education spending, % of GDP	4.8
Doctors per 1,000 pop.	2.8	Enrolment, %: primary	114
Hospital beds per 1,000 pop.	1.6	secondary	90
Improved-water source access,		tertiary	26
% of pop.	94		

Society

No. of households	27.6m	Colour TVs per 100 households	95.3
Av. no. per household	3.9	Telephone lines per 100 pop.	17.6
Marriages per 1,000 pop.	5.5	Mobile telephone subscribers	
Divorces per 1,000 pop.	0.8	per 100 pop.	76.2
Cost of living, Dec. 2010		Broadband subs per 100 pop.	8.8
New York = 100	84	Internet hosts per 1,000 pop.	126.1

MOROCCO

Area	446,550 sq km	Capital	Rabat
Arable as % of total land	18	Currency	Dirham (Dh)

People

Population	32.0m	Life expectancy: men	70.2 yrs
Pop. per sq km	71.6	women	74.8 yrs
Av. ann. growth		Adult literacy	56.1%
in pop. 2010–15	1.00%	Fertility rate (per woman)	2.4
Pop. under 15	28.0%	Urban population	58.2%
Pop. over 60	8.1%		per 1,000 pop.
No. of men per 100 women	96.2	Crude birth rate	20.2
Human Development Index	56.7	Crude death rate	5.8

The economy

GDP	Dh736bn	GDP per head	$2,810
GDP	$91.4bn	GDP per head in purchasing	
Av. ann. growth in real		power parity (USA=100)	9.8
GDP 2004–09	4.8%	Economic freedom index	59.6

Origins of GDP

	% of total
Agriculture	16
Industry, of which:	29
manufacturing	16
Services	55

Components of GDP

	% of total
Private consumption	57
Public consumption	18
Investment	36
Exports	29
Imports	-39

Structure of employment

	% of total		% of labour force
Agriculture	41	Unemployed 2009	10.0
Industry	22	Av. ann. rate 1995–2009	13.4
Services	37		

Energy

	m TOE		
Total output	0.6	Net energy imports as %	
Total consumption	15.0	of energy use	96
Consumption per head,			
kg oil equivalent	474		

Inflation and finance

		av. ann. increase 2004–09	
Consumer price			
inflation 2010	1.0%	Narrow money (M1)	12.5%
Av. ann. inflation 2005–10	2.2%	Broad money	14.0%
Money market rate, 2010	3.29%		

Exchange rates

	end 2010		2010
Dh per $	8.36	Effective rates	2005 = 100
Dh per SDR	12.87	– nominal	99.1
Dh per €	11.17	– real	96.6

Trade

Principal exports		Principal imports	
	$bn fob		*$bn cif*
Clothing & textiles	2.2	Capital goods	7.9
Phosphoric acid	1.0	Fuel & lubricants	6.7
Fertilisers	0.7	Semi-finished goods	6.7
Electrical cables & wires	0.6	Consumer goods	6.5
Phosphate rock	0.6	Food, drink & tobacco	3.0
Total incl. others	**14.0**	Total incl. others	**32.9**

Main export destinations		Main origins of imports	
	% of total		*% of total*
Spain	20.7	France	17.1
France	18.9	Spain	14.9
India	4.6	China	7.5
Italy	3.7	Italy	6.8

Balance of payments, reserves and debt, $bn

Visible exports fob	14.0	Change in reserves	0.8
Visible imports fob	-30.4	Level of reserves	
Trade balance	-16.4	end Dec.	23.6
Invisibles inflows	13.3	No. months of import cover	7.1
Invisibles outflows	-9.3	Official gold holdings, m oz	0.7
Net transfers	7.1	Foreign debt	23.8
Current account balance	-5.4	– as % of GDP	23
– as % of GDP	-5.9	– as % of total exports	65
Capital balance	1.5	Debt service ratio	13
Overall balance	-4.4		

Health and education

Health spending, % of GDP	5.5	Education spending, % of GDP	5.6
Doctors per 1,000 pop.	0.6	Enrolment, %: primary	107
Hospital beds per 1,000 pop.	1.1	secondary	56
Improved-water source access,		tertiary	12
% of pop.	81		

Society

No. of households	6.3m	Colour TVs per 100 households	82.4
Av. no. per household	5.1	Telephone lines per 100 pop.	11.0
Marriages per 1,000 pop.	...	Mobile telephone subscribers	
Divorces per 1,000 pop.	...	per 100 pop.	79.1
Cost of living, Dec. 2010		Broadband subs per 100 pop.	1.5
New York = 100	73	Internet hosts per 1,000 pop.	8.7

NETHERLANDS

Area[a]	41,526 sq km	Capital	Amsterdam
Arable as % of total land	31	Currency	Euro (€)

People

Population	16.6m	Life expectancy: men	78.5 yrs
Pop. per sq km	400.0	women	82.6 yrs
Av. ann. growth		Adult literacy	...
in pop. 2010–15	0.37%	Fertility rate (per woman)	1.8
Pop. under 15	17.6%	Urban population	82.9%
Pop. over 60	21.9%		per 1,000 pop.
No. of men per 100 women	98.5	Crude birth rate	11.3
Human Development Index	89.0	Crude death rate	8.8

The economy

GDP	€570bn	GDP per head	$47,920
GDP	$792bn	GDP per head in purchasing	
Av. ann. growth in real		power parity (USA=100)	88.5
GDP 2004–09	1.4%	Economic freedom index	74.7

Origins of GDP

	% of total
Agriculture	2
Industry, of which:	24
manufacturing	13
Services	74

Components of GDP

	% of total
Private consumption	46
Public consumption	29
Investment	18
Exports	69
Imports	-62

Structure of employment

	% of total		% of labour force
Agriculture	3	Unemployed 2009	3.4
Industry	18	Av. ann. rate 1995–2009	4.0
Services	79		

Energy

	m TOE		
Total output	66.5	Net energy imports as %	
Total consumption	79.7	of energy use	16
Consumption per head,			
kg oil equivalent	4,845		

Inflation and finance

		av. ann. increase 2004–09	
Consumer price			
inflation 2010	1.3%	Euro area:	
Av. ann. inflation 2005–10	1.5%	Narrow money (M1)	9.0%
Deposit rate, households, 2010	3.44%	Broad money	7.3%
		Household saving rate, 2010	6.6%

Exchange rates

	end 2010		2010
€ per $	0.75	Effective rates	2005 = 100
€ per SDR	1.15	– nominal	97.8
		– real	97.1

Trade

Principal exports	$bn fob	Principal imports	$bn cif
Machinery & transport equip.	147.4	Machinery & transport equip.	137.0
Mineral fuels & lubricants	70.0	Mineral fuels & lubricants	71.9
Chemicals & related products	65.8	Chemicals & related products	51.5
Food, drink & tobacco	65.6	Food, drink & tobacco	42.2
Total incl. others	**431.8**	Total incl. others	**382.4**

Main export destinations	% of total	Main origins of imports	% of total
Germany	29.7	Germany	19.5
Belgium	14.6	China	13.5
France	10.7	Belgium	10.1
United Kingdom	9.4	United States	9.0
ETU27	77.4	EU27	49.0

Balance of payments, reserves and aid, $bn

Visible exports fob	424.8	Overall balance	7.0
Visible imports fob	-373.7	Change in reserves	10.9
Trade balance	51.1	Level of reserves	
Invisibles inflows	180.5	end Dec.	39.5
Invisibles outflows	-184.7	No. months of import cover	0.7
Net transfers	-10.3	Official gold holdings, m oz	19.7
Current account balance	36.6	Aid given	6.43
– as % of GDP	4.6	– as % of GDP	0.82
Capital balance	-48.3		

Health and education

Health spending, % of GDP	10.8	Education spending, % of GDP	5.3
Doctors per 1,000 pop.	3.9	Enrolment, %: primary	107
Hospital beds per 1,000 pop.	4.4	secondary	121
Improved-water source access,		tertiary	61
% of pop.	100		

Society

No. of households	7.3m	Colour TVs per 100 households	99.1
Av. no. per household	2.3	Telephone lines per 100 pop.	44.1
Marriages per 1,000 pop.	4.1	Mobile telephone subscribers	
Divorces per 1,000 pop.	2.0	per 100 pop.	127.7
Cost of living, Dec. 2010		Broadband subs per 100 pop.	35.6
New York = 100	97	Internet hosts per 1,000 pop.	819.0

a Includes water.

NEW ZEALAND

Area	270,534 sq km	Capital	Wellington
Arable as % of total land	2	Currency	New Zealand dollar (NZ$)

People

Population	4.3m	Life expectancy: men		79.1 yrs
Pop. per sq km	16.1		women	82.8 yrs
Av. ann. growth		Adult literacy		...
in pop. 2010–15	1.10%	Fertility rate (per woman)		2.1
Pop. under 15	20.2%	Urban population		86.2%
Pop. over 60	18.2%			per 1,000 pop.
No. of men per 100 women	96.5	Crude birth rate		14.9
Human Development Index	90.7	Crude death rate		7.2

The economy

GDP	NZ$188bn	GDP per head	$29,350
GDP	$127bn	GDP per head in purchasing	
Av. ann. growth in real		power parity (USA=100)	63.0
GDP 2004–09	1.0%	Economic freedom index	82.3

Origins of GDP

	% of total
Agriculture & mining	5
Industry	24
Services	71

Components of GDP

	% of total
Private consumption	60
Public consumption	20
Investment	18
Exports	28
Imports	-27

Structure of employment

	% of total		% of labour force
Agriculture	7	Unemployed 2009	6.1
Industry	22	Av. ann. rate 1995–2009	5.4
Services	71		

Energy

	m TOE		
Total output	14.9	Net energy imports as %	
Total consumption	16.9	of energy use	12
Consumption per head,			
kg oil equivalent	3,967		

Inflation and finance

		av. ann. increase 2004–09	
Consumer price			
inflation 2010	1.8%	Narrow money (M1)	-1.2%
Av. ann. inflation 2005–10	2.7%	Broad money	8.2%
Money market rate, 2010	2.61%		

Exchange rates

	end 2010		2010
NZ$ per $	1.30	Effective rates	2005 = 100
NZ$ per SDR	2.00	– nominal	93.3
NZ$ per €	1.74	– real	97.5

Trade

Principal exports		Principal imports	
	$bn fob		*$bn cif*
Dairy produce	5.6	Machinery & equipment	6.0
Meat	3.5	Mineral fuels	4.3
Forestry products	2.2	Transport equipment	2.3
Mineral fuels	1.3		
Total incl. others	**25.6**	Total incl. others	**28.8**

Main export destinations		Main origins of imports	
	% of total		*% of total*
Australia	23.0	Australia	18.4
China	10.0	China	15.1
United States	9.1	United States	10.8
Japan	7.1	Japan	7.4

Balance of payments, reserves and aid, $bn

Visible exports fob	25.3	Overall balance	3.7
Visible imports fob	-24.0	Change in reserves	4.5
Trade balance	1.3	Level of reserves	
Invisibles inflows	10.6	end Dec.	15.6
Invisibles outflows	-15.8	No. months of import cover	4.7
Net transfers	0.3	Official gold holdings, m oz	0.0
Current account balance	-3.6	Aid given	0.31
– as % of GDP	-2.9	– as % of GDP	0.28
Capital balance	3.8		

Health and education

Health spending, % of GDP	9.7	Education spending, % of GDP	6.1
Doctors per 1,000 pop.	2.3	Enrolment, %: primary	101
Hospital beds per 1,000 pop.	6.0	secondary	119
Improved-water source access,		tertiary	78
% of pop.	100		

Society

No. of households	1.5m	Colour TVs per 100 households	98.6
Av. no. per household	2.9	Telephone lines per 100 pop.	43.8
Marriages per 1,000 pop.	4.7	Mobile telephone subscribers	
Divorces per 1,000 pop.	2.7	per 100 pop.	110.2
Cost of living, Dec. 2010		Broadband subs per 100 pop.	23.0
New York = 100	101	Internet hosts per 1,000 pop.	639.6

NIGERIA

Area	923,768 sq km	Capital	Abuja
Arable as % of total land	41	Currency	Naira (N)

People

Population	154.7m	Life expectancy: men	48.6 yrs
Pop. per sq km	171.5	women	49.7 yrs
Av. ann. growth		Adult literacy	60.8%
in pop. 2010–15	2.50%	Fertility rate (per woman)	5.6
Pop. under 15	42.4%	Urban population	49.8%
Pop. over 60	4.9%		per 1,000 pop.
No. of men per 100 women	102.5	Crude birth rate	40.4
Human Development Index	42.3	Crude death rate	15.3

The economy

GDP	N25,761bn	GDP per head	$1,120
GDP	$173bn	GDP per head in purchasing	
Av. ann. growth in real		power parity (USA=100)	4.8
GDP 2004–09	6.3%	Economic freedom index	56.7

Origins of GDP

Components of GDP

	% of total		% of total
Agriculture	33	Private consumption	65
Industry, of which:	41	Public consumption	6
manufacturing	3	Investment	8
Services	27	Exports	43
		Imports	-22

Structure of employment

	% of total		% of labour force
Agriculture	...	Unemployed 2001	3.9
Industry	...	Av. ann. rate 1995–2001	3.7
Services	...		

Energy

	m TOE		
Total output	226.8	Net energy imports as %	
Total consumption	111.2	of energy use	-104
Consumption per head,			
kg oil equivalent	735		

Inflation and finance

Consumer price		av. ann. increase 2004–09	
inflation 2010	13.7%	Narrow money (M1)	27.6%
Av. ann. inflation 2005–10	10.1%	Broad money	35.2%
Treasury bill rate 2010	3.88%		

Exchange rates

	end 2010		2010
N per $	150.66	Effective rates	2005 = 100
N per SDR	232.02	– nominal	83.6
N per €	201.31	– real	121.2

Trade

Principal exports		Principal imports	
	$bn fob		*$bn cif*
Mineral products, incl oil & gas	74.3	Machinery & transport equip.	12.9
Vehicle parts	1.9	Manufactured goods	6.7
Rubber & plastics	1.0	Chemicals	3.4
		Food & live animals	2.4
Total incl. others	**80.7**	Total incl. others	**27.8**

Main export destinations		Main origins of imports	
	% of total		*% of total*
United States	34.2	China	13.9
India	9.8	United States	9.3
Brazil	9.1	Netherlands	8.6
Spain	6.8	United Kingdom	4.9

Balance of payments, reserves and debt, $bn

Visible exports fob	59.3	Change in reserves	-8.1
Visible imports fob	-30.3	Level of reserves	
Trade balance	29.0	end Dec.	45.5
Invisibles inflows	3.3	No. months of import cover	9.3
Invisibles outflows	-28.6	Official gold holdings, m oz	0.7
Net transfers	18.0	Foreign debt	7.9
Current account balance	21.7	– as % of GDP	4
– as % of GDP	12.5	– as % of total exports	8
Capital balance	6.6	Debt service ratio	1
Overall balance	-10.5		

Health and education

Health spending, % of GDP	5.8	Education spending, % of GDP	...
Doctors per 1,000 pop.	0.4	Enrolment, %: primary	93
Hospital beds per 1,000 pop.	0.5	secondary	30
Improved-water source access,		tertiary	10
% of pop.	58		

Society

No. of households	31.4m	Colour TVs per 100 households	33.5
Av. no. per household	4.9	Telephone lines per 100 pop.	1.0
Marriages per 1,000 pop.	...	Mobile telephone subscribers	
Divorces per 1,000 pop.	...	per 100 pop.	48.2
Cost of living, Dec. 2010		Broadband subs per 100 pop.	0.1
New York = 100	73	Internet hosts per 1,000 pop.	...

NORWAY

Area	323,878 sq km	Capital	Oslo
Arable as % of total land	3	Currency	Norwegian krone (Nkr)

People

Population	4.8m	Life expectancy: men		79.2 yrs
Pop. per sq km	12.7	women		83.4 yrs
Av. ann. growth		Adult literacy		...
in pop. 2010–15	1.09%	Fertility rate (per woman)		1.9
Pop. under 15	18.8%	Urban population		79.4%
Pop. over 60	21.1%			per 1,000 pop.
No. of men per 100 women	100.1	Crude birth rate		12.6
Human Development Index	93.8	Crude death rate		8.5

The economy

GDP	Nkr2,401bn	GDP per head	$79,090
GDP	$382bn	GDP per head in purchasing	
Av. ann. growth in real		power parity (USA=100)	122.2
GDP 2004–09	1.4%	Economic freedom index	70.3

Origins of GDP

	% of total
Agriculture	1
Industry, of which:	40
manufacturing	10
Services	59

Components of GDP

	% of total
Private consumption	43
Public consumption	22
Investment	20
Exports	42
Imports	-27

Structure of employment

	% of total		% of labour force
Agriculture	3	Unemployed 2009	3.2
Industry	21	Av. ann. rate 1995–2009	3.7
Services	76		

Energy

	m TOE		
Total output	219.7	Net energy imports as %	
Total consumption	29.7	of energy use	-640
Consumption per head,			
kg oil equivalent	6,222		

Inflation and finance

Consumer price		av. ann. increase 2004–09	
inflation 2010	2.4%	Narrow money (M1)	...
Av. ann. inflation 2005–10	2.3%	Broad money	9.5%
Interbank rate, 2010	2.50%	Household saving rate, 2010	7.2%

Exchange rates

	end 2010		2010
Nkr per $	5.86	Effective rates	2005 = 100
Nkr per SDR	9.03	– nominal	101.3
Nkr per €	7.83	– real	102.4

Trade

Principal exports		Principal imports	
	$bn fob		$bn cif
Mineral fuels & lubricants	78.4	Machinery & transport equip.	27.8
Machinery & transport equip.	13.5	Manufactured goods	10.3
Manufactured goods	10.1	Chemicals & mineral products	6.9
Food & beverages	7.4	Food & beverages	5.0
Total incl. others	**120.8**	Total incl. others	**69.3**

Main export destinations		Main origins of imports	
	% of total		% of total
United Kingdom	24.3	Sweden	13.7
Germany	13.4	Germany	12.7
Netherlands	10.9	China	7.7
France	8.5	Denmark	6.7
Sweden	5.8	United States	6.1
United States	4.8	United Kingdom	5.9
EU27	80.0	EU27	66.7

Balance of payments, reserves and aid, $bn

Visible exports fob	121.9	Overall balance	-17.1
Visible imports fob	-67.5	Change in reserves	-2.1
Trade balance	54.4	Level of reserves	
Invisibles inflows	65.8	end Dec.	48.9
Invisibles outflows	-65.7	No. months of import cover	4.4
Net transfers	-4.4	Official gold holdings, m oz	0.0
Current account balance	50.1	Aid given	4.09
– as % of GDP	13.1	– as % of GDP	1.06
Capital balance	-71.9		

Health and education

Health spending, % of GDP	9.7	Education spending, % of GDP	6.8
Doctors per 1,000 pop.	4.0	Enrolment, %: primary	99
Hospital beds per 1,000 pop.	3.3	secondary	112
Improved-water source access,		tertiary	73
% of pop.	100		

Society

No. of households	2.1m	Colour TVs per 100 households	98.4
Av. no. per household	2.3	Telephone lines per 100 pop.	37.1
Marriages per 1,000 pop.	5.2	Mobile telephone subscribers	
Divorces per 1,000 pop.	2.1	per 100 pop.	111.4
Cost of living, Dec. 2010		Broadband subs per 100 pop.	34.0
New York = 100	142	Internet hosts per 1,000 pop.	737.9

PAKISTAN

Area	803,940 sq km	Capital	Islamabad
Arable as % of total land	26	Currency	Pakistan rupee (PRs)

People

Population	180.8m	Life expectancy: men		67.6 yrs
Pop. per sq km	218.1		women	68.3 yrs
Av. ann. growth		Adult literacy		55.5%
in pop. 2010–15	1.80%	Fertility rate (per woman)		3.7
Pop. under 15	36.6%	Urban population		35.9%
Pop. over 60	6.2%			per 1,000 pop.
No. of men per 100 women	103.4	Crude birth rate		28.1
Human Development Index	49.0	Crude death rate		6.4

The economy

GDP	PRs12,739bn	GDP per head	$960
GDP	$162bn	GDP per head in purchasing	
Av. ann. growth in real		power parity (USA=100)	5.7
GDP 2004–09	4.9%	Economic freedom index	55.1

Origins of GDP

	% of total
Agriculture	22
Industry, of which:	24
manufacturing	17
Services	54

Components of GDP

	% of total
Private consumption	80
Public consumption	8
Investment	19
Exports	13
Imports	-20

Structure of employment

	% of total		% of labour force
Agriculture	44	Unemployed 2008	5.0
Industry	21	Av. ann. rate 1995–2008	6.3
Services	35		

Energy

	m TOE		
Total output	63.3	Net energy imports as %	
Total consumption	82.8	of energy use	24
Consumption per head,			
kg oil equivalent	499		

Inflation and finance

		av. ann. increase 2004–09	
Consumer price			
inflation 2010	13.9%	Narrow money (M1)	10.1%
Av. ann. inflation 2005–10	12.6%	Broad money (M2)	14.3%
Money market rate, 2010	11.69%		

Exchange rates

	end 2010		2010
PRs per $	85.74	Effective rates	2005 = 100
PRs per SDR	132.00	– nominal	64.2
PRs per €	114.57	– real	106.8

Trade[a]

Principal exports[a]

	$bn fob
Rice	2.0
Cotton fabrics	1.9
Bedwear	1.7
Knitwear	1.7
Cotton yard & thread	1.1
Total incl. others	**17.6**

Principal imports[a]

	$bn fob
Mineral fuels	10.1
Machinery & transport equip.	8.0
Chemicals	5.2
Manufactured goods	3.5
Food & live animals	2.3
Total incl. others	**34.7**

Main export destinations[a]

	% of total
United States	18.1
United Arab Emirates	8.4
Afghanistan	7.7
China	5.6
United Kingdom	5.3

Main origins of imports[a]

	% of total
China	11.9
Saudi Arabia	11.0
United Arab Emirates	10.9
Kuwait	5.7
United States	5.7

Balance of payments, reserves and debt, $bn

Visible exports fob	18.3	Change in reserves	4.9
Visible imports fob	-28.5	Level of reserves	
Trade balance	-10.2	end Dec.	14.0
Invisibles inflows	4.5	No. months of import cover	4.3
Invisibles outflows	-10.7	Official gold holdings, m oz	2.1
Net transfers	12.8	Foreign debt	53.7
Current account balance	-3.6	– as % of GDP	24
– as % of GDP	-2.2	– as % of total exports	157
Capital balance	5.9	Debt service ratio	15
Overall balance	1.7		

Health and education

Health spending, % of GDP	2.6	Education spending, % of GDP	2.7
Doctors per 1,000 pop.	0.8	Enrolment, %: primary	85
Hospital beds per 1,000 pop.	0.6	secondary	33
Improved-water source access,		tertiary	5
% of pop.	90		

Society

No. of households	25.1	Colour TVs per 100 households	36.6
Av. no. per household	7.2	Telephone lines per 100 pop.	2.0
Marriages per 1,000 pop.	...	Mobile telephone subscribers	
Divorces per 1,000 pop.	...	per 100 pop.	52.2
Cost of living, Dec. 2010		Broadband subs per 100 pop.	0.2
New York = 100	43	Internet hosts per 1,000 pop.	1.8

a Fiscal year ending June 30, 2009.

PERU

Area	1,285,216 sq km	Capital	Lima
Arable as % of total land	3	Currency	Nuevo Sol (New Sol)

People

Population	29.2m	Life expectancy:	men	71.6 yrs
Pop. per sq km	22.6		women	76.9 yrs
Av. ann. growth		Adult literacy		89.6%
in pop. 2010–15	1.07%	Fertility rate (per woman)		2.6
Pop. under 15	29.9%	Urban population		76.9%
Pop. over 60	8.7%			per 1,000 pop.
No. of men per 100 women	100.4	Crude birth rate		21.3
Human Development Index	72.3	Crude death rate		5.5

The economy

GDP	New Soles 393bn	GDP per head	$4,470
GDP	$130bn	GDP per head in purchasing	
Av. ann. growth in real		power parity (USA=100)	18.8
GDP 2004–09	6.8%	Economic freedom index	68.6

Origins of GDP

	% of total
Agriculture	7
Industry, of which:	34
manufacturing	14
Services	59

Components of GDP

	% of total
Private consumption	64
Public consumption	10
Investment	22
Exports	24
Imports	-20

Structure of employment

	% of total		% of labour force
Agriculture	9	Unemployed 2008	6.8
Industry	42	Av. ann. rate 1995–2008	7.7
Services	49		

Energy

	m TOE		
Total output	12.3	Net energy imports as %	
Total consumption	14.7	of energy use	16
Consumption per head,			
kg oil equivalent	510		

Inflation and finance

		av. ann. increase 2004–09	
Consumer price			
inflation 2010	1.5%	Narrow money (M1)	16.3%
Av. ann. inflation 2005–10	2.8%	Broad money	15.2%
Money market rate, 2010	2.98%		

Exchange rates

	end 2010		2010
New Soles per $	2.81	Effective rates	2005 = 100
New Soles per SDR	4.33	– nominal	...
New Soles per €	3.75	– real	...

Trade

Principal exports		Principal imports	
	$bn fob		*$bn fob*
Gold	6.8	Intermediate goods	10.1
Copper	5.9	Capital goods	6.8
Fishmeal	1.7	Consumer goods	4.0
Zinc	1.2	Other goods	0.1
Total incl. others	**27.0**	Total	**21.0**

Main export destinations		Main origins of imports	
	% of total		*% of total*
United States	17.5	United States	21.6
China	15.2	China	16.5
Switzerland	14.8	Brazil	8.4
Canada	8.6	Ecuador	5.3

Balance of payments, reserves and debt, $bn

Visible exports fob	26.9	Change in reserves	2.0
Visible imports fob	-21.0	Level of reserves	
Trade balance	5.9	end Dec.	33.2
Invisibles inflows	5.1	No. months of import cover	11.5
Invisibles outflows	-13.6	Official gold holdings, m oz	1.1
Net transfers	2.9	Foreign debt	29.6
Current account balance	0.2	– as % of GDP	23
– as % of GDP	0.2	– as % of total exports	78
Capital balance	2.6	Debt service ratio	12
Overall balance	1.9		

Health and education

Health spending, % of GDP	4.6	Education spending, % of GDP	2.7
Doctors per 1,000 pop.	0.9	Enrolment, %: primary	109
Hospital beds per 1,000 pop.	1.4	secondary	89
Improved-water source access,		tertiary	34
% of pop.	82		

Society

No. of households	7.1m	Colour TVs per 100 households	66.2
Av. no. per household	4.1	Telephone lines per 100 pop.	10.2
Marriages per 1,000 pop.	2.7	Mobile telephone subscribers	
Divorces per 1,000 pop.	...	per 100 pop.	84.7
Cost of living, Dec. 2010		Broadband subs per 100 pop.	2.8
New York = 100	71	Internet hosts per 1,000 pop.	9.0

PHILIPPINES

Area	300,000 sq km	Capital	Manila
Arable as % of total land	18	Currency	Philippine peso (P)

People

Population	92.0m	Life expectancy: men	70.7 yrs
Pop. per sq km	310.9	women	75.2 yrs
Av. ann. growth		Adult literacy	95.4%
in pop. 2010–15	1.73%	Fertility rate (per woman)	3.3
Pop. under 15	33.5%	Urban population	48.9%
Pop. over 60	6.7%		per 1,000 pop.
No. of men per 100 women	100.7	Crude birth rate	25.9
Human Development Index	63.8	Crude death rate	4.7

The economy

GDP	P7,679bn	GDP per head	$1,750
GDP	$161bn	GDP per head in purchasing	
Av. ann. growth in real		power parity (USA=100)	7.7
GDP 2004–09	4.4%	Economic freedom index	56.2

Origins of GDP		Components of GDP	
	% of total		% of total
Agriculture	7	Private consumption	74
Industry, of which:	34	Public consumption	11
manufacturing	14	Investment	15
Services	59	Exports	32
		Imports	-31

Structure of employment

	% of total		% of labour force
Agriculture	36	Unemployed 2009	7.5
Industry	15	Av. ann. rate 1995–2009	9.2
Services	49		

Energy

	m TOE		
Total output	23.3	Net energy imports as %	
Total consumption	41.1	of energy use	43
Consumption per head,			
kg oil equivalent	455		

Inflation and finance

Consumer price		av. ann. increase 2006–09	
inflation 2010	3.8%	Narrow money (M1)	...
Av. ann. inflation 2005–10	5.1%	Broad money	9.4%
Money market rate, 2010	4.20%		

Exchange rates

	end 2010		2010
P per $	43.89	Effective rates	2005 = 100
P per SDR	67.58	– nominal	109.9
P per €	58.65	– real	127.6

Trade

Principal exports		Principal imports	
	$bn fob		*$bn fob*
Electrical & electronic		Capital goods	12.9
equipment	22.2	Mineral fuels	7.3
Clothing	1.5	Chemicals	4.2
Coconut oil	0.6	Manufactured goods	3.2
Petroleum products	0.3		
Total incl. others	**38.3**	Total incl. others	**45.3**

Main export destinations		Main origins of imports	
	% of total		*% of total*
United States	18.1	Japan	12.7
Japan	16.7	United States	12.1
Netherlands	9.7	China	9.0
Hong Kong	8.6	Singapore	8.7
China	7.8	South Korea	7.0

Balance of payments, reserves and debt, $bn

Visible exports fob	37.5	Change in reserves	6.7
Visible imports fob	-46.4	Level of reserves	
Trade balance	-8.9	end Dec.	44.2
Invisibles inflows	15.8	No. months of import cover	8.7
Invisibles outflows	-14.3	Official gold holdings, m oz	5.0
Net transfers	16.0	Foreign debt	62.9
Current account balance	8.6	– as % of GDP	35
– as % of GDP	5.3	– as % of total exports	90
Capital balance	-0.8	Debt service ratio	19
Overall balance	6.4		

Health and education

Health spending, % of GDP	3.8	Education spending, % of GDP	2.8
Doctors per 1,000 pop.	1.0	Enrolment, %: primary	110
Hospital beds per 1,000 pop.	1.0	secondary	82
Improved-water source access,		tertiary	29
% of pop.	91		

Society

No. of households	19.1m	Colour TVs per 100 households	90.3
Av. no. per household	4.8	Telephone lines per 100 pop.	7.4
Marriages per 1,000 pop.	6.3	Mobile telephone subscribers	
Divorces per 1,000 pop.	...	per 100 pop.	100.3
Cost of living, Dec. 2010		Broadband subs per 100 pop.	1.9
New York = 100	58	Internet hosts per 1,000 pop.	5.1

POLAND

Area	312,683 sq km	Capital	Warsaw
Arable as % of total land	41	Currency	Zloty (Zl)

People

Population	38.1m	Life expectancy: men	72.3 yrs
Pop. per sq km	118.4	women	80.4 yrs
Av. ann. growth		Adult literacy	99.5
in pop. 2010–15	0.06%	Fertility rate (per woman)	1.3
Pop. under 15	14.8%	Urban population	61.0%
Pop. over 60	19.4%		per 1,000 pop.
No. of men per 100 women	93.2	Crude birth rate	10.2
Human Development Index	79.5	Crude death rate	10.5

The economy

GDP	Zl1,342bn	GDP per head	$11,270
GDP	$430bn	GDP per head in purchasing	
Av. ann. growth in real		power parity (USA=100)	41.1
GDP 2004–09	4.7%	Economic freedom index	64.1

Origins of GDP		Components of GDP	
	% of total		% of total
Agriculture	4	Private consumption	61
Industry, of which:	30	Public consumption	19
manufacturing	16	Investment	20
Services	66	Exports	39
		Imports	-39

Structure of employment

	% of total		% of labour force
Agriculture	15	Unemployed 2009	8.2
Industry	31	Av. ann. rate 1995–2009	14.0
Services	54		

Energy

	m TOE		
Total output	71.4	Net energy imports as %	
Total consumption	97.9	of energy use	27
Consumption per head,			
kg oil equivalent	2,567		

Inflation and finance

Consumer price		av. ann. increase 2004–09	
inflation 2010	2.7%	Narrow money (M1)	16.4%
Av. ann. inflation 2005–10	2.9%	Broad money	13.8%
Money market rate, 2010	3.08%	Household saving rate, 2010	6.5%

Exchange rates

	end 2010		2010
Zl per $	2.96	Effective rates	2005 = 100
Zl per SDR	4.56	– nominal	102.1
Zl per €	3.96	– real	103.9

Trade

Principal exports		Principal imports	
	$bn fob		*$bn cif*
Machinery & transport equipment	57.7	Machinery & transport equipment	51.4
Manufactured goods	43.9	Manufactured goods	40.8
Foodstuffs & live animals	12.7	Chemicals & products	20.4
Total incl. others	**136.7**	Total incl. others	**149.6**

Main export destinations		Main origins of imports	
	% of total		*% of total*
Germany	26.1	Germany	28.1
France	6.9	Russia	8.5
Italy	6.8	Italy	6.6
United Kingdom	6.4	France	5.4
EU27	79.3	EU27	72.0

Balance of payments, reserves and debt, $bn

Visible exports fob	142.1	Change in reserves	17.3
Visible imports fob	-146.4	Level of reserves	
Trade balance	-4.4	end Dec.	79.5
Invisibles inflows	36.3	No. months of import cover	4.9
Invisibles outflows	-48.1	Official gold holdings, m oz	3.3
Net transfers	6.5	Foreign debt	169.0
Current account balance	-9.6	– as % of GDP	56
– as % of GDP	-2.2	– as % of total exports	134
Capital balance	43.9	Debt service ratio	29
Overall balance	14.8	Aid given	0.37
		% of GDP	0.09

Health and education

Health spending, % of GDP	7.1	Education spending, % of GDP	4.9
Doctors per 1,000 pop.	2.2	Enrolment, %: primary	97
Hospital beds per 1,000 pop.	6.7	secondary	100
Improved-water source access, % of pop.	100	tertiary	69

Society

No. of households	14.4m	Colour TVs per 100 households	97.6
Av. no. per household	2.6	Telephone lines per 100 pop.	25.2
Marriages per 1,000 pop.	5.3	Mobile telephone subscribers	
Divorces per 1,000 pop.	1.7	per 100 pop.	117.7
Cost of living, Dec. 2010		Broadband subs per 100 pop.	12.9
New York = 100	82	Internet hosts per 1,000 pop.	296.6

PORTUGAL

Area	88,940 sq km	Capital	Lisbon
Arable as % of total land	12	Currency	Euro (€)

People

Population	10.7m	Life expectancy: men	76.1 yrs
Pop. per sq km	116.1	women	82.6 yrs
Av. ann. growth		Adult literacy	94.9%
in pop. 2010–15	0.25%	Fertility rate (per woman)	1.4
Pop. under 15	15.2%	Urban population	60.7%
Pop. over 60	23.6%		per 1,000 pop.
No. of men per 100 women	94.0	Crude birth rate	9.8
Human Development Index	79.5	Crude death rate	10.5

The economy

GDP	€168bn	GDP per head	$21,900
GDP	$233bn	GDP per head in purchasing	
Av. ann. growth in real		power parity (USA=100)	54.2
GDP 2004–09	0.4%	Economic freedom index	64.0

Origins of GDP		Components of GDP	
	% of total		% of total
Agriculture	2	Private consumption	67
Industry, of which:	23	Public consumption	21
manufacturing	13	Investment	20
Services	75	Exports	28
		Imports	-36

Structure of employment

	% of total		% of labour force
Agriculture	12	Unemployed 2009	9.5
Industry	29	Av. ann. rate 1995–2009	6.4
Services	59		

Energy

	m TOE		
Total output	4.4	Net energy imports as %	
Total consumption	24.2	of energy use	82
Consumption per head,			
kg oil equivalent	2,274		

Inflation and finance

Consumer price		av. ann. increase 2004–09	
inflation 2010	1.4%	Euro area:	
Av. ann. inflation 2005–10	1.7%	Narrow money (M1)	9.0%
Deposit rate, h'holds, 2010	1.48%	Broad money	7.3%
		Household saving rate[a], 2010	9.8%

Exchange rates

	end 2010		2010
€ per $	0.75	Effective rates	2005 = 100
€ per SDR	1.15	– nominal	101.4
		– real	99.4

Trade

Principal exports		Principal imports	
	$bn fob		*$bn cif*
Machinery & transport equip.	11.7	Machinery & transport equip.	20.7
Food, drink & tobacco	4.8	Mineral fuels & lubricants	8.8
Chemicals & related products	3.2	Food, drink & tobacco	8.7
Raw materials	2.2	Chemicals & related products	8.6
Total incl. others	**44.3**	Total incl. others	**71.6**

Main export destinations		Main origins of imports	
	% of total		*% of total*
Spain	27.3	Spain	32.7
Germany	12.9	Germany	13.3
France	12.4	France	8.4
Italy	7.1	Italy	5.8
United Kingdom	5.8	Netherlands	5.5
EU27	74.9	EU27	78.0

Balance of payments, reserves and debt, $bn

Visible exports fob	44.5	Overall balance	1.1
Visible imports fob	-68.9	Change in reserves	3.8
Trade balance	-24.4	Level of reserves	
Invisibles inflows	33.8	end Dec.	15.8
Invisibles outflows	-36.4	No. months of import cover	1.8
Net transfers	3.0	Official gold holdings, m oz	12.3
Current account balance	-24.0	Aid given	0.51
– as % of GDP	-10.3	– as % of GDP	0.23
Capital balance	24.4		

Health and education

Health spending, % of GDP	11.3	Education spending, % of GDP	5.2
Doctors per 1,000 pop.	3.7	Enrolment, %: primary	115
Hospital beds per 1,000 pop.	3.4	secondary[b]	104
Improved-water source access,		tertiary	60
% of pop.	99		

Society

No. of households	4.1m	Colour TVs per 100 households	99.2
Av. no. per household	2.6	Telephone lines per 100 pop.	39.7
Marriages per 1,000 pop.	4.8	Mobile telephone subscribers	
Divorces per 1,000 pop.	2.5	per 100 pop.	148.8
Cost of living, Dec. 2010		Broadband subs per 100 pop.	17.4
New York = 100	84	Internet hosts per 1,000 pop.	316.3

a Gross.
b Includes training for unemployed.

ROMANIA

Area	237,500 sq km	Capital	Bucharest
Arable as % of total land	38	Currency	Leu (RON)

People

Population	21.3m	Life expectancy: men	70.3 yrs
Pop. per sq km	90.1	women	77.2 yrs
Av. ann. growth		Adult literacy	97.6%
in pop. 2010–15	-0.26%	Fertility rate (per woman)	1.3
Pop. under 15	15.2%	Urban population	57.5%
Pop. over 60	20.3%		per 1,000 pop.
No. of men per 100 women	94.3	Crude birth rate	10.2
Human Development Index	76.7	Crude death rate	12.6

The economy

GDP	RON491bn	GDP per head	$7,500
GDP	$161bn	GDP per head in purchasing	
Av. ann. growth in real		power parity (USA=100)	31.1
GDP 2004–09	3.6%	Economic freedom index	64.7

Origins of GDP

	% of total
Agriculture	7
Industry, of which:	26
manufacturing	22
Services	67

Components of GDP

	% of total
Private consumption	61
Public consumption	15
Investment	31
Exports	33
Imports	-40

Structure of employment

	% of total		% of labour force
Agriculture	29	Unemployed 2009	6.9
Industry	32	Av. ann. rate 1995–2009	6.9
Services	40		

Energy

	m TOE		
Total output	28.8	Net energy imports as %	
Total consumption	39.4	of energy use	27
Consumption per head,			
kg oil equivalent	1,830		

Inflation and finance

		av. ann. increase 2004–09	
Consumer price inflation 2010	6.1%	Narrow money (M1)	39.0%
Av. ann. inflation 2005–10	6.2%	Broad money	25.1%
Money market rate, 2010	5.44%		

Exchange rates

	end 2010		2010
RON per $	3.21	Effective rates	2005 = 100
RON per SDR	4.94	– nominal	85.6
RON per €	4.29	– real	103.8

Trade

Principal exports		Principal imports	
	$bn fob		$bn cif
Machinery & equipment		Machinery & equipment	
(incl. transport)	10.7	(incl. transport)	14.6
Basic metals & products	4.1	Chemical products	6.0
Textiles & apparel	4.1	Textiles & products	5.4
Minerals, fuels & lubricants	2.5	Minerals, fuels & lubricants	3.8
Total incl. others	**40.6**	Total incl. others	**54.3**

Main export destinations		Main origins of imports	
	% of total		% of total
Germany	18.8	Germany	17.4
Italy	15.5	Italy	11.8
France	8.2	Hungary	8.5
Turkey	5.0	France	6.2
EU27	74.3	EU27	73.3

Balance of payments, reserves and debt, $bn

Visible exports fob	40.7	Change in reserves	6.0
Visible imports fob	-50.2	Level of reserves	
Trade balance	-9.5	end Dec.	45.8
Invisibles inflows	11.4	No. months of import cover	8.4
Invisibles outflows	-14.9	Official gold holdings, m oz	3.3
Net transfers	-7.3	Foreign debt	117.5
Current account balance	-20.3	– as % of GDP	53
– as % of GDP	-4.5	– as % of total exports	166
Capital balance	2.7	Debt service ratio	31
Overall balance	-6.4		

Health and education

Health spending, % of GDP	5.4	Education spending, % of GDP	4.3
Doctors per 1,000 pop.	1.9	Enrolment, %: primary	100
Hospital beds per 1,000 pop.	6.5	secondary	92
Improved-water source access,		tertiary	66
% of pop.	57		

Society

No. of households	7.5m	Colour TVs per 100 households	93.9
Av. no. per household	2.9	Telephone lines per 100 pop.	25.0
Marriages per 1,000 pop.	6.4	Mobile telephone subscribers	
Divorces per 1,000 pop.	1.7	per 100 pop.	119.4
Cost of living, Dec. 2010		Broadband subs per 100 pop.	13.2
New York = 100	59	Internet hosts per 1,000 pop.	116.7

RUSSIA

Area	17,075,400 sq km	Capital	Moscow
Arable as % of total land	7	Currency	Rouble (Rb)

People

Population	140.9m	Life expectancy: men		61.9 yrs
Pop. per sq km	8.4		women	74.1 yrs
Av. ann. growth		Adult literacy		99.6%
in pop. 2010–15	-0.12%	Fertility rate (per woman)		1.4
Pop. under 15	15.0%	Urban population		73.2%
Pop. over 60	18.1%			per 1,000 pop.
No. of men per 100 women	86.1	Crude birth rate		11.4
Human Development Index	71.9	Crude death rate		15.1

The economy

GDP	Rb39,101bn	GDP per head	$8,680
GDP	$1,232bn	GDP per head in purchasing	
Av. ann. growth in real		power parity (USA=100)	41.2
GDP 2004–09	3.9%	Economic freedom index	50.5

Origins of GDP		Components of GDP	
	% of total		% of total
Agriculture	5	Private consumption	54
Industry, of which:	33	Public consumption	20
manufacturing	15	Investment	19
Services	62	Exports	28
		Imports	-20

Structure of employment

	% of total		% of labour force
Agriculture	9	Unemployed 2009	8.2
Industry	29	Av. ann. rate 1995–2009	9.1
Services	62		

Energy

	m TOE		
Total output	1,253.9	Net energy imports as %	
Total consumption	686.8	of energy use	-83
Consumption per head,			
kg oil equivalent	4,838		

Inflation and finance

Consumer price		av. ann. increase 2004–09	
inflation 2010	6.9%	Narrow money (M1)	21.3%
Av. ann. inflation 2005–10	10.2%	Broad money	29.8%
Money market rate, 2010	3.07%		

Exchange rates

	end 2010		2010
Rb per $	30.48	Effective rates	2005 = 100
Rb per SDR	46.94	– nominal	89.6
Rb per 7	40.73	– real	125.8

Trade

Principal exports		Principal imports	
	$bn fob		*$bn fob*
Fuels	203.0	Machinery & equipment	72.6
Metals	38.7	Food & agricultural products	30.1
Chemicals	18.7	Chemicals	27.9
Machinery & equipment	17.9	Metals	11.3
Total incl. others	**301.7**	Total incl. others	**167.3**

Main export destinations		Main origins of imports	
	% of total		*% of total*
Netherlands	11.6	United States	13.7
Italy	6.7	China	12.6
China	5.3	Germany	5.4
Germany	3.9	Ukraine	5.2

Balance of payments, reserves and debt, $bn

Visible exports fob	303.4	Change in reserves	11.9
Visible imports fob	-191.8	Level of reserves	
Trade balance	111.6	end Dec.	438.9
Invisibles inflows	75.6	No. months of import cover	16.1
Invisibles outflows	-134.9	Official gold holdings, m oz	20.9
Net transfers	-2.9	Foreign debt	381.3
Current account balance	49.4	– as % of GDP	26
– as % of GDP	4.0	– as % of total exports	74
Capital balance	-44.3	Debt service ratio	18
Overall balance	3.4		

Health and education

Health spending, % of GDP	5.4	Education spending, % of GDP	3.9
Doctors per 1,000 pop.	4.4	Enrolment, %: primary	97
Hospital beds per 1,000 pop.	9.6	secondary	85
Improved-water source access,		tertiary	77
% of pop.	96		

Society

No. of households	52.8m	Colour TVs per 100 households	96.8
Av. no. per household	2.7	Telephone lines per 100 pop.	32.2
Marriages per 1,000 pop.	8.0	Mobile telephone subscribers	
Divorces per 1,000 pop.	3.8	per 100 pop.	163.6
Cost of living, Dec. 2010		Broadband subs per 100 pop.	9.2
New York = 100	97	Internet hosts per 1,000 pop.	84.0

SAUDI ARABIA

Area	2,200,000 sq km	Capital	Riyadh
Arable as % of total land	2	Currency	Riyal (SR)

People

Population	25.7m	Life expectancy:	men	71.9 yrs
Pop. per sq km	12.8		women	76.3 yrs
Av. ann. growth		Adult literacy		85.5%
in pop. 2010–15	2.65%	Fertility rate (per woman)		3.0
Pop. under 15	31.9%	Urban population		82.1%
Pop. over 60	4.6%			per 1,000 pop.
No. of men per 100 women	124.0	Crude birth rate		22.1
Human Development Index	75.2	Crude death rate		3.6

The economy

GDP	SR1,409bn	GDP per head	$14,800
GDP	$376bn	GDP per head in purchasing	
Av. ann. growth in real		power parity (USA=100)	51.1
GDP 2004–09	3.1%	Economic freedom index	66.2

Origins of GDP

	% of total
Agriculture	3
Industry, of which:	51
manufacturing	10
Services	46

Components of GDP

	% of total
Private consumption	38
Public consumption	25
Investment	26
Exports	54
Imports	-43

Structure of employment

	% of total		% of labour force
Agriculture	5	Unemployed 2008	5.0
Industry	20	Av. ann. rate 1995–2008	4.7
Services	75		

Energy

	m TOE		
Total output	579.0	Net energy imports as %	
Total consumption	161.6	of energy use	-258
Consumption per head,			
kg oil equivalent	6,514		

Inflation and finance

Consumer price		av. ann. increase 2004–09	
inflation 2010	5.3%	Narrow money (M1)	14.6%
Av. ann. inflation 2005–10	5.3%	Broad money	16.4%
Money market rate, Nov. 2010	0.73%		

Exchange rates

	end 2010		2010
SR per $	3.75	Effective rates	2005 = 100
SR per SDR	5.78	– nominal	92.8
SRE per €	5.01	– real	104.5

Trade

Principal exports		Principal imports	
	$bn fob		$bn cif
Crude oil	142.2	Machinery & transport equip.	44.1
Refined petroleum products	20.9	Foodstuffs	14.2
		Chemicals & metal products	8.3
Total incl. others	**192.3**	Total incl. others	**89.5**

Main export destinations		Main origins of imports	
	% of total		% of total
Japan	15.4	United States	12.8
China	12.5	China	10.7
South Korea	12.3	United Kingdom	4.9
United States	10.4	South Korea	4.6

Balance of payments, reserves and aid, $bn

Visible exports fob	192.3	Overall balance	-32.6
Visible imports fob	-87.1	Change in reserves	-31.6
Trade balance	105.2	Level of reserves	
Invisibles inflows	29.4	end Dec.	415.0
Invisibles outflows	-84.7	No. months of import cover	29.0
Net transfers	-27.2	Official gold holdings, m oz	10.4
Current account balance	22.8	Aid given	3.13
– as % of GDP	6.1	– as % of GDP	0.83
Capital balance	-19.0		

Health and education

Health spending, % of GDP	5.0	Education spending, % of GDP	5.6
Doctors per 1,000 pop.	1.0	Enrolment, %: primary	99
Hospital beds per 1,000 pop.	1.9	secondary	97
Improved-water source access,		tertiary	33
% of pop.	96		

Society

No. of households	4.7m	Colour TVs per 100 households	98.0
Av. no. per household	5.4	Telephone lines per 100 pop.	16.2
Marriages per 1,000 pop.	4.6	Mobile telephone subscribers	
Divorces per 1,000 pop.	1.0	per 100 pop.	174.4
Cost of living, Dec. 2010		Broadband subs per 100 pop.	5.2
New York = 100	66	Internet hosts per 1,000 pop.	18.8

SINGAPORE

Area	639 sq km	Capital	Singapore
Arable as % of total land	1	Currency	Singapore dollar (S$)

People

Population	4.7m	Life expectancy: men		78.5 yrs
Pop. per sq km	7,447.2		women	83.4 yrs
Av. ann. growth		Adult literacy		94.7%
in pop. 2010–15	3.52%	Fertility rate (per woman)		1.3
Pop. under 15	15.6%	Urban population		100.0%
Pop. over 60	16.0%			per 1,000 pop.
No. of men per 100 women	101.7	Crude birth rate		8.9
Human Development Index	84.6	Crude death rate		6.0

The economy

GDP	S$265bn	GDP per head	$36,540
GDP	$182bn	GDP per head in purchasing	
Av. ann. growth in real		power parity (USA=100)	110.1
GDP 2004–09	5.0%	Economic freedom index	87.2

Origins of GDP		Components of GDP	
	% of total		% of total
Agriculture	0	Private consumption	43
Industry, of which:	26	Public consumption	10
manufacturing	19	Investment	29
Services	74	Exports	221
		Imports	-203

Structure of employment

	% of total		% of labour force
Agriculture	0	Unemployed 2009	5.9
Industry	23	Av. ann. rate 1995–2009	4.2
Services	77		

Energy

	m TOE		
Total output	0.0	Net energy imports as %	
Total consumption	18.5	of energy use	100
Consumption per head,			
kg oil equivalent	3,828		

Inflation and finance

Consumer price		av. ann. increase 2004–09	
inflation 2010	2.8%	Narrow money (M1)	16.2%
Av. ann. inflation 2005–10	2.6%	Broad money	12.4%
Money market rate, 2010	0.56%		

Exchange rates

	end 2010		2010
S$ per $	1.29	Effective rates	2005 = 100
S$ per SDR	1.98	– nominal	114.6
S$ per 7	1.72	– real	114.8

Trade

Principal exports		Principal imports	
	$bn fob		*$bn cif*
Electronic components & parts	62.7	Machinery & transport equip.	117.5
Mineral fuels	53.9	Mineral fuels	61.2
Chemicals & products	32.1	Manufactured products	17.9
Manufactured products	18.9	Misc. manufactured articles	17.1
Total incl. others	**269.5**	Total incl. others	**245.6**

Main export destinations		Main origins of imports	
	% of total		*% of total*
Hong Kong	11.6	Malaysia	11.6
Malaysia	11.4	United States	11.6
China	9.7	China	10.5
United States	6.5	Japan	7.6
Japan	4.5	Taiwan	5.2
Australia	3.9	France	3.4
Thailand	3.7	Thailand	3.3

Balance of payments, reserves and debt, $bn

Visible exports fob	273.4	Change in reserves	13.6
Visible imports fob	-243.2	Level of reserves	
Trade balance	30.2	end Dec.	187.8
Invisibles inflows	143.7	No. months of import cover	5.9
Invisibles outflows	-138.2	Official gold holdings, m oz	...
Net transfers	-3.0	Foreign debt	14.0
Current account balance	32.6	– as % of GDP	11
– as % of GDP	17.9	– as % of total exports	5
Capital balance	-20.6	Debt service ratio	1
Overall balance	11.8		

Health and education

Health spending, % of GDP	3.9	Education spending, % of GDP	3.0
Doctors per 1,000 pop.	1.8	Enrolment, %: primary	...
Hospital beds per 1,000 pop.	2.3	secondary	...
Improved-water source access,		tertiary	...
% of pop.	100		

Society

No. of households	1.2m	Colour TVs per 100 households	99.4
Av. no. per household	5.2	Telephone lines per 100 pop.	40.7
Marriages per 1,000 pop.	5.1	Mobile telephone subscribers	
Divorces per 1,000 pop.	1.9	per 100 pop.	145.2
Cost of living, Dec. 2010		Broadband subs per 100 pop.	24.7
New York = 100	129	Internet hosts per 1,000 pop.	213.0

SLOVAKIA

Area	49,035 sq km	Capital	Bratislava
Arable as % of total land	29	Currency	Euro (€)

People

Population	5.4m	Life expectancy:	men	71.8 yrs
Pop. per sq km	111.4		women	79.3 yrs
Av. ann. growth		Adult literacy		...
in pop. 2010–15	0.17%	Fertility rate (per woman)		1.3
Pop. under 15	15.2%	Urban population		55.0%
Pop. over 60	17.7%			per 1,000 pop.
No. of men per 100 women	94.6	Crude birth rate		10.1
Human Development Index	81.8	Crude death rate		10.1

The economy

GDP	€63.1bn	GDP per head	$16,180
GDP	$87.6bn	GDP per head in purchasing	
Av. ann. growth in real		power parity (USA=100)	49.0
GDP 2004–09	5.2%	Economic freedom index	69.5

Origins of GDP

	% of total
Agriculture	3
Industry, of which:	35
Manufacturing	19
Services	63

Components of GDP

	% of total
Private consumption	47
Public consumption	20
Investment	38
Exports	99
Imports	-104

Structure of employment

	% of total		% of labour force
Agriculture	4	Unemployed 2009	12.1
Industry	40	Av. ann. rate 1995–2009	14.7
Services	56		

Energy

	m TOE		
Total output	6.4	Net energy imports as %	
Total consumption	18.3	of energy use	65
Consumption per head,			
kg oil equivalent	3,385		

Inflation and finance

Consumer price		av. ann. increase 2004–09	
inflation 2010	1.0%	Narrow money	9.0%
Av. ann. inflation 2005–10	2.9%	Broad money	7.3%
Deposit rate, h'holds, 2010	1.60%	Household saving rate, 2010	3.8%

Exchange rates

	end 2010		2010
€ per $	0.75	Effective rates	2005 = 100
€ per SDR	1.15	– nominal	128.11
		– real	131.04

Trade

Principal exports	$bn fob	Principal imports	$bn fob
Machinery & transport equipment	30.5	Machinery & transport equipment	23.1
Semi-manufactures	10.4	Semi-manufactures	8.2
Other manufactured goods	5.8	Fuels	6.4
Chemicals	2.5	Chemicals	5.2
Total incl. others	55.6	Total incl. others	54.5

Main export destinations	% of total	Main origins of imports	% of total
Germany	19.8	Czech Republic	19.8
Czech Republic	13.5	Germany	17.8
France	7.7	Russia	8.9
Hungary	7.3	Hungary	7.5
EU27	85.8	EU27	74.7

Balance of payments, reserves and debt, $bn

Visible exports fob	55.5	Change in reserves	-17.0
Visible imports fob	-53.8	Level of reserves	
Trade balance	1.7	end Dec.	1.8
Invisibles inflows	9.0	No. months of import cover	0.3
Invisibles outflows	-12.6	Official gold holdings, m oz	1.0
Net transfers	-1.0	Foreign debt	22.0
Current account balance	-2.8	– as % of GDP	36
– as % of GDP	-3.2	– as % of total exports	49
Capital balance	5.4	Debt service ratio	13
Overall balance	-0.2	Aid given	0.08
		% of GDP	0.09

Health and education

Health spending, % of GDP	8.5	Education spending, % of GDP	3.6
Doctors per 1,000 pop.	3.0	Enrolment, %: primary	103
Hospital beds per 1,000 pop.	6.8	secondary	92
Improved-water source access,		tertiary	54
% of pop.	100		

Society

No. of households	2.3m	Colour TVs per 100 households	99.2
Av. no. per household	2.4	Telephone lines per 100 pop.	22.6
Marriages per 1,000 pop.	5.2	Mobile telephone subscribers	
Divorces per 1,000 pop.	2.3	per 100 pop.	101.7
Cost of living, Dec. 2010		Broadband subs per 100 pop.	14.3
New York = 100	...	Internet hosts per 1,000 pop.	245.0

SLOVENIA

Area	20,253 sq km	Capital	Ljubljana
Arable as % of total land	9	Currency	Euro (€)

People

Population	2.0m	Life expectancy: men	75.4 yrs
Pop. per sq km	100.2	women	82.6 yrs
Av. ann. growth		Adult literacy	99.7%
in pop. 2010–15	0.27%	Fertility rate (per woman)	1.4
Pop. under 15	13.8%	Urban population	49.5%
Pop. over 60	22.4%		per 1,000 pop.
No. of men per 100 women	95.7	Crude birth rate	9.8
Human Development Index	82.8	Crude death rate	10.2

The economy

GDP	€34.9bn	GDP per head	$23,730
GDP	$48.5bn	GDP per head in purchasing	
Av. ann. growth in real		power parity (USA=100)	59.0
GDP 2004–09	2.4%	Economic freedom index	64.6

Origins of GDP		**Components of GDP**	
	% of total		% of total
Agriculture	2	Private consumption	55
Industry, of which:	34	Public consumption	20
manufacturing	22	Investment	23
Services	64	Exports	59
		Imports	-57

Structure of employment

	% of total		% of labour force
Agriculture	10	Unemployed 2009	5.9
Industry	34	Av. ann. rate 1995–2009	6.4
Services	56		

Energy

	m TOE		
Total output	3.7	Net energy imports as %	
Total consumption	7.7	of energy use	53
Consumption per head,			
kg oil equivalent	3,827		

Inflation and finance

Consumer price		av. ann. increase 2004–09	
inflation 2010	1.8%	Euro area:	
Av. ann. inflation 2005–10	2.9%	Narrow money (M1)	9.0%
Money market rate, 2010	0.57%	Broad money	7.3%

Exchange rates

	end 2010		2010
€ per $	0.75	Effective rates	2005 = 100
€ per SDR	1.15	– nominal	...
		– real	...

Trade

Principal exports		Principal imports	
	$bn fob		*$bn fob*
Machinery & transport equip.	9.0	Machinery & transport equip.	7.6
Manufactures	4.6	Manufactures	4.4
Chemicals	3.7	Chemicals	3.2
Miscellaneous manufactures	2.7	Miscellaneous manufactures	2.6
Total incl. others	**22.3**	Total incl. others	**23.9**

Main export destinations		Main origins of imports	
	% of total		*% of total*
Germany	22.7	Germany	18.4
Italy	13.3	Italy	17.7
Croatia	9.1	Austria	13.1
France	8.6	France	5.5
Austria	8.5	Croatia	4.8
Hungary	4.4	Hungary	3.8
EU27	69.3	EU27	73.3

Balance of payments, reserves and debt, $bn

Visible exports fob	22.5	Change in reserves	0.1
Visible imports fob	-23.5	Level of reserves	
Trade balance	-1.0	end Dec.	1.1
Invisibles inflows	6.9	No. months of import cover	0.4
Invisibles outflows	-6.5	Official gold holdings, m oz	0.1
Net transfers	-0.2	Foreign debt[a]	21.4
Current account balance	-0.7	– as % of GDP[a]	55
– as % of GDP	-1.5	– as % of total exports[a]	80
Capital balance	0.4	Debt service ratio[a]	19
Overall balance	0.1		

Health and education

Health spending, % of GDP	9.1	Education spending, % of GDP	5.7
Doctors per 1,000 pop.	2.4	Enrolment, %: primary	97
Hospital beds per 1,000 pop.	4.6	secondary	97
Improved-water source access,		tertiary	87
% of pop.	99		

Society

No. of households	0.7m	Colour TVs per 100 households	96.7
Av. no. per household	2.8	Telephone lines per 100 pop.	51.2
Marriages per 1,000 pop.	3.3	Mobile telephone subscribers	
Divorces per 1,000 pop.	1.1	per 100 pop.	104.0
Cost of living, Dec. 2010		Broadband subs per 100 pop.	23.7
New York = 100	...	Internet hosts per 1,000 pop.	89.6

a 2006

SOUTH AFRICA

Area	1,225,815 sq km	Capital	Pretoria
Arable as % of total land	12	Currency	Rand (R)

People

Population	50.1m	Life expectancy: men	51.8 yrs
Pop. per sq km	41.1	women	53.8 yrs
Av. ann. growth		Adult literacy	88.7%
in pop. 2010–15	0.96%	Fertility rate (per woman)	2.6
Pop. under 15	30.3%	Urban population	61.7%
Pop. over 60	7.3%		per 1,000 pop.
No. of men per 100 women	98.1	Crude birth rate	21.9
Human Development Index	59.7	Crude death rate	15.1

The economy

GDP	R2,408bn	GDP per head	$5,790
GDP	$285bn	GDP per head in purchasing	
Av. ann. growth in real		power parity (USA=100)	22.4
GDP 2004–09	3.6%	Economic freedom index	62.7

Origins of GDP		Components of GDP	
	% of total		% of total
Agriculture	3	Private consumption	60
Industry, of which:	31	Public consumption	21
manufacturing	15	Investment	19
Services	66	Exports	27
		Imports	-28

Structure of employment

	% of total		% of labour force
Agriculture	9	Unemployed 2009	23.8
Industry	26	Av. ann. rate 1995–2009	24.9
Services	65		

Energy

	m TOE		
Total output	163.0	Net energy imports as %	
Total consumption	134.5	of energy use	-21
Consumption per head,			
kg oil equivalent	2,756		

Inflation and finance

Consumer price		av. ann. increase 2004–09	
inflation 2010	4.3%	Narrow money (M1)	13.8%
Av. ann. inflation 2005–10	6.9%	Broad money	16.5%
Money market rate, 2010	6.19%		

Exchange rates

	end 2010		2010
R per $	6.63	Effective rates	2005 = 100
R per SDR	10.21	– nominal	85.7
R per €	8.86	– real	107.1

Trade

Principal exports		Principal imports	
	$bn fob		*$bn cif*
Platinum	6.8	Petrochemicals	10.3
Gold	6.3	Motor vehicle components	3.6
Coal	4.2	Petroleum oils & other	2.5
Ferro-alloys	2.8	Cars & other vehicles	2.4
Car & other components	0.8	Telecoms components	0.3
Total incl. others	**62.9**	Total incl. others	**64.7**

Main export destinations		Main origins of imports	
	% of total		*% of total*
Japan	8.9	China	19.6
United States	7.9	Germany	12.8
Germany	6.6	United States	8.4
United Kingdom	6.1	Saudi Arabia	5.5

Balance of payments, reserves and debt, $bn

Visible exports fob	66.5	Change in reserves	5.5
Visible imports fob	-66.0	Level of reserves	
Trade balance	0.5	end Dec.	39.6
Invisibles inflows	16.0	No. months of import cover	5.2
Invisibles outflows	-25.2	Official gold holdings, m oz	4.0
Net transfers	-2.7	Foreign debt	42.1
Current account balance	-11.3	– as % of GDP	15
– as % of GDP	-4.0	– as % of total exports	44
Capital balance	16.3	Debt service ratio	9
Overall balance	4.2		

Health and education

Health spending, % of GDP	8.5	Education spending, % of GDP	5.4
Doctors per 1,000 pop.	0.7	Enrolment, %: primary	101
Hospital beds per 1,000 pop.	2.8	secondary	94
Improved-water source access,		tertiary	...
% of pop.	91		

Society

No. of households	13.7m	Colour TVs per 100 households	67.7
Av. no. per household	3.7	Telephone lines per 100 pop.	8.6
Marriages per 1,000 pop.	3.9	Mobile telephone subscribers	
Divorces per 1,000 pop.	1.0	per 100 pop.	92.7
Cost of living, Dec. 2010		Broadband subs per 100 pop.	1.0
New York = 100	83	Internet hosts per 1,000 pop.	83.5

SOUTH KOREA

Area	99,274 sq km	Capital	Seoul
Arable as % of total land	16	Currency	Won (W)

People

Population	48.3m	Life expectancy: men	76.6 yrs
Pop. per sq km	484.1	women	83.2 yrs
Av. ann. growth		Adult literacy	...
in pop. 2010–15	0.48%	Fertility rate (per woman)	1.3
Pop. under 15	16.2%	Urban population	83.0%
Pop. over 60	15.6%		per 1,000 pop.
No. of men per 100 women	99.4	Crude birth rate	10.0
Human Development Index	87.7	Crude death rate	6.3

The economy

GDP	W1,063trn	GDP per head	$17,080
GDP	$833bn	GDP per head in purchasing	
Av. ann. growth in real		power parity (USA=100)	58.9
GDP 2004–09	3.3%	Economic freedom index	69.8

Origins of GDP		Components of GDP	
	% of total		% of total
Agriculture	3	Private consumption	54
Industry, of which:	37	Public consumption	16
manufacturing	28	Investment	26
Services	61	Exports	50
		Imports	-46

Structure of employment

	% of total		% of labour force
Agriculture	7	Unemployed 2009	3.6
Industry	26	Av. ann. rate 1995–2009	3.7
Services	67		

Energy

	m TOE		
Total output	44.7	Net energy imports as %	
Total consumption	226.9	of energy use	80
Consumption per head,			
kg oil equivalent	4,669		

Inflation and finance

Consumer price		av. ann. increase 2004–09	
inflation 2010	2.9%	Narrow money (M1)	9.0%
Av. ann. inflation 2005–10	3.0%	Broad money	7.0%
Money market rate, 2010	2.16%	Household saving rate, 2010	4.3%

Exchange rates

	end 2010		2010
W per $	1,135	Effective rates	2005 = 100
W per SDR	1,748	– nominal	...
W per €	1,516	– real	...

Trade

Principal exports		Principal imports	
	$bn fob		*$bn cif*
Information & communications		Crude petroleum	54.3
products	36.7	Machinery & equipment	30.4
Chemicals	34.2	Chemicals	26.2
Machinery & equipment	32.4	Semiconductors	24.2
Semiconductors	32.0		
Total incl. others	**363.5**	Total incl. others	**323.1**

Main export destinations		Main origins of imports	
	% of total		*% of total*
China	23.9	China	16.8
United States	10.4	Japan	15.3
Japan	6.0	United States	9.0
Hong Kong	5.4	Germany	3.8

Balance of payments, reserves and debt, $bn

Visible exports fob	373.6	Change in reserves	68.9
Visible imports fob	-317.5	Level of reserves	
Trade balance	56.1	end Dec.	270.4
Invisibles inflows	74.2	No. months of import cover	8.0
Invisibles outflows	-86.9	Official gold holdings, m oz	0.5
Net transfers	-0.8	Foreign debt	259.0
Current account balance	42.7	– as % of GDP	45
– as % of GDP	5.1	– as % of total exports	83
Capital balance	26.5	Debt service ratio	10
Overall balance	69.1	Aid given	0.82
		% of GDP	0.10

Health and education

Health spending, % of GDP	6.5	Education spending, % of GDP	4.2
Doctors per 1,000 pop.	2.0	Enrolment, %: primary	105
Hospital beds per 1,000 pop.	7.1	secondary	98
Improved-water source access,		tertiary	98
% of pop.	98		

Society

No. of households	17.8m	Colour TVs per 100 households	96.6
Av. no. per household	2.7	Telephone lines per 100 pop.	53.7
Marriages per 1,000 pop.	6.6	Mobile telephone subscribers	
Divorces per 1,000 pop.	4.5	per 100 pop.	100.7
Cost of living, Dec. 2010		Broadband subs per 100 pop.	34.8
New York = 100	100	Internet hosts per 1,000 pop.	6.1

SPAIN

Area	504,782 sq km	Capital	Madrid
Arable as % of total land	25	Currency	Euro (€)

People

Population	44.9m	Life expectancy: men	78.6 yrs
Pop. per sq km	91.1	women	84.7 yrs
Av. ann. growth		Adult literacy	97.7%
in pop. 2010–15	1.20%	Fertility rate (per woman)	1.4
Pop. under 15	14.9%	Urban population	77.4%
Pop. over 60	22.4%		per 1,000 pop.
No. of men per 100 women	97.5	Crude birth rate	10.9
Human Development Index	86.3	Crude death rate	8.9

The economy

GDP	€1,051bn	GDP per head	$31,770
GDP	$1,460bn	GDP per head in purchasing	
Av. ann. growth in real		power parity (USA=100)	69.9
GDP 2004–09	1.6%	Economic freedom index	70.2

Origins of GDP

	% of total
Agriculture	3
Industry, of which:	26
manufacturing	13
Services	71

Components of GDP

	% of total
Private consumption	56
Public consumption	21
Investment	24
Exports	23
Imports	-26

Structure of employment

	% of total		% of labour force
Agriculture	4	Unemployed 2009	18.0
Industry	28	Av. ann. rate 1995–2009	14.3
Services	68		

Energy

	m TOE		
Total output	30.4	Net energy imports as %	
Total consumption	138.8	of energy use	78
Consumption per head,			
kg oil equivalent	3,047		

Inflation and finance

Consumer price		av. ann. increase 2004–09	
inflation 2010	1.9%	Euro area:	
Av. ann. inflation 2005–10	2.4%	Narrow money (M1)	9.0%
Money market rate, 2010	0.45%	Broad money	7.3%
		Household saving rate[a], 2010	13.1%

Exchange rates

	end 2010		2010
€ per $	0.75	Effective rates	2005 = 100
€ per SDR	1.15	– nominal	103.5
		– real	106.0

Trade

Principal exports		**Principal imports**	
	$bn fob		*$bn cif*
Machinery & transport equip.	75.9	Machinery & transport equip.	88.2
Food, drink & tobacco	30.9	Mineral fuels & lubricants	45.6
Chemicals & related products	29.4	Chemicals & related products	40.1
Mineral fuels & lubricants	12.0	Food, drink & tobacco	28.1
Total incl. others	**220.9**	Total incl. others	**290.8**

Main export destinations		**Main origins of imports**	
	% of total		*% of total*
France	19.9	Germany	14.2
Germany	11.6	France	12.9
Portugal	9.5	Italy	7.4
Italy	8.7	China	5.7
EU 27	68.8	EU 27	61.5

Balance of payments, reserves and aid, $bn

Visible exports fob	224.0	Overall balance	6.0
Visible imports fob	-286.8	Change in reserves	7.8
Trade balance	-62.8	Level of reserves	
Invisibles inflows	179.6	end Dec.	28.0
Invisibles outflows	-186.3	No. months of import cover	0.7
Net transfers	-10.9	Official gold holdings, m oz	9.1
Current account balance	-80.4	Aid given	6.58
– as % of GDP	-5.5	– as % of GDP	0.46
Capital balance	91.4		

Health and education

Health spending, % of GDP	9.7	Education spending, % of GDP	4.3
Doctors per 1,000 pop.	3.6	Enrolment, %: primary	107
Hospital beds per 1,000 pop.	3.2	secondary	120
Improved-water source access,		tertiary	71
% of pop.	100		

Society

No. of households	17.4m	Colour TVs per 100 households	99.7
Av. no. per household	2.6	Telephone lines per 100 pop.	45.3
Marriages per 1,000 pop.	4.7	Mobile telephone subscribers	
Divorces per 1,000 pop.	1.1	per 100 pop.	113.8
Cost of living, Dec. 2010		Broadband subs per 100 pop.	21.6
New York = 100	107	Internet hosts per 1,000 pop.	89.0

a Gross.

SWEDEN

Area	449,964 sq km	Capital	Stockholm
Arable as % of total land	6	Currency	Swedish krona (Skr)

People

Population	9.2m	Life expectancy: men	79.6 yrs
Pop. per sq km	20.8	women	83.6 yrs
Av. ann. growth		Adult literacy	...
in pop. 2010–15	0.76%	Fertility rate (per woman)	1.9
Pop. under 15	16.5%	Urban population	84.7%
Pop. over 60	25.0%		per 1,000 pop.
No. of men per 100 women	99.2	Crude birth rate	11.9
Human Development Index	88.5	Crude death rate	9.8

The economy

GDP	Skr3,108bn	GDP per head	$43,650
GDP	$406bn	GDP per head in purchasing	
Av. ann. growth in real		power parity (USA=100)	81.3
GDP 2004–09	0.9%	Economic freedom index	71.9

Origins of GDP		Components of GDP	
	% of total		% of total
Agriculture	2	Private consumption	49
Industry, of which:	25	Public consumption	28
manufacturing	16	Investment	17
Services	73	Exports	49
		Imports	-42

Structure of employment

	% of total		% of labour force
Agriculture	2	Unemployed 2009	8.3
Industry	22	Av. ann. rate 1995–2009	6.6
Services	76		

Energy

	m TOE		
Total output	33.2	Net energy imports as %	
Total consumption	49.6	of energy use	33
Consumption per head,			
kg oil equivalent	5,379		

Inflation and finance

Consumer price		av. ann. increase 2004–09	
inflation 2010	1.2%	Narrow money	11.4%
Av. ann. inflation 2005–10	1.5%	Broad money	10.0%
Repurchase rate, end 2010	1.25%	Household saving rate, 2010	10.8%

Exchange rates

	end 2010		2010
Skr per $	6.71	Effective rates	2005 = 100
Skr per SDR	10.33	– nominal	103.3
Skr per €	8.97	– real	100.5

Trade

Principal exports		Principal imports	
	$bn fob		*$bn cif*
Machinery & transport equipment	49.6	Machinery & transport equipment	42.1
Chemicals & related products	17.2	Chemicals & related products	14.8
Mineral fuels & lubricants	8.4	Fuels & lubricants	13.5
Raw materials	8.0	Food, drink & tobacco	11.3
Total incl. others	**131.0**	Total incl. others	**120.3**

Main export destinations		Main origins of imports	
	% of total		*% of total*
Norway	10.6	Germany	18.0
Germany	10.2	Denmark	8.9
United Kingdom	7.4	Norway	8.7
Denmark	7.3	Netherlands	6.1
Finland	6.4	United Kingdom	5.5
EU27	58.5	EU27	68.1

Balance of payments, reserves and aid, $bn

Visible exports fob	134.9	Overall balance	15.2
Visible imports fob	-120.9	Change in reserves	17.5
Trade balance	14.0	Level of reserves	
Invisibles inflows	105.2	end Dec.	47.3
Invisibles outflows	-82.7	No. months of import cover	2.8
Net transfers	-5.1	Official gold holdings, m oz	4.0
Current account balance	31.5	Aid given	4.55
– as % of GDP	7.7	– as % of GDP	1.12
Capital balance	7.6		

Health and education

Health spending, % of GDP	9.9	Education spending, % of GDP	6.6
Doctors per 1,000 pop.	3.5	Enrolment, %: primary	95
Hospital beds per 1,000 pop.	...	secondary	103
Improved-water source access, % of pop.	100	tertiary	71

Society

No. of households	4.5m	Colour TVs per 100 households	97.9
Av. no. per household	2.0	Telephone lines per 100 pop.	55.7
Marriages per 1,000 pop.	5.0	Mobile telephone subscribers	
Divorces per 1,000 pop.	2.3	per 100 pop.	125.9
Cost of living, Dec. 2010		Broadband subs per 100 pop.	31.8
New York = 100	105	Internet hosts per 1,000 pop.	515.4

SWITZERLAND

Area	41,293 sq km	Capital	Berne
Arable as % of total land	10	Currency	Swiss franc (SFr)

People

Population	7.6m	Life expectancy: men	80.2 yrs
Pop. per sq km	185.6	women	84.7 yrs
Av. ann. growth		Adult literacy	...
in pop. 2010–15	0.66%	Fertility rate (per woman)	1.5
Pop. under 15	15.2%	Urban population	73.6%
Pop. over 60	23.3%		per 1,000 pop.
No. of men per 100 women	96.7	Crude birth rate	9.9
Human Development Index	87.4	Crude death rate	8.5

The economy

GDP	SFr535bn	GDP per head	$63,630
GDP	$492bn	GDP per head in purchasing	
Av. ann. growth in real		power parity (USA=100)	98.3
GDP 2004–09	2.0%	Economic freedom index	81.9

Origins of GDP		Components of GDP	
	% of total		% of total
Agriculture	1	Private consumption	58
Industry, of which:	27	Public consumption	11
manufacturing	19	Investment	20
Services	72	Exports	52
		Imports	-41

Structure of employment

	% of total		% of labour force
Agriculture	4	Unemployed 2009	4.1
Industry	24	Av. ann. rate 1995–2009	3.6
Services	72		

Energy

	m TOE		
Total output	12.7	Net energy imports as %	
Total consumption	26.7	of energy use	52
Consumption per head,			
kg oil equivalent	3,491		

Inflation and finance

Consumer price		av. ann. increase 2004–09	
inflation 2010	0.7%	Narrow money (M1)	10.2%
Av. ann. inflation 2005–10	0.9%	Broad money	5.1%
Money market rate, 2010	0.04%	Household saving rate, 2010	10.1%

Exchange rates

	end 2010		2010
SFr per $	0.94	Effective rates	2005 = 100
SFr per SDR	1.45	– nominal	120.9
SFr per €	1.26	– real	113.8

Trade

Principal exports	$bn	Principal imports	$bn
Chemicals	65.9	Chemicals	32.1
Machinery, equipment & electronics	31.0	Machinery, equipment & electronics	27.0
Precision instruments, watches & jewellery	29.8	Precision instruments, watches & jewellery	14.1
Metals & metal manufactures	9.6	Motor vehicles	13.8
Total incl. others	**166.8**	Total incl. others	**147.9**

Main export destinations	% of total	Main origins of imports	% of total
Germany	19.9	Germany	34.3
United States	10.4	Italy	11.3
France	8.7	France	9.8
Italy	8.7	United States	6.1
United Kingdom	5.2	Netherlands	4.8
Japan	3.9	Austria	4.5
Spain	3.6	United Kingdom	3.9
EU 27	59.8	EU27	77.9

Balance of payments, reserves and aid, $bn

Visible exports fob	206.1	Overall balance	48.1
Visible imports fob	-204.7	Change in reserves	60.3
Trade balance	1.4	Level of reserves	
Invisibles inflows	170.3	end Dec.	134.4
Invisibles outflows	-120.4	No. months of import cover	5.0
Net transfers	-12.3	Official gold holdings, m oz	33.4
Current account balance	39.0	Aid given	2.31
– as % of GDP	7.9	– as % of GDP	0.45
Capital balance	34.4		

Health and education

Health spending, % of GDP	11.3	Education spending, % of GDP	5.2
Doctors per 1,000 pop.	3.9	Enrolment, %: primary	103
Hospital beds per 1,000 pop.	2.9	secondary	96
Improved-water source access, % of pop.	100	tertiary	49

Society

No. of households	3.6m	Colour TVs per 100 households	94.6
Av. no. per household	2.2	Telephone lines per 100 pop.	61.8
Marriages per 1,000 pop.	5.1	Mobile telephone subscribers	
Divorces per 1,000 pop.	2.7	per 100 pop.	122.3
Cost of living, Dec. 2010		Broadband subs per 100 pop.	35.5
New York = 100	127	Internet hosts per 1,000 pop.	666.1

TAIWAN

Area	36,179 sq km	Capital	Taipei
Arable as % of total land	25	Currency	Taiwan dollar (T$)

People

Population	23.0m	Life expectancy:[a] men	75.5 yrs
Pop. per sq km	635.7	women	81.4 yrs
Av. ann. growth		Adult literacy	96.1%
in pop. 2010–15	0.40%	Fertility rate (per woman)	1.2
Pop. under 15	16.7%	Urban population	...
Pop. over 60	14.5%		per 1,000 pop.
No. of men per 100 women	101	Crude birth rate	9.0
Human Development Index	...	Crude death rate[a]	7.0

The economy

GDP	T$12,513bn	GDP per head	$16,330
GDP	$378bn	GDP per head in purchasing	
Av. ann. growth in real		power parity (USA=100)	64.3
GDP 2004–09	2.9%	Economic freedom index	70.8

Origins of GDP		Components of GDP	
	% of total		% of total
Agriculture	2	Private consumption	61
Industry, of which:	30	Public consumption	13
manufacturing	25	Investment	18
Services	69	Exports	63
		Imports	-54

Structure of employment

	% of total		% of labour force
Agriculture	5	Unemployed 2009	5.9
Industry	37	Av. ann. rate 1995–2009	3.8
Services	59		

Energy

	m TOE		
Total output	...	Net energy imports as %	
Total consumption	...	of energy use	...
Consumption per head,			
kg oil equivalent	...		

Inflation and finance

Consumer price			av. ann. increase 2004–09
inflation 2010	1.0%	Narrow money (M1)	7.4%
Av. ann. inflation 2005–10	1.2%	Broad money	5.1%
Interbank rate, end 2010	1.03%		

Exchange rates

	end 2010		2010
T$ per $	29.17	Effective rates	2005 = 100
T$ per SDR	44.92	– nominal	...
T$ per €	39.05	– real	...

Trade

Principal exports		Principal imports	
	$bn fob		$bn cif
Electronic products	95.2	Intermediate goods	132.5
Basic metals	19.4	Capital goods	25.9
Plastics & plastic articles	16.5	Consumer goods	16.1
Precision instruments, clocks			
& watches	16.1		
Total incl. others	**203.7**	Total incl. others	**174.4**

Main export destinations		Main origins of imports	
	% of total		% of total
China	28.0	Japan	20.9
Hong Kong	15.2	China	14.1
United States	12.2	United States	10.5
Japan	7.5	South Korea	6.1

Balance of payments, reserves and debt, $bn

Visible exports fob	203.4	Change in reserves	56.5
Visible imports fob	-172.8	Level of reserves	
Trade balance	30.6	end Dec.	348.2
Invisibles inflows	51.3	No. months of import cover	19.9
Invisibles outflows	-37.6	Official gold holdings, m oz	0.0
Net transfers	-2.2	Foreign debt	55.0
Current account balance	42.1	– as % of GDP	21
– as % of GDP	11.1	– as % of total exports	31
Capital balance	13.5	Debt service ratio	4
Overall balance	54.1	Aid given	0.41
		% of GDP	0.13

Health and education

Health spending, % of GDP	...	Education spending, % of GDP	...
Doctors per 1,000 pop.	1.7	Enrolment, %: primary	...
Hospital beds per 1,000 pop.	6.7	secondary	...
Improved-water source access,		tertiary	...
% of pop.	...		

Society

No. of households	7.6m	Colour TVs per 100 households	99.4
Av. no. per household	3.0	Telephone lines per 100 pop.	63.2
Marriages per 1,000 pop.	7.3	Mobile telephone subscribers	
Divorces per 1,000 pop.	3.6	per 100 pop.	116.7
Cost of living, Dec. 2010		Broadband subs per 100 pop.	21.4
New York = 100	85	Internet hosts per 1,000 pop.	259.6

a 2002 estimate.

THAILAND

Area	513,115 sq km	Capital	Bangkok
Arable as % of total land	30	Currency	Baht (Bt)

People

Population	67.8m	Life expectancy: men	67.1 yrs
Pop. per sq km	134.7	women	72.8 yrs
Av. ann. growth		Adult literacy	93.5%
in pop. 2010–15	0.71%	Fertility rate (per woman)	1.6
Pop. under 15	21.5%	Urban population	34.0%
Pop. over 60	11.7%		per 1,000 pop.
No. of men per 100 women	96.7	Crude birth rate	12.9
Human Development Index	65.4	Crude death rate	9.1

The economy

GDP	Bt9,051bn	GDP per head	$3,890
GDP	$264bn	GDP per head in purchasing	
Av. ann. growth in real		power parity (USA=100)	17.4
GDP 2004–09	2.9%	Economic freedom index	64.7

Origins of GDP

Components of GDP

	% of total		% of total
Agriculture	12	Private consumption	54
Industry, of which:	43	Public consumption	13
manufacturing	34	Investment	22
Services	45	Exports	68
		Imports	-58

Structure of employment

	% of total		% of labour force
Agriculture	42	Unemployed 2009	1.2
Industry	21	Av. ann. rate 1995–2009	1.7
Services	37		

Energy

	m TOE		
Total output	63.9	Net energy imports as %	
Total consumption	107.2	of energy use	40
Consumption per head,			
kg oil equivalent	1,591		

Inflation and finance

		av. ann. increase 2004–09	
Consumer price			
inflation 2010	3.3%	Narrow money (M1)	7.2%
Av. ann. inflation 2005–10	2.9%	Broad money	7.3%
Money market rate, 2010	1.25%		

Exchange rates

	end 2010		2010
Bt per $	30.15	Effective rates	2005 = 100
Bt per SDR	46.43	– nominal	...
Bt per €	40.29	– real	...

Trade

Principal exports		Principal imports	
	$bn fob		*$bn cif*
Machinery & mech. appliances	21.5	Fuel & lubricants	24.8
Integrated circuits & parts	13.2	Minerals & metal products	15.9
Vehicle parts & accessories	12.0	Electronic parts	12.7
Electrical appliances	10.7	Industry machinery, tools	
		& parts	9.6
Total incl. others	**152.0**	Total incl. others	**134.8**

Main export destinations		Main origins of imports	
	% of total		*% of total*
United States	10.9	Japan	18.7
China	10.6	China	12.7
Japan	10.3	United States	6.4
Hong Kong	6.2	United Arab Emirates	6.3

Balance of payments, reserves and debt, $bn

Visible exports fob	150.7	Change in reserves	27.4
Visible imports fob	-118.0	Level of reserves	
Trade balance	32.7	end Dec.	138.4
Invisibles inflows	35.8	No. months of import cover	9.8
Invisibles outflows	-51.1	Official gold holdings, m oz	2.7
Net transfers	4.5	Foreign debt	58.8
Current account balance	21.9	– as % of GDP	22
– as % of GDP	8.3	– as % of total exports	28
Capital balance	-2.7	Debt service ratio	7
Overall balance	24.1	Aid given	0.04
		– as % of GDP	0.02

Health and education

Health spending, % of GDP	4.3	Education spending, % of GDP	4.1
Doctors per 1,000 pop.	0.3	Enrolment, %: primary	88
Hospital beds per 1,000 pop.	7.0	secondary	77
Improved-water source access,		tertiary	45
% of pop.	98		

Society

No. of households	18.3m	Colour TVs per 100 households	96.6
Av. no. per household	3.5	Telephone lines per 100 pop.	10.6
Marriages per 1,000 pop.	4.3	Mobile telephone subscribers	
Divorces per 1,000 pop.	1.1	per 100 pop.	97.3
Cost of living, Dec. 2010		Broadband subs per 100 pop.	1.5
New York = 100	86	Internet hosts per 1,000 pop.	28.1

TURKEY

Area	779,452 sq km	Capital	Ankara
Arable as % of total land	28	Currency	Turkish Lira (YTL)

People

Population	74.8m	Life expectancy: men	70.3 yrs
Pop. per sq km	92.8	women	75.2 yrs
Av. ann. growth		Adult literacy	90.8%
in pop. 2010–15	1.31%	Fertility rate (per woman)	2.2
Pop. under 15	26.4%	Urban population	69.6%
Pop. over 60	9.0%		per 1,000 pop.
No. of men per 100 women	99.5	Crude birth rate	18.7
Human Development Index	67.9	Crude death rate	6.1

The economy

GDP	YTL953bn	GDP per head	$8,220
GDP	$615bn	GDP per head in purchasing	
Av. ann. growth in real		power parity (USA=100)	29.7
GDP 2004–09	3.1%	Economic freedom index	64.2

Origins of GDP		Components of GDP	
	% of total		% of total
Agriculture	9	Private consumption	72
Industry, of which:	26	Public consumption	15
manufacturing	17	Investment	15
Services	65	Exports	23
		Imports	-24

Structure of employment

	% of total		% of labour force
Agriculture	26	Unemployed 2009	14.0
Industry	26	Av. ann. rate 1995–2009	9.2
Services	48		

Energy

	m TOE		
Total output	29.0	Net energy imports as %	
Total consumption	98.5	of energy use	71
Consumption per head,			
kg oil equivalent	1,333		

Inflation and finance

Consumer price		av. ann. increase 2004–09	
inflation 2010	8.6%	Narrow money (M1)	30.1%
Av. ann. inflation 2005–10	8.9%	Broad money	21.5%
Money market rate, 2010	5.81%		

Exchange rates

	end 2010		2010
YTL per $	1.54	Effective rates	2005 = 100
YTL per SDR	2.37	– nominal	...
YTL per €	2.06	– real	...

Trade

Principal exports		Principal imports	
	$bn fob		$bn cif
Textiles & clothing	19.2	Mechanical machinery	21.4
Iron & steel	15.1	Chemicals	12.5
Transport equipment	12.9	Fuels	10.8
Agricultural products	10.3	Transport equipment	16.4
Total incl. others	**102.1**	Total incl. others	**140.9**

Main export destinations		Main origins of imports	
	% of total		% of total
Germany	9.6	Russia	13.8
France	6.1	Germany	10.0
Italy	5.8	China	9.0
United Kingdom	5.8	United States	6.1
Iraq	5.0	Italy	5.4
EU27	45.9	EU27	40.5

Balance of payments, reserves and debt, $bn

Visible exports fob	109.6	Change in reserves	1.3
Visible imports fob	-134.5	Level of reserves	
Trade balance	-24.9	end Dec.	74.9
Invisibles inflows	38.4	No. months of import cover	5.5
Invisibles outflows	-30.2	Official gold holdings, m oz	3.7
Net transfers	2.3	Foreign debt	251.4
Current account balance	-14.4	– as % of GDP	35
– as % of GDP	-2.3	– as % of total exports	144
Capital balance	10.5	Debt service ratio	42
Overall balance	0.9	Aid given	0.71
		% of GDP	0.11

Health and education

Health spending, % of GDP	6.7	Education spending, % of GDP	3.7
Doctors per 1,000 pop.	1.5	Enrolment, %: primary	99
Hospital beds per 1,000 pop.	2.9	secondary	82
Improved-water source access,		tertiary	38
% of pop.	99		

Society

No. of households	18.2m	Colour TVs per 100 households	93.2
Av. no. per household	3.9	Telephone lines per 100 pop.	22.1
Marriages per 1,000 pop.	6.3	Mobile telephone subscribers	
Divorces per 1,000 pop.	0.8	per 100 pop.	83.9
Cost of living, Dec. 2010		Broadband subs per 100 pop.	8.5
New York = 100	103	Internet hosts per 1,000 pop.	53.5

UKRAINE

Area	603,700 sq km	Capital	Kiev
Arable as % of total land	56	Currency	Hryvnya (UAH)

People

Population	45.7m	Life expectancy: men	63.9 yrs
Pop. per sq km	75.3	women	74.3 yrs
Av. ann. growth		Adult literacy	99.7%
in pop. 2010–15	-0.64%	Fertility rate (per woman)	1.4
Pop. under 15	13.9%	Urban population	68.8%
Pop. over 60	20.9%		per 1,000 pop.
No. of men per 100 women	85.2	Crude birth rate	10.4
Human Development Index	71.0	Crude death rate	16.1

The economy

GDP	UAH915bn	GDP per head	$2,470
GDP	$114bn	GDP per head in purchasing	
Av. ann. growth in real		power parity (USA=100)	13.7
GDP 2004–09	0.7%	Economic freedom index	45.8

Origins of GDP		Components of GDP	
	% of total		% of total
Agriculture	8	Private consumption	65
Industry, of which:	29	Public consumption	19
manufacturing	18	Investment	17
Services	62	Exports	46
		Imports	-48

Structure of employment

	% of total		% of labour force
Agriculture	17	Unemployed 2009	8.8
Industry	24	Av. ann. rate 1995–2009	8.7
Services	59		

Energy

	m TOE		
Total output	81.3	Net energy imports as %	
Total consumption	136.1	of energy use	40
Consumption per head,			
kg oil equivalent	2,943		

Inflation and finance

Consumer price		av. ann. increase 2004–09	
inflation 2010	9.4%	Narrow money (M1)	28.4%
Av. ann. inflation 2005–10	14.3%	Broad money	31.1%
Money market rate, 2010	3.42%		

Exchange rates

	end 2010		2010
UAH per $	7.96	Effective rates	2005 = 100
UAH per SDR	12.26	– nominal	63.3
UAH per €	10.64	– real	100.7

Trade

Principal exports		Principal imports	
	$bn fob		*$bn cif*
Non-precious metals	12.8	Fuels & mineral products	15.7
Food & agricultural produce	9.5	Machinery & equipment	9.1
Machinery & equipment	6.9	Chemicals	5.3
Fuels & mineral products	3.9	Food & agricultural produce	4.9
Chemicals	2.5		
Total incl. others	**39.7**	Total incl. others	**45.4**

Main export destinations		Main origins of imports	
	% of total		*% of total*
Russia	21.4	Russia	29.6
Turkey	5.4	Germany	8.6
Italy	3.6	China	6.1
Kazakhstan	3.6	Poland	4.9
Belarus	3.2	Kazakhstan	4.6

Balance of payments, reserves and debt, $bn

Visible exports fob	40.4	Change in reserves	-5.0
Visible imports fob	-44.7	Level of reserves	
Trade balance	-4.3	end Dec.	26.5
Invisibles inflows	18.3	No. months of import cover	5.0
Invisibles outflows	-18.6	Official gold holdings, m oz	0.9
Net transfers	2.7	Foreign debt	93.2
Current account balance	-1.7	– as % of GDP	62
– as % of GDP	-1.5	– as % of total exports	123
Capital balance	-10.3	Debt service ratio	36
Overall balance	-11.7		

Health and education

Health spending, % of GDP	7.0	Education spending, % of GDP	5.3
Doctors per 1,000 pop.	3.1	Enrolment, %: primary	98
Hospital beds per 1,000 pop.	8.6	secondary	94
Improved-water source access,		tertiary	79
% of pop.	98		

Society

No. of households	20.0m	Colour TVs per 100 households	94.9
Av. no. per household	2.3	Telephone lines per 100 pop.	28.5
Marriages per 1,000 pop.	5.7	Mobile telephone subscribers	
Divorces per 1,000 pop.	3.5	per 100 pop.	121.1
Cost of living, Dec. 2010		Broadband subs per 100 pop.	4.2
New York = 100	71	Internet hosts per 1,000 pop.	31.6

UNITED ARAB EMIRATES

Area	83,600 sq km	Capital	Abu Dhabi
Arable as % of total land	1	Currency	Dirham (AED)

People

Population	4.6m	Life expectancy: men	77.3 yrs
Pop. per sq km	89.9	women	79.5 yrs
Av. ann. growth		Adult literacy	90.0%
in pop. 2010–15	12.26%	Fertility rate (per woman)	1.9
Pop. under 15	19.1%	Urban population	84.1%
Pop. over 60	2.0%		per 1,000 pop.
No. of men per 100 women	228.3	Crude birth rate	14.0
Human Development Index	81.5	Crude death rate	1.5

The economy

GDP	AED846bn	GDP per head	$50,070
GDP	$230bn	GDP per head in purchasing	
Av. ann. growth in real		power parity (USA=100)	125.6
GDP 2004–09	5.1%	Economic freedom index	67.8

Origins of GDP		Components of GDP	
	% of total		% of total
Agriculture	2	Private consumption	46
Industry, of which:	61	Public consumption	10
manufacturing	12	Investment	20
Services	38	Exports	87
		Imports	-64

Structure of employment

	% of total		% of labour force
Agriculture	8	Unemployed 2005	3.1
Industry	22	Av. ann. rate 1995–2005	2.4
Services	70		

Energy

			m TOE
Total output	180.5	Net energy imports as %	
Total consumption	58.4	of energy use	-209
Consumption per head,			
kg oil equivalent	13,030		

Inflation and finance

Consumer price		av. ann. increase 2004–09	
inflation 2010	0.9%	Narrow money (M1)	22.6%
Av. ann. inflation 2005–10	6.9%	Broad money	24.4%
Interbank rate, end 2009	1.89%		

Exchange rates

	end 2010		2010
AED per $	3.67	Effective rates	2005 = 100
AED per SDR	5.66	– nominal	95.5
AED per €	4.90	– real	...

Trade

Principal exports		Principal imports	
	$bn fob		*$bn cif*
Re-exports	79.9	Machinery & electrical equip.	29.4
Crude oil	54.1	Precious stones & metals	27.6
Gas	8.5	Vehicles & other transp. equip.	15.6
		Base metals & related products	11.2
Total incl. others	**191.8**	Total incl. others	**170.5**

Main export destinations		Main origins of imports	
	% of total		*% of total*
Japan	17.5	China	15.0
South Korea	11.9	India	13.5
Thailand	7.2	United States	8.8
India	6.9	Germany	6.1

Balance of payments, reserves and debt, $bn

Visible exports fob	192.2	Change in reserves	4.4
Visible imports fob	-150.0	Level of reserves	
Trade balance	42.1	end Dec.	36.1
Invisibles, net	-24.1	No. months of import cover	2.3
Net transfers	-10.2	Official gold holdings, m oz	0.0
Current account balance	7.8	Foreign debt	85.0
– as % of GDP	3.4	– as % of GDP	49
Capital balance	2.3	– as % of total exports	56
Overall balance	-6.1	Debt service ratio	8
		Aid given	0.83
		% of GDP	0.33

Health and education

Health spending, % of GDP	2.8	Education spending, % of GDP	1.2
Doctors per 1,000 pop.	2.0	Enrolment, %: primary	105
Hospital beds per 1,000 pop.	1.9	secondary	95
Improved-water source access,		tertiary	30
% of pop.	100		

Society

No. of households	0.7m	Colour TVs per 100 households	99.9
Av. no. per household	6.3	Telephone lines per 100 pop.	34.0
Marriages per 1,000 pop.	3.6	Mobile telephone subscribers	
Divorces per 1,000 pop.	1.0	per 100 pop.	232.1
Cost of living, Dec. 2010		Broadband subs per 100 pop.	15.0
New York = 100	76	Internet hosts per 1,000 pop.	81.0

UNITED KINGDOM

Area	242,534 sq km	Capital	London
Arable as % of total land	25	Currency	Pound (£)

People

Population	61.6m	Life expectancy:	men	77.8 yrs
Pop. per sq km	255.4		women	82.3 yrs
Av. ann. growth		Adult literacy		...
in pop. 2010–15	0.60%	Fertility rate (per woman)		1.8
Pop. under 15	17.4%	Urban population		79.6%
Pop. over 60	22.7%			per 1,000 pop.
No. of men per 100 women	96.8	Crude birth rate		12.2
Human Development Index	84.9	Crude death rate		9.8

The economy

GDP	£1,396bn	GDP per head	$35,170
GDP	$2,175bn	GDP per head in purchasing	
Av. ann. growth in real		power parity (USA=100)	76.4
GDP 2004–09	0.5%	Economic freedom index	74.5

Origins of GDP		Components of GDP	
	% of total		% of total
Agriculture	1	Private consumption	65
Industry, of which:	21	Public consumption	23
manufacturing	11	Investment	14
Services	78	Exports	11
		Imports	-14

Structure of employment

	% of total		% of labour force
Agriculture	1	Unemployed 2009	7.7
Industry	21	Av. ann. rate 1995–2009	5.9
Services	78		

Energy

	m TOE		
Total output	166.7	Net energy imports as %	
Total consumption	208.5	of energy use	20
Consumption per head,			
kg oil equivalent	3,395		

Inflation and finance

			av. ann. increase 2004–09
Consumer price			
inflation 2010	4.6%	Narrow money	...
Av. ann. inflation 2005–10	3.1%	Broad money (M4)	12.1%
Money market rate, 2010	0.49%	Household saving rate[a], 2010	5.4%

Exchange rates

	end 2010		2010
£ per $	0.64	Effective rates	2005 = 100
£ per SDR	1.02	– nominal	79.7
£ per €	0.86	– real	84.8

Trade

Principal exports		Principal imports	
	$bn fob		*$bn fob*
Machinery & transport equip.	108.1	Machinery & transport equip.	146.4
Chemicals & related products	71.5	Chemicals & related products	61.0
Mineral fuels & lubricants	39.2	Food, drink & tobacco	48.9
Food, drink & tobacco	22.1	Mineral fuels & lubricants	48.2
Total incl. others	**354.6**	Total incl. others	**482.9**

Main export destinations		Main origins of imports	
	% of total		*% of total*
United States	14.6	Germany	12.9
Germany	11.0	United States	9.7
Netherlands	8.0	China	8.9
France	7.8	France	7.0
Ireland	6.9	Netherlands	6.7
EU27	55.1	EU27	52.9

Balance of payments, reserves and aid, $bn

Visible exports fob	356.4	Overall balance	9.6
Visible imports fob	-484.9	Change in reserves	13.5
Trade balance	-128.6	Level of reserves	
Invisibles inflows	508.6	end Dec.	66.6
Invisibles outflows	-394.3	No. months of import cover	0.9
Net transfers	-22.8	Official gold holdings, m oz	10.0
Current account balance	-37.1	Aid given	11.49
– as % of GDP	-1.7	– as % of GDP	0.52
Capital balance	76.3		

Health and education

Health spending, % of GDP	9.3	Education spending, % of GDP	5.5
Doctors per 1,000 pop.	2.7	Enrolment, %: primary	106
Hospital beds per 1,000 pop.	3.3	secondary	99
Improved-water source access,		tertiary	57
% of pop.	100		

Society

No. of households	27.2m	Colour TVs per 100 households	99.1
Av. no. per household	2.3	Telephone lines per 100 pop.	52.2
Marriages per 1,000 pop.	5.1	Mobile telephone subscribers	
Divorces per 1,000 pop.	3.0	per 100 pop.	130.6
Cost of living, Dec. 2010		Broadband subs per 100 pop.	29.6
New York = 100	113	Internet hosts per 1,000 pop.	135.4

a Gross.

UNITED STATES

Area	9,372,610 sq km	Capital	Washington DC
Arable as % of total land	19	Currency	US dollar ($)

People

Population	314.7m	Life expectancy: men	77.7 yrs
Pop. per sq km	32.2	women	82.1 yrs
Av. ann. growth		Adult literacy	...
in pop. 2010–15	0.89%	Fertility rate (per woman)	2.1
Pop. under 15	20.2%	Urban population	82.3%
Pop. over 60	18.2%		per 1,000 pop.
No. of men per 100 women	97.4	Crude birth rate	14.0
Human Development Index	90.2	Crude death rate	7.8

The economy

GDP	$14,119bn	GDP per head	$45,990
Av. ann. growth in real		GDP per head in purchasing	
GDP 2004–09	1.0%	power parity (USA=100)	100
		Economic freedom index	77.8

Origins of GDP		Components of GDP	
	% of total		% of total
Agriculture	1	Private consumption	71
Industry, of which:	21	Public consumption	17
manufacturing	13	Non-government investment	14
Services[a]	77	Exports	11
		Imports	-14

Structure of employment

	% of total		% of labour force
Agriculture	1	Unemployed 2009	9.3
Industry	21	Av. ann. rate 1995–2009	5.3
Services	78		

Energy

	m TOE		
Total output	1,706	Net energy imports as %	
Total consumption	2,284	of energy use	25
Consumption per head,			
kg oil equivalent	7,503		

Inflation and finance

Consumer price		av. ann. increase 2004–09	
inflation 2010	1.6%	Narrow money	4.2%
Av. ann. inflation 2005–10	2.2%	Broad money	7.2%
Fed funds rate, 2010	0.18%	Household saving rate, 2010	5.8%

Exchange rates

	end 2010		2010
$ per SDR	1.54	Effective rates	2005 = 100
$ per €	1.34	– nominal	90.0
		– real	89.6

Trade

Principal exports		Principal imports	
	$bn fob		*$bn fob*
Capital goods, excl. vehicles	390.4	Industrial supplies	461.2
Industrial supplies	296.3	Consumer goods,	
Consumer goods,		excl. vehicles	428.4
excl. vehicles	150.0	Capital goods, excl. vehicles	369.3
Vehicles & products	81.6	Vehicles & products	160.0
Total incl. others	**1,056.0**	Total incl. others	**1,559.6**

Main export destinations		Main origins of imports	
	% of total		*% of total*
Canada	19.4	China	19.8
Mexico	12.2	Canada	14.6
China	6.6	Mexico	11.4
Japan	4.8	Japan	6.3
United Kingdom	4.3	Germany	4.7
Germany	4.1	United Kingdom	3.1
EU27	20.9	EU27	17.9

Balance of payments, reserves and aid, $bn

Visible exports fob	1,073	Overall balance	52
Visible imports fob	1,577	Change in reserves	110.0
Trade balance	-504	Level of reserves	
Invisibles inflows	1,086	end Dec.	404.1
Invisibles outflows	-836	No. months of import cover	2.0
Net transfers	-125	Official gold holdings, m oz	261.5
Current account balance	-378	Aid given	28.83
– as % of GDP	-2.7	– as % of GDP	0.21
Capital balance	268		

Health and education

Health spending, % of GDP	16.2	Education spending, % of GDP	5.5
Doctors per 1,000 pop.	2.8	Enrolment, %: primary	99
Hospital beds per 1,000 pop.	3.1	secondary	94
Improved-water source access,		tertiary	83
% of pop.	99		

Society

No. of households	118.5m	Colour TVs per 100 households	99.0
Av. no. per household	2.6	Telephone lines per 100 pop.	44.8
Marriages per 1,000 pop.	7.1	Mobile telephone subscribers	
Divorces per 1,000 pop.	3.2	per 100 pop.	90.8
Cost of living, Dec. 2010		Broadband subs per 100 pop.	25.8
New York = 100	100	Internet hosts per 1,000 pop.[b]	1,415.3

a Including utilities.
b Includes all hosts ending ".com", ".net" and ".org" which exaggerates the numbers.

VENEZUELA

Area	912,050 sq km	Capital	Caracas
Arable as % of total land	3	Currency	Bolivar (Bs)

People

Population	28.6m	Life expectancy:	men	71.8 yrs
Pop. per sq km	31.8		women	77.7 yrs
Av. ann. growth		Adult literacy		95.2%
in pop. 2010–15	1.67%	Fertility rate (per woman)		2.6
Pop. under 15	29.5%	Urban population		93.4%
Pop. over 60	8.6%			per 1,000 pop.
No. of men per 100 women	100.7	Crude birth rate		21.4
Human Development Index	69.6	Crude death rate		5.2

The economy

GDP	Bs700bn	GDP per head	$11,490
GDP	$326bn	GDP per head in purchasing	
Av. ann. growth in real		power parity (USA=100)	26.8
GDP 2004–09	5.8%	Economic freedom index	37.6

Origins of GDP

	% of total
Agriculture	4
Industry, of which:	37
manufacturing	...
Services	59

Components of GDP

	% of total
Private consumption	64
Public consumption	13
Investment	25
Exports	18
Imports	-20

Structure of employment

	% of total		% of labour force
Agriculture	9	Unemployed 2009	7.6
Industry	23	Av. ann. rate 1995–2009	11.8
Services	68		

Energy

	m TOE		
Total output	180.7	Net energy imports as %	
Total consumption	64.1	of energy use	-182
Consumption per head,			
kg oil equivalent	2,295		

Inflation and finance

Consumer price		av. ann. increase 2004–08	
inflation 2010	29.1%	Narrow money	56.3%
Av. ann. inflation 2005–10	24.1%	Broad money	44.3%
Money market rate, 2010	5.36%		

Exchange rates

	end 2010		2010
Bs per $	2.59	Effective rates	2005 = 100
Bs per SDR	3.99	– nominal	75.5
Bs per €	3.46	– real	108.5

Trade

Principal exports		Principal imports	
	$bn fob		*$bn fob*
Oil	54.2	Intermediate goods	21.6
Non-oil	3.4	Capital goods	10.0
		Consumer goods	9.2
Total	**57.6**	Total	**40.9**

Main export destinations		Main origins of imports	
	% of total		*% of total*
United States	37.8	United States	24.6
Netherlands Antilles	5.8	Colombia	10.7
China	4.9	Brazil	7.8
Spain	4.3	Mexico	7.6

Balance of payments, reserves and debt, $bn

Visible exports fob	57.6	Change in reserves	-8.7
Visible imports fob	-38.4	Level of reserves	
Trade balance	19.2	end Dec.	34.3
Invisibles inflows	4.3	No. months of import cover	7.8
Invisibles outflows	-14.6	Official gold holdings, m oz	11.6
Net transfers	-0.3	Foreign debt	54.5
Current account balance	8.6	– as % of GDP	19
– as % of GDP	2.6	– as % of total exports	66
Capital balance	-14.6	Debt service ratio	6
Overall balance	-10.8		

Health and education

Health spending, % of GDP	5.8	Education spending, % of GDP	3.7
Doctors per 1,000 pop.	1.7	Enrolment, %: primary	103
Hospital beds per 1,000 pop.	1.3	secondary	82
Improved-water source access,		tertiary	79
% of pop.	83		

Society

No. of households	6.4m	Colour TVs per 100 households	92.4
Av. no. per household	4.5	Telephone lines per 100 pop.	24.0
Marriages per 1,000 pop.	2.5	Mobile telephone subscribers	
Divorces per 1,000 pop.	0.9	per 100 pop.	98.4
Cost of living, Dec. 2010		Broadband subs per 100 pop.	4.7
New York = 100	92	Internet hosts per 1,000 pop.	14.1

VIETNAM

Area	331,114 sq km	Capital	Hanoi
Arable as % of total land	20	Currency	Dong (D)

People

Population	88.1m	Life expectancy: men		73.3 yrs
Pop. per sq km	264.9		women	77.4 yrs
Av. ann. growth		Adult literacy		92.8%
in pop. 2010–15	1.10%	Fertility rate (per woman)		1.9
Pop. under 15	25.1%	Urban population		30.4%
Pop. over 60	6.7%			per 1,000 pop.
No. of men per 100 women	97.7	Crude birth rate		17.2
Human Development Index	57.2	Crude death rate		5.5

The economy

GDP	D1,658trn	GDP per head	$1,110
GDP	$97.2bn	GDP per head in purchasing	
Av. ann. growth in real		power parity (USA=100)	6.4
GDP 2004–09	7.3%	Economic freedom index	51.6

Origins of GDP		Components of GDP	
	% of total		% of total
Agriculture	21	Private consumption	66
Industry, of which:	40	Public consumption	6
manufacturing	20	Investment	38
Services	39	Exports	68
		Imports	-79

Structure of employment

	% of total		% of labour force
Agriculture	52	Unemployed 2004	2.1
Industry	18	Av. ann. rate 2003–04	2.3
Services	30		

Energy

	m TOE		
Total output	71.4	Net energy imports as %	
Total consumption	59.4	of energy use	-20
Consumption per head,			
kg oil equivalent	689		

Inflation and finance

Consumer price		av. ann. increase 2004–09	
inflation 2010	8.9%	Narrow money (M1)	23.3
Av. ann. inflation 2005–10	10.8%	Broad money	31.0
Refinancing rate, Aug. 2010	100%		

Exchange rates

	end 2010		2010
D per $	20,566	Effective rates	2005 = 100
D per SDR	31,672	– nominal	...
D per €	29,781	– real	...

Trade

Principal exports		Principal imports	
	$bn fob		*$bn cif*
Textiles & garments	9.1	Machinery & equipment	12.1
Crude oil	6.2	Petroleum products	6.2
Fisheries products	4.2	Steel	5.3
Footwear	4.1	Textiles	4.2
Total incl. others	**57.1**	Total incl. others	**69.9**

Main export destinations		Main origins of imports	
	% of total		*% of total*
United States	19.9	China	23.5
Japan	11.0	Japan	10.7
China	8.6	South Korea	10.0
Switzerland	4.4	Thailand	6.5
Australia	4.0	Singapore	6.1
Singapore	3.6	United States	4.3
South Korea	3.6	Malaysia	3.6

Balance of payments, reserves and debt, $bn

Visible exports fob	57.1	Change in reserves	-7.4
Visible imports fob	-65.4	Level of reserves	
Trade balance	-8.3	end Dec.	16.8
Invisibles inflows	6.4	No. months of import cover	2.6
Invisibles outflows	-10.8	Official gold holdings, m oz	0.0
Net transfers	6.4	Foreign debt	28.7
Current account balance	-6.3	– as % of GDP	27
– as % of GDP	-6.5	– as % of total exports	34
Capital balance	11.9	Debt service ratio	2
Overall balance	-7.8		

Health and education

Health spending, % of GDP	7.2	Education spending, % of GDP	5.3
Doctors per 1,000 pop.	1.2	Enrolment, %: primary	...
Hospital beds per 1,000 pop.	2.6	secondary	...
Improved-water source access,		tertiary	...
% of pop.	94		

Society

No. of households	19.8m	Colour TVs per 100 households	89.7
Av. no. per household	4.4	Telephone lines per 100 pop.	19.8
Marriages per 1,000 pop.	5.7	Mobile telephone subscribers	
Divorces per 1,000 pop.	0.2	per 100 pop.	111.5
Cost of living, Dec. 2010		Broadband subs per 100 pop.	3.7
New York = 100	64	Internet hosts per 1,000 pop.	1.4

ZIMBABWE

Area	390,759 sq km	Capital	Harare
Arable as % of total land	10	Currency	Zimbabwe dollar (Z$)

People

Population	12.5m	Life expectancy: men		50.5 yrs
Pop. per sq km	32.5		women	49.8 yrs
Av. ann. growth		Adult literacy		91.4%
in pop. 2010–15	0.00%	Fertility rate (per woman)		3.5
Pop. under 15	39.5%	Urban population		38.3%
Pop. over 60	5.8%			per 1,000 pop.
No. of men per 100 women	97.2	Crude birth rate		29.4
Human Development Index	14.0	Crude death rate		12.9

The economy

GDP[a]	$5.6bn	GDP per head[a]	$450
Av. ann. growth in real		GDP per head in purchasing	
GDP 2004–09	-4.5%	power parity (USA=100)	0.7
		Economic freedom index	22.1

Origins of GDP		Components of GDP	
	% of total		% of total
Agriculture	18	Private consumption	113
Industry, of which:	29	Public consumption	14
manufacturing	17	Investment	2
Services	53	Exports	36
		Imports	-65

Structure of employment

	% of total		% of labour force
Agriculture	...	Unemployed 2004	4.2
Industry	...	Av. ann. rate 1997–2004	6.4
Services	...		

Energy

	m TOE		
Total output	8.5	Net energy imports as %	
Total consumption	9.5	of energy use	10
Consumption per head,			
kg oil equivalent	763		

Inflation[a] and finance

Consumer price		av. ann. increase 2004–07	
inflation 2010	3.0%	Narrow money (M1)	3,857%
Av. ann. inflation 2005–10	28,118%	Broad money	3,628%
Treasury bill rate, 2007	248.8%		

Exchange rates

	end 2010		2010
Z$ per $	...	Effective rates	2005 = 100
Z$ per SDR	...	– nominal	...
Z$ per €	...	– real	...

Trade

Principal exports		Principal imports	
	$bn fob		*$bn cif*
Manufactures	0.8	Manufactures	1.7
Agricultural raw materials	0.5	Food	0.6
Ores & minerals	0.5	Fuels	0.4
Food	0.4	Ores & minerals	0.1
Total incl. others	**2.3**	Total incl. others	**2.9**

Main export destinations		Main origins of imports	
	% of total		*% of total*
South Africa	12.8	South Africa	60.9
Congo-Kinshasa	11.5	China	5.7
Botswana	11.4	Botswana	3.7
China	7.9	Zambia	3.2
Zambia	6.3	United States	3.0

Balance of payments[a], reserves[a] and debt, $bn

Visible exports fob	1.6	Change in reserves	0.4
Visible imports fob	-3.2	Level of reserves	
Trade balance	-1.6	end Dec.	0.4
Invisibles, net	-0.4	No. months of import cover	1.1
Net private transfers	0.7	Official gold holdings, m oz	0.0
Current account balance	-1.3	Foreign debt	5.0
– as % of GDP	-25.4	– as % of GDP[b]	380
Capital balance	1.1	– as % of total exports	335
Overall balance	0.0	Debt service ratio[ab]	94

Health and education

Health spending, % of GDP	8.9	Education spending, % of GDP	4.7
Doctors per 1,000 pop.	0.2	Enrolment, %: primary	104
Hospital beds per 1,000 pop.	3.0	secondary	41
Improved-water source access,		tertiary	...
% of pop.	82		

Society

No. of households	3.5m	Colour TVs per 100 households	...
Av. no. per household	3.6	Telephone lines per 100 pop.	3.1
Marriages per 1,000 pop.	...	Mobile telephone subscribers	
Divorces per 1,000 pop.	...	per 100 pop.	23.9
Cost of living, Dec. 2010		Broadband subs per 100 pop.	0.2
New York = 100	...	Internet hosts per 1,000 pop.	2.4

a Estimates.
b 2008

EURO AREA[a]

Area	2,573,704 sq km	Capital	–
Arable as % of total land	25	Currency	Euro (€)

People

Population	325.8m	Life expectancy: men	78.1 yrs
Pop. per sq km	126.6	women	84.1 yrs
Av. ann. growth		Adult literacy	...
in pop. 2010–15	2.25%	Fertility rate (per woman)	1.5
Pop. under 15	15.4%	Urban population	72.8%
Pop. over 60	23.8%		per 1,000 pop.
No. of men per 100 women	96.1	Crude birth rate	10.1
Human Development Index	86.7	Crude death rate	9.9

The economy

GDP	€9,272bn	GDP per head	$38,080
GDP	$12,446bn	GDP per head in purchasing	
Av. ann. growth in real		power parity (USA=100)	74.5
GDP 2004–09	0.8%	Economic freedom index	67.6

Origins of GDP		Components of GDP	
	% of total		% of total
Agriculture	2	Private consumption	58
Industry, of which:	24	Public consumption	22
manufacturing	15	Investment	19
Services	74	Exports	36
		Imports	-35

Structure of employment

	% of total		% of labour force
Agriculture	4	Unemployed 2009	9.4
Industry	28	Av. ann. rate 1995–2009	9.1
Services	69		

Energy

	m TOE		
Total output	463.1	Net energy imports as %	
Total consumption	1,226.5	of energy use	62
Consumption per head,			
kg oil equivalent	3,763		

Inflation and finance

Consumer price		av. ann. increase 2004–09	
inflation 2010	1.6%	Narrow money (M1)	9.0%
Av. ann. inflation 2005–10	1.9%	Broad money	7.3%
Interbank rate, 2010	0.44%	Household saving rate, 2010	11.1%

Exchange rates

	end 2010		2010
€ per $	0.75	Effective rates	2005 = 100
€ per SDR	1.15	– nominal	100.0
		– real	94.5

Trade[b]

Principal exports		Principal imports	
	$bn fob		*$bn cif*
Machinery & transport equip.	633.4	Machinery & transport equip.	476.6
Manufactures	359.9	Manufactures	411.5
Chemicals	272.4	Mineral fuels & lubricants	404.1
Mineral fuels & lubricants	87.2	Chemicals	156.6
Food, drink & tobacco	79.7	Food, drink & tobacco	102.6
Raw materials	38.7	Raw materials	65.8
Total incl. others	**1,524.5**	Total incl. others	**1,670.5**

Main export destinations		Main origins of imports	
	% of total		*% of total*
United States	18.7	China	17.9
Switzerland	8.1	United States	13.3
China	7.5	Russia	9.6
Russia	6.0	Switzerland	6.2
Turkey	4.0	Norway	5.7
Norway	3.4	Japan	4.7

Balance of payments, reserves and aid, $bn

Visible exports fob	1,802	Overall balance	19
Visible imports fob	-1,745	Change in reserves	138.7
Trade balance	57	Level of reserves	
Invisibles inflows	1,218	end Dec.	661.1
Invisibles outflows	-1,212	No. months of import cover	2.7
Net transfers	-128	Official gold holdings, m oz	347.2
Current account balance	-65	Aid given[c]	48.7
– as % of GDP	-0.5	– as % of GDP[c]	0.39
Capital balance	105		

Health and education

Health spending, % of GDP	10.7	Education spending, % of GDP	4.9
Doctors per 1,000 pop.	3.8	Enrolment, %: primary	...
Hospital beds per 1,000 pop.	5.8	secondary	...
Improved-water source access,		tertiary	...
% of pop.	100		

Society

No. of households	130.5	Colour TVs per 100 households	97.6
Av. no. per household	2.39	Telephone lines per 100 pop.	48.4
Marriages per 1,000 pop.	4.5	Mobile telephone subscribers	
Divorces per 1,000 pop.	2.0	per 100 pop.	122.8
Cost of living, Dec. 2010		Broadband subs per 100 pop.	26.2
New York = 100	...	Internet hosts per 1,000 pop.	309.4

---

a Data generally refer to the 16 EU members that had adopted the euro before
   December 31 2009: Austria, Belgium, Cyprus, Finland, France, Germany, Greece,
   Ireland, Italy, Luxembourg, Malta, Netherlands, Portugal, Slovakia, Slovenia and
   Spain.
b EU27, excluding intra-trade.
c Excluding Cyprus and Malta.

WORLD

Area	148,698,382 sq km	Capital	...
Arable as % of total land	11	Currency	...

People

Population	6,829.4m	Life expectancy:	men	67.1 yrs
Pop. per sq km	45.4		women	71.6 yrs
Av. ann. growth		Adult literacy		82.4%
in pop. 2010–15	1.16%	Fertility rate (per woman)		2.5
Pop. under 15	26.9%	Urban population		50.4%
Pop. over 60	11.0%			per 1,000 pop.
No. of men per 100 women	101.7	Crude birth rate		20.0
Human Development Index	62.4	Crude death rate		8.2

The economy

GDP	$58.3trn	GDP per head	$8,600
Av. ann. growth in real		GDP per head in purchasing	
GDP 2004–09	3.5%	power parity (USA=100)	23.2
		Economic freedom index	57.1

Origins of GDP		Components of GDP	
	% of total		% of total
Agriculture	3	Private consumption	62
Industry, of which:	27	Public consumption	19
manufacturing	17	Investment	19
Services	70	Exports	24
		Imports	-24

Structure of employment[a]

	% of total		% of labour force
Agriculture	...	Unemployed 2009	8.1
Industry	...	Av. ann. rate 1995–2009	6.7
Services	...		

Energy

	m TOE		
Total output	12,358	Net energy imports as %	
Total consumption	11,899	of energy use	-4
Consumption per head,			
kg oil equivalent	1,835		

Inflation and finance

Consumer price		av. ann. increase 2004–09	
inflation 2010	3.4%	Narrow money (M1)[a]	6.7%
Av. ann. inflation 2005–10	3.4%	Broad money[a]	7.5%
LIBOR $ rate, 3-month, 2010	0.34%	Household saving rate, 2009[a]	7.6%

Trade

World exports

	$bn fob		$bn fob
Manufactures	8,745	Ores & minerals	500
Fuels	1,499	Agricultural raw materials	250
Food	999	Total incl. others	**12,492**

Main export destinations

	% of total
United States	12.0
China	7.4
Germany	7.2
France	4.6
United Kingdom	4.1
Japan	4.0

Main origins of imports

	% of total
China	11.4
Germany	8.7
United States	8.2
Japan	5.0
France	3.9
Netherlands	3.5

Balance of payments, reserves and aid, $bn

Visible exports fob	12,416	Overall balance	0
Visible imports fob	12,189	Change in reserves	1,362
Trade balance	227	Level of reserves	
Invisibles inflows	6,335	end Dec.	9,603
Invisibles outflows	-6,248	No. months of import cover	6
Net transfers	-1	Official gold holdings, m oz	977
Current account balance	313	Aid given[b]	126.7
– as % of GDP	0.5	– as % of GDP[b]	0.30
Capital balance	-249		

Health and education

Health spending, % of GDP	10.0	Education spending, % of GDP	4.4
Doctors per 1,000 pop.	1.4	Enrolment, %: primary	107
Hospital beds per 1,000 pop.	2.9	secondary	67
Improved-water source access,		tertiary	26
% of pop.	61		

Society

No. of households	...	TVs per 100 households	...
Av. no. per household	...	Telephone lines per 100 pop.	19.0
Marriages per 1,000 pop.	...	Mobile telephone subscribers	
Divorces per 1,000 pop.	...	per 100 pop.	68.3
Cost of living, Dec. 2010		Broadband subs per 100 pop.	6.8
New York = 100	...	Internet hosts per 1,000 pop.	119.4

a OECD countries.
b OECD, non-OECD Europe and Middle East countries.

Glossary

Balance of payments The record of a country's transactions with the rest of the world. The **current account** of the balance of payments consists of: visible trade (goods); "invisible" trade (services and income); private transfer payments (eg, remittances from those working abroad); official transfers (eg, payments to international organisations, famine relief). Visible imports and exports are normally compiled on rather different definitions to those used in the trade statistics (shown in principal imports and exports) and therefore the statistics do not match. The **capital account** consists of long- and short-term transactions relating to a country's assets and liabilities (eg, loans and borrowings). The **current and capital accounts**, plus an errors and omissions item, make up the **overall balance. Changes in reserves** include gold at market prices and are shown without the practice often followed in balance of payments presentations of reversing the sign.

Big Mac index A light-hearted way of looking at exchange rates. If the dollar price of a burger at McDonald's in any country is higher than the price in the United States, converting at market exchange rates, then that country's currency could be thought to be over-valued against the dollar and vice versa.

Body-mass index A measure for assessing obesity – weight in kilograms divided by height in metres squared. An index of 30 or more is regarded as an indicator of obesity; 25 to 29.9 as over-weight. Guidelines vary for men and for women and may be adjusted for age.

CFA Communauté Financière Africaine. Its members, most of the francophone African nations, share a common currency, the CFA franc, pegged to the euro.

Cif/fob Measures of the value of merchandise trade. Imports include the cost of "carriage, insurance and freight" (cif) from the exporting country to the importing. The value of exports does not include these elements and is recorded

"free on board" (fob). Balance of payments statistics are generally adjusted so that both exports and imports are shown fob; the cif elements are included in invisibles.

Crude birth rate The number of live births in a year per 1,000 population. The crude rate will automatically be relatively high if a large proportion of the population is of childbearing age.

Crude death rate The number of deaths in a year per 1,000 population. Also affected by the population's age structure.

Debt, foreign Financial obligations owed by a country to the rest of the world and repayable in foreign currency. **The debt service ratio** is debt service (principal repayments plus interest payments) expressed as a percentage of the country's earnings from exports of goods and services.

Economic Freedom Index The ranking includes data on labour and business freedom as well as trade policy, taxation, monetary policy, the banking system, foreign-investment rules, property rights, the amount of economic output consumed by the government, regulation policy, the size of the black market and the extent of wage and price controls.

Effective exchange rate The nominal index measures a currency's depreciation (figures below 100) or appreciation (figures over 100) from a base date against a trade-weighted basket of the currencies of the country's main trading partners. The real effective exchange rate reflects adjustments for relative movements in prices or costs.

EU European Union. Members are: Austria, Belgium, Bulgaria, Cyprus, Czech Republic, Denmark, Estonia, Finland, France, Germany, Greece, Hungary, Ireland, Italy, Latvia, Lithuania, Luxembourg, Malta, Netherlands, Poland, Portugal, Romania, Slovakia, Slovenia, Spain, Sweden and the United Kingdom.

Euro area The 17 euro area members of the EU are Austria, Belgium, Cyprus, Finland, France, Germany, Greece, Ireland, Italy, Luxembourg, Malta, Netherlands, Portugal, Slovakia, Slovenia and Spain. Estonia joined on January 1 2011. Their common currency is the euro, which came into circulation on January 1 2002.

Fertility rate The average number of children born to a woman who completes her childbearing years.

G7 Group of seven countries: United States, Japan, Germany, United Kingdom, France, Italy and Canada.

GDP Gross domestic product. The sum of all output produced by economic activity within a country. GNP (gross national product) and GNI (gross national income) include net income from abroad eg, rent, profits.

Household saving rate Household savings as % of disposable household income.

Import cover The number of months of imports covered by reserves ie, reserves ÷ $\frac{1}{12}$ annual imports (visibles and invisibles).

Inflation The annual rate at which prices are increasing. The most common measure and the one shown here is the increase in the consumer price index.

Internet hosts Websites and other computers that sit permanently on the internet.

Life expectancy The average length of time a baby born today can expect to live.

Literacy is defined by UNESCO as the ability to read and write a simple sentence, but definitions can vary from country to country.

Median age Divides the age distribution into two halves. Half of the population is above and half below the median age.

Money supply A measure of the "money" available to buy goods and services.

Various definitions exist. The measures shown here are based on definitions used by the IMF and may differ from measures used nationally. Narrow money (M1) consists of cash in circulation and demand deposits (bank deposits that can be withdrawn on demand). "Quasi-money" (time, savings and foreign currency deposits) is added to this to create broad money.

OECD Organisation for Economic Co-operation and Development. The "rich countries" club was established in 1961 to promote economic growth and the expansion of world trade. It is based in Paris and now has 34 members.

Official reserves The stock of gold and foreign currency held by a country to finance any calls that may be made for the settlement of foreign debt.

Opec Organisation of Petroleum Exporting Countries. Set up in 1960 and based in Vienna, Opec is mainly concerned with oil pricing and production issues. Members are: Algeria, Ecuador, Indonesia, Iran, Iraq, Kuwait, Libya, Nigeria, Qatar, Saudi Arabia, United Arab Emirates and Venezuela.

PPP Purchasing power parity. PPP statistics adjust for cost of living differences by replacing normal exchange rates with rates designed to equalise the prices of a standard "basket"of goods and services. These are used to obtain PPP estimates of GDP per head. PPP estimates are shown on an index, taking the United States as 100.

Real terms Figures adjusted to exclude the effect of inflation.

SDR Special drawing right. The reserve currency, introduced by the IMF in 1970, was intended to replace gold and national currencies in settling international transactions. The IMF uses SDRs for book-keeping purposes and issues them to member countries. Their value is based on a basket of the US dollar (with a weight of 44%), the euro (34%), the Japanese yen (11%) and the pound sterling (11%).

List of countries

Wherever data is available, the world rankings consider 194
countries: all those which had (in 2009) or have recently had a
population of at least 1m or a GDP of at least $1bn. Here is a list of
them.

	Population	GDP	GDP per head	Area '000 sq	Median age
	m, 2009	$bn, 2009	$PPP, 2009	km	yrs, 2010
Afghanistan	28.20	14.5	1,320	652	16.6
Albania	3.20	12.0	8,720	29	30.0
Algeria	34.90	140.6	8,170	2,382	26.2
Andorra	0.08	3.7[a]	43,770	0.4	40.0
Angola	18.50	75.5	5,810	1,247	16.6
Antigua & Barbuda	0.09	1.1	18,780	0.4	30.0
Argentina	40.30	307.2	14,540	2,767	30.4
Armenia	3.10	8.7	5,280	30	32.1
Aruba	0.10	2.6	23,150	0.2	38.3
Australia	21.30	924.8	39,540	7,682	36.9
Austria	8.40	381.1	38,820	84	41.8
Azerbaijan	8.80	43.0	9,640	87	29.5
Bahamas	0.30	7.4	20,310	14	30.9
Bahrain	0.80	20.6	35,170[a]	0.7	30.1
Bangladesh	162.20	89.4	1,420	144	24.2
Barbados	0.30	3.6	12,830	0.4	37.5
Belarus	9.60	49.0	13,040	208	38.3
Belgium	10.60	471.2	36,310	31	41.2
Belize	0.30	1.4	6,630	23	21.8
Benin	8.90	6.7	1,510	113	17.9
Bermuda	0.07	5.7	125,290	0.1	42.4
Bhutan	0.70	1.3	5,110	47	24.6
Bolivia	9.90	17.3	4,420	1,099	21.7
Bosnia	3.80	17.0	8,580	51	39.4
Botswana	2.00	11.8	13,380	581	22.9
Brazil	193.70	1,594.5	10,370	8,512	29.1
British Virgin Islands	0.02	1.3	57,630	0.2	29.5
Brunei	0.40	10.7	51,210[a]	6	28.9
Bulgaria	7.50	48.7	13,870	111	41.6
Burkina Faso	15.80	8.1	1,190	274	17.1
Burundi	8.30	1.3	390	28	20.2
Cambodia	14.80	10.4	1,920	181	22.9
Cameroon	19.50	22.2	2,210	475	19.3
Canada	33.60	1,336.1	37,810	9,971	39.9
Cape Verde	0.50	1.5	3,640	4	22.8
Cayman Islands	0.05	3.1	60,530	0.3	38.7
Central African Republic	4.40	2.0	760	622	19.4
Chad	11.20	6.8	1,300	1,284	17.1
Channel Islands	0.15	11.5[a]	51,930[ab]	0.2	42.6
Chile	17.00	163.7	14,310	757	32.1
China	1345.80	4,985.5	6,830	9,561	34.5
Colombia	45.70	234.0	8,960	1,142	26.8

	Population	GDP	GDP per head	Area	Median age
	m, 2009	$bn, 2009	$PPP, 2009	'000 sq km	yrs, 2010
Congo-Brazzaville	3.70	9.6	4,240	342	19.6
Congo-Kinshasa	66.00	10.6	320	2,345	16.7
Costa Rica	4.60	29.2	11,110	51	28.4
Côte d'Ivoire	21.10	23.3	1,700	322	19.2
Croatia	4.40	63.0	19,990	57	41.5
Cuba	11.20	62.7[a]	5,360	111	38.4
Cyprus	0.90	25.0	38,050	9	34.2
Czech Republic	10.40	190.3	25,580	79	39.4
Denmark	5.50	309.6	37,720	43	40.6
Djibouti	0.90	1.0	2,320	23	21.4
Dominican Republic	10.10	46.8	8,430	48	25.1
Ecuador	13.60	57.2	8,270	272	25.5
Egypt	83.00	188.4	5,670	1,000	24.4
El Salvador	6.20	21.1	6,630	21	23.2
Equatorial Guinea	0.70	10.4	31,780	28	20.3
Eritrea	5.10	1.9	580	117	19.0
Estonia	1.30	19.1	19,690	45	39.7
Ethiopia	82.80	28.5	930	1,134	18.7
Faroe Islands	0.05	2.2	32,800[ab]	1	35.6
Fiji	0.80	2.8	4,530	18	26.4
Finland	5.30	238.0	35,270	338	42.0
France	62.30	2,649.4[c]	33,670	544	39.9
French Guiana	0.23	4.6[a]	18,150	90	24.3
French Polynesia	0.30	4.5	19,950	3	29.1
Gabon	1.50	11.1	14,420	268	21.6
Gambia, The	1.70	0.7	1,420	11	17.8
Georgia	4.30	10.7	4,770	70	37.3
Germany	82.20	3,330.0	36,340	358	44.3
Ghana	23.80	26.2	1,550	239	20.5
Greece	11.20	329.9	29,620	132	41.4
Greenland	0.06	1.3	19,990	2,176	29.6
Guadeloupe	0.50	12.8[a]	25,170[a]	2	36.8
Guam	0.20	2.8[ab]	15,000[ab]	0.5	29.2
Guatemala	14.00	37.3	4,720	109	18.9
Guinea	10.10	4.1	1,050	246	18.3
Guinea-Bissau	1.60	0.8	1,070	36	19.0
Guyana	0.80	2.0	3,240	215	23.8
Haiti	10.00	6.5	1,150	28	21.5
Honduras	7.50	14.3	3,840	112	21.0
Hong Kong	7.00	210.6	43,230	1	41.8
Hungary	10.00	129.0	20,310	93	39.8
Iceland	0.30	12.1	36,800	103	34.8
India	1198.00	1,377.3	3,300	3,287	25.1
Indonesia	230.00	540.3	4,200	1,904	27.8
Iran	74.20	331.0	11,560	1,648	27.1
Iraq	30.70	65.8	3,550	438	18.3
Ireland	4.50	227.2	40,700	70	34.7

	Population	GDP	GDP per head	Area '000 sq	Median age
	m, 2009	$bn, 2009	$PPP, 2009	km	yrs, 2010
Israel	7.20	195.4	27,660	21	30.1
Italy	59.90	2,112.8	32,430	301	43.2
Jamaica	2.70	12.1	7,630	11	27.0
Japan	127.20	5,069.0	32,420	378	44.7
Jordan	6.30	25.1	5,600	89	20.7
Kazakhstan	15.60	115.3	11,510	2,717	29.0
Kenya	39.80	29.4	1,570	583	18.5
Kosovo	1.80	5.4	2,360	11	28.7
Kuwait	3.00	109.5	48,630[a]	18	28.2
Kyrgyzstan	5.50	4.6	2,280	199	23.8
Laos	6.30	5.9	2,260	237	21.5
Latvia	2.20	26.2	16,440	64	40.2
Lebanon	4.20	34.5	13,070	10	29.1
Lesotho	2.10	1.6	1,470	30	20.3
Liberia	4.00	0.9	400	111	18.2
Libya	6.40	62.4	16,500	1,760	25.9
Lithuania	3.30	37.2	17,310	65	39.3
Luxembourg	0.50	52.3	83,820	3	38.9
Macau	0.56	21.7	60,150	0.02	37.6
Macedonia	2.00	9.2	11,160	26	35.9
Madagascar	19.60	8.6	1,000	587	18.2
Malawi	15.30	4.7	790	118	16.9
Malaysia	27.50	193.1	14,010	333	26.0
Maldives	0.30	1.5	5,480	0.3	24.6
Mali	13.00	9.0	1,190	1,240	16.3
Malta	0.40	8.0	24,810	0.3	39.5
Martinique	0.40	12.6[a]	27,810[a]	1	39.4
Mauritania	3.30	3.0	193	1,031	19.8
Mauritius	1.30	8.6	12,840	2	32.4
Mexico	109.60	874.8	14,260	1,973	26.6
Moldova	3.60	5.4	2,850	34	35.2
Mongolia	2.70	4.2	3,520	1,565	25.4
Montenegro	0.60	4.1	13,090	14	35.9
Morocco	32.00	91.4	4,490	447	26.3
Mozambique	22.90	9.8	890	799	17.8
Myanmar	50.00	35.2	380	677	28.2
Namibia	2.20	9.3	6,410	824	21.2
Nepal	29.30	12.5	1,160	147	21.4
Netherlands	16.60	792.1	40,680	42	40.7
Netherlands Antilles	0.20	4.0	20,340	1	37.9
New Caledonia	0.30	9.3	37,120	19	30.3
New Zealand	4.30	126.7	28,990	271	36.6
Nicaragua	5.70	6.1	2,640	130	22.1
Niger	15.30	5.4	690	1,267	15.5
Nigeria	154.70	173.0	2,200	924	18.5
North Korea	23.90	12.0	500	121	32.9
Norway	4.80	381.8	56,210	324	38.7

	Population	GDP	GDP per head	Area '000 sq	Median age
	m, 2009	$bn, 2009	$PPP, 2009	km	yrs, 2010
Oman	2.80	46.1	25,460[a]	310	25.3
Pakistan	180.80	162.0	2,610	804	21.7
Panama	3.50	24.7	13,060	77	27.3
Papua New Guinea	6.70	7.9	2,280	463	20.4
Paraguay	6.30	14.2	4,520	407	23.1
Peru	29.20	130.3	8,630	1,285	25.6
Philippines	92.00	161.2	3,540	300	22.2
Poland	38.10	430.1	18,910	313	38.0
Portugal	10.70	232.9	24,920	89	41.0
Puerto Rico	4.00	98.5	16,110	9	34.4
Qatar	1.40	98.3	91,380	11	31.6
Réunion	0.80	21.3[a]	22,980[a]	3	29.9
Romania	21.30	161.1	14,280	238	38.5
Russia	140.90	1,231.9	18,930	17,075	37.9
Rwanda	10.00	5.2	1,140	26	18.7
St. Lucia	0.16	0.9	9,610	0.6	27.4
Saudi Arabia	25.70	375.8	23,480	2,200	25.9
Senegal	12.50	12.8	1,820	197	17.8
Serbia	9.90	43.0	11,890	88	37.6
Sierra Leone	5.70	1.9	810	72	18.4
Singapore	4.70	182.2	50,630	0.6	37.6
Slovakia	5.40	87.6	22,880	49	36.9
Slovenia	2.00	48.5	27,130	20	41.7
Somalia	9.10	2.0	210	638	17.5
South Africa	50.10	285.4	10,280	1,226	24.9
South Korea	48.30	832.5	27,100	99	37.9
Spain	44.90	1,460.3	32,150	505	40.1
Sri Lanka	20.20	42.0	4,770	66	30.7
Sudan	42.30	54.7	2,210	2,506	19.7
Suriname	0.50	3.3	7,460[a]	164	27.6
Swaziland	1.20	3.0	5,000	17	19.5
Sweden	9.20	406.1	37,380	450	40.7
Switzerland	7.60	491.9	45,220	41	41.4
Syria	21.90	52.2	4,730	185	21.1
Taiwan	23.00	377.5	31,770	36	38.0
Tajikistan	7.00	5.0	1,970	143	20.4
Tanzania	43.70	21.4	1,360	945	17.5
Thailand	67.80	263.8	8,000	513	34.2
Timor-Leste	1.10	0.6	810	15	16.6
Togo	6.60	2.9	850	57	19.7
Trinidad & Tobago	1.30	21.2	25,570	5	30.8
Tunisia	10.30	39.6	8,270	164	28.9
Turkey	74.80	614.6	13,670	779	28.3
Turkmenistan	5.10	19.9	7,240	488	24.5
Uganda	32.70	16.0	1,220	241	15.7
Ukraine	45.70	113.5	6,320	604	39.3
United Arab Emirates	4.60	230.3	57,740	84	30.1

	Population m, 2009	GDP $bn, 2009	GDP per head $PPP, 2009	Area '000 sq km	Median age yrs, 2010
United Kingdom	61.60	2,174.5	35,160	243	39.8
United States	314.70	14,119.0	45,990	9,373	36.9
Uruguay	3.40	31.5	13,190	176	33.7
Uzbekistan	27.50	32.1	2,880	447	24.2
Venezuela	28.60	326.1	12,320	912	26.1
Vietnam	88.10	97.2	2,950	331	28.2
Virgin Islands (US)	0.11	1.6[ab]	14,500[ab]	0.4	38.8
West Bank & Gaza	4.30	6.6[ab]	2,900[ab]	6	18.1
Yemen	23.60	26.4	2,470	528	17.4
Zambia	12.90	12.8	1,430	753	16.7
Zimbabwe	12.50	5.6	320	391	19.3
Euro area (16)	325.80	12,446.2	34,280	2,497	41.8
World	6,829.40	58,259.8	10,690	148,698	29.2

a Latest available year.
b Estimate.
c Including French Guiana, Guadeloupe, Martinique and Réunion.

Sources

Academy of Motion Picture Arts and Sciences
AFM Research
Airports Council International, *Worldwide Airport Traffic Report*

Bloomberg
BP, *Statistical Review of World Energy*
Business Software Alliance

CAF, *The World Giving Index*
CB Richard Ellis, *Global MarketView Office Occupancy Costs*
Central Banking Publications, *Central Bank Directory 2011*
Central banks
Central Intelligence Agency, *The World Factbook*
CIRFS, *International Rayon and Synthetic Fibres Committee*
Corporate Resources Group, *Quality of Living Report*

The Economist
www.economist.com
Economist Intelligence Unit, *Cost of Living Survey*; *Country Forecasts*; *Country Reports*; *Democracy index*; *E-readiness rankings*; *Global Outlook – Business Environment Rankings*
ERC Statistics International, *World Cigarette Report*
Euromonitor, *International Marketing Data and Statistics*; *European Marketing Data and Statistics*
Eurostat, *Statistics in Focus*

Facebook
Food and Agriculture Organisation

The Heritage Foundation, *Index of Economic Freedom*

IFPI

IMD, *World Competitiveness Yearbook*
IMF, *International Financial Statistics*; *World Economic Outlook*
International Centre for Prison Studies, *World Prison Brief*
International Cocoa Organisation, *Quarterly Bulletin of Cocoa Statistics*
International Coffee Organisation (data as of April 2011)
International Cotton Advisory Committee, *April Bulletin*
International Diabetes Federation, *Diabetes Atlas*
International Grains Council
International Institute for Strategic Studies, *Military Balance*
International Labour Organisation
International Obesity Task Force
International Rubber Study Group, *Rubber Statistical Bulletin*
International Sugar Organisation, *Statistical Bulletin*
International Tea Committee
International Telecommunication Union, *ITU Indicators*
International Union of Railways
International Wool Trade Organisation
Inter-Parliamentary Union

Johnson Matthey

McDonald's

National statistics offices
Network Wizards
Nobel Foundation

OECD, *Development Assistance Committee Report*; *Economic Outlook*; *Environmental Data*; *Revenue Statistics*
www.olympic.org

Reporters Without Borders, *Press Freedom Index*
Reuters Thomson

Space.com
Standard & Poor's *Emerging Stock Markets Factbook*

Taiwan Statistical Data Book
The Times, *Atlas of the World*
Transparency International

UN, *Demographic Yearbook*; *Global Refugee Trends*; *Review of Maritime Transport*; *State of World Population Report*; *Survey on Crime Trends*; *World Contraceptive Use*; *World Population Database*; *World Population Prospects*; *World Urbanisation Prospects*
UNAIDS, *Report on the Global AIDS Epidemic*
UNCTAD, *Review of Maritime Transport*; *World Investment Report*

UNCTAD/WTO Internati Centre
UN Development Progr *Human Development*
UNESCO, Institute for S
Unicef, *Child Poverty in Perspective*
US Census Bureau
US Department of Agric
University of Michigan, to the Universe websit

WHO, *Global Tuberculosi Global Immunisation D World Health Statistics*
World Bank, *Doing Busin Global Development Fi World Development Ind World Development Rep*
World Bureau of Metal St *World Metal Statistics*
World Economic Forum/H University, *Global Competitiveness Report*
World Resources Institute *Resources*
World Tourism Organisati *Yearbook of Tourism Sta*
World Trade Organisation *Report*